Romances of the White Man's Burden

Romances of the White Man's Burden

Race, Empire, and the Plantation in American Literature, 1880–1936

Jeremy Wells

Vanderbilt University Press

Nashville

© 2011 by Vanderbilt University Press
Nashville, Tennessee 37235
All rights reserved
First printing 2011

This book is printed on acid-free paper
made from 30% post-consumer recycled content.
Manufactured in the United States of America

Library of Congress Cataloging-in-Publication Data

Wells, Jeremy, 1971–
Romances of the white man's burden : race, empire,
and the plantation in American literature 1880–1936 /
Jeremy Wells.
    p. cm.
Includes bibliographical references and index.
ISBN 978-0-8265-1756-2 (cloth edition : alk. paper)
1. American literature—Southern States—History and
criticism. 2. American fiction—19th century—History
and criticism. 3. American fiction—20th century—
History and criticism. 4. Southern States—Intellectual
life—19th century. 5. Southern States—Intellectual
life—20th century. 6. Southern States—In literature.
7. Race in literature. 8. Plantation life in literature.
9. Imperialism in literature. I. Title.
PS261.W45 2011
813'.509355—dc22
2010028334

For my parents

Contents

Acknowledgments

My first word of thanks goes to Sandra Gunning, whose warm and expert guidance at the University of Michigan enabled an early version of this project to come into being. It has assumed a very different shape during the intervening years, with only a handful of observations about Thomas Dixon surviving into the present book (and these primarily because Patricia Yaeger especially liked the language used to convey them; her encouragement to care about voice is a piece of advice I have come to value greatly). Yet the examples of these and the other teachers who guided my research into American literature, race studies, and postcolonial theory at Michigan—June Howard, Kerry Larson, Kevin K. Gaines, Anne Ruggles Gere, and especially Simon Gikandi—have always been before me as I pursued this project.

Grants from the University of Michigan's Rackham Graduate School, the Andrew Mellon Foundation, and the Jacob K. Javits Fellowship Program funded portions of the early research that led to this project. A fellowship funded by the Woodrow Wilson Foundation and Indiana University allowed me to conceptualize a project specifically about the plantation. A grant from Southern Illinois University–Carbondale's Office of Research Development and Administration supported the research that led to Chapter 1. Stephanie Graves at SIUC's Morris Library; Kathy Shoemaker and Elizabeth Chase at Emory University's Robert W. Woodruff Library; Jane Westenfeld, Cynthia Burton, and Linda Ernst at Allegheny College's Pelletier Library; Rebecca Cape at Indiana University's Lilly Library; Lain Shakespeare at the Wren's Nest Museum in Atlanta; Lanelle Frost at the Uncle Remus Museum in Eatonton; and Diana Lachatanere at the Schomburg Center for Research in Black Culture helped me to locate a number of the texts and images that make this study in part a work of cultural history.

A number of colleagues have offered helpful feedback on this project. Many more have provided the professional guidance that has made it possible. Edward Brunner in particular has offered both; his routine discovery of obscure texts related to my research—and more generally his ceaseless enthusiasm for the project—have proved sustaining. David Anthony has likewise offered valuable criticism, helping me to see especially how the point of Thomas Dixon was as much his banality as his singularity. George Boulukos, Kevin Dettmar, and Elizabeth Klaver helped me to think about how the project might be framed for larger audiences. George Hutchinson, David Nordloh, Janet Sorensen, Steve Watt, and Eugene Kintgen made my time at Indiana especially valuable. Bob Hamblin and Chris Rieger have been great neighbors in southeast Missouri. Kathleen Diffley and Ben Slote have been supportive from different quadrants in the Midwest. All have helped me to understand how the plantation resonates beyond the U.S. Southeast.

Cecelia Tichi and Teresa Goddu inspired me as an undergraduate to want to pursue the study of American literature as a career. That it is Vanderbilt University Press that is publishing this book is thus especially rewarding. Eli Bortz has been an exceptionally patient and supportive editor throughout, and the suggestions provided by John Mayfield and the additional anonymous reader and editorial board members have made this a much more current and comprehensive project than it would have been otherwise.

The idea for *Romances of the White Man's Burden* first announced itself when, at Indiana, I was allowed to develop a course on empire and Englishness in the twentieth-century novel. As a counterpoint to Conrad's *Heart of Darkness*, I thought I might teach Kipling's *Kim*. As part of my research into *Kim*, I discovered that Kipling admired and indeed corresponded with Joel Chandler Harris. The research into southern culture I had done before seemed suddenly to belong to a much larger universe. The fact that students at Indiana and SIUC responded to these connections made me want to pursue this project. When I say that the book profits from what my students have taught me, I thus express a feeling of gratitude that I hope came through in the classroom.

The support of friends and family has kept me going, especially that supplied by Zack McMillin, Clay Hensley, Doree Wells, Mary Winiarski, and the late Ed Winiarski. I thank my parents, Ann and Stan Wells, for being heroic, not least in the many cross-country car trips they have taken over the past year to watch Zachary. What they supposed was mere grandparenting I perceive as evidence once again of my own extraordinary fortune as a son. To Zachary himself I say thank you for discovering patience while still insisting on being brilliantly distracting. To Amy I owe more than I know how to express. She read every word I wrote at least twice, and since many of these were produced in what turned out to be false starts or wayward drifts, she has labored enormously to help me see this through. The metaphor of burden suggests itself but in the end seems inadequate, since what she proves is my inspiration.

Introduction

White Southern Men and the Burden of Empire

In a very bad novel published in 1907 and titled *Love Is the Sum of It All: A Plantation Romance*, the former Confederate soldier turned popular writer George Cary Eggleston wondered whether the old plantations of the antebellum South might provide evidence that nature intended the United States to dominate the world:

> Perhaps . . . inequality belongs to nature's scheme of progress for the human race, by means of a certain struggle for existence and survival of the fittest. Certain it is that the cultured ease of this old Southern life gave to the American people—yes, and to the whole world, for the whole world has benefited by it—the work of Washington and Jefferson and Patrick Henry and John Marshall and James Madison and the rest. Is not every man living under American institutions, or under the inspiration of those institutions in other lands . . . the better off because Washington and Jefferson and Madison and the rest had the ease and leisure in which to ripen their minds and do the thinking that created this republic and its institutions? . . . Isn't nature's scheme best, after all—the scheme of struggle with the reward of advantage for those who win the struggle?[1]

Eggleston's vision of a "whole world . . . the better off" because a Virginia plantocracy had once had time to think brings together images that circulated widely in late nineteenth- and early twentieth-century U.S. cultural discourse—images of old plantations, founding fathers, expanding empires, and evolved societies—and incorporates them into an explanation of human history remarkable for its compactness if for nothing else. Borrowing from social Darwinists ideas about the "fitness" and competitiveness of particular cultural groups, he depicts the planter class of the early Republic as the winners of humanity's long "struggle" to evolve. He interprets their victory, moreover, as a sign that nature now intends, through them, the uplift of everyone else. Imag-

1

ining American "institutions" and "inspiration" projecting into "other lands," he develops an imagery that could rightly be called imperial—one that might have reminded his 1907 readers of the figures of speech used less than a decade earlier to justify the United States' annexation of Hawaii and its military expeditions in Cuba, the Philippines, Colombia, and elsewhere. Yet even as it proceeds toward the ends of the earth and into realms of the foreign, Eggleston's vision of expanding American power remains rooted in the familiar. His picture of an "old Southern life" filled with "leisure" and "cultured ease" and made possible by what the passage takes for granted—slave labor—would have called to readers' minds the hundreds of similar portraits of plantation life that, since the end of Reconstruction thirty years earlier, had filled the pages of the nation's periodicals and found their way into dozens of books, achieving, one might say, a form of cultural conquest of their own.

    This book is about those images. It is about the fact that visions of the old plantation became so prevalent in U.S. print culture during the decades following Reconstruction that, in 1888—two decades, almost, before Eggleston would imagine "the whole world" an extension of the plantation South—another novelist, Albion W. Tourgée of Ohio, was moved to observe that "American fiction of to-day . . . is predominantly Southern in type and character" and that "the South" therefore seemed suddenly to have become "the seat of intellectual empire in America." The statement was exaggerated but not outrageous. The volume of plantation fiction, nonfiction, and poetry issuing from national magazine and book publishers had risen steadily since the middle 1870s and dramatically since about 1885. By 1888 it seemed to Tourgée to have become a "flood": an overflow of "novels, poems, and all forms of literature" that "to the Northern man, whose belief in averages is so profound . . . seems quite unaccountable."[2] In March of that year alone, for example, readers could have encountered stories and poems involving plantation themes and settings in *Scribner's*, the *Century*, *Peterson's*, the *Cosmopolitan*, the *Christian Union*, *Godey's Lady's Book*, *Ballou's*, and the *New Princeton Review*. Readers of that month's *Harper's* were treated to "A Visit to a Colonial Estate," a travel piece describing the plantation home of Robert E. Lee Jr., son of the late Confederate general, while readers of the March *Chautauquan* were offered a tour of "The Homes of Some Southern Authors" and shown several plantations that had been purchased or improved with the proceeds from their owners' recent book sales—evidence that, for some writers, rehabilitating the old plantation had become more than a metaphorical affair.[3] Readers who may have wanted still more representations of plantation life in 1888 could have filled entire shelves with the books on the subject published during just the previous two years, among them Thomas Nelson Page and A. C. Gordon's *Befo' de War: Echoes in Negro Dialect* (1888); Page's *Two Little Confederates* (1888) and *In Ole Virginia* (1887); Joel Chandler Harris and Eli Shepherd's *Songs and Ballads of the Old Plantation* (1888); Harris's *Free Joe and Other Georgian Sketches* (1887); Grace King's *Monsieur Motte* (1888); Amélie Rives's *Virginia of Virginia* (1888); Susan Dabney Smedes's *Memorials of a Southern Planter* (1887); and—not least, in terms of the insight it affords into how popular the plantation had become by the late 1880s—an illustrated collection of sheet music titled *The Old Plantation Melodies* (1888) that repackaged the plantation ballads of Stephen Foster and others as "genuine American folk-lore songs . . . that defy age."[4]

Foster's "My Old Kentucky Home" (1850), "Old Folks at Home" (1851), and "Massa's in the Cold, Cold Ground" (1852), all of which were included in *The Old Plantation Melodies*, were compositions from more than three decades earlier. All offered portraits of slaves or former slaves "longing for de old plantation," as Foster had phrased it in "Old Folks at Home," and all had contributed to a store of images that, by 1888, had long since become cultural clichés: images of "darkies" professing to be "happy as de day am long" while "pickin' on de old banjo" or going on hunts for "the possum and the coon"; images of older slaves mourning the passing of a master "cayse he was so kind" or recollecting happier times spent wandering "round de little farm"; and so on. Such ideas had resonated powerfully with U.S. audiences during the years *prior* to Emancipation, at a time when the southern plantation system, though it showed signs of strain, still very much existed. It is little wonder, then, that they continued to resonate once slavery had come to an end and "the old plantation" had indeed become a place accessible only in memory or imagination.

It is remarkable, however, that the resonance seemed actually to increase as the nineteenth century came to an end, with such works as Francis Hopkinson Smith's *Colonel Carter of Cartersville* (1891) and Thomas Nelson Page's *Red Rock* (1898) numbering among the more popular American novels of the 1890s. It is more remarkable still that it continued well into the twentieth century, long after most of those who might actually have known life on an old plantation had gone the way of Foster's "old massa . . . in de cold, cold ground." Yet what is most noteworthy about the proliferation of plantation images underway during these decades is how it coincided with the emergence of a new *interpretation* of the old plantation, a new explanation of how and why it mattered to the ever larger, more geographically dispersed audiences that, with the passage of each decade, were less and less likely to have any real ties to the plantation South. Page, one of the foremost figures in the postbellum plantation fiction movement and someone who actually did possess deep connections to a southern plantocracy—he was the descendant of not one but two of the First Families of Virginia—captured this new sense of the significance of the institution in 1892, when he wrote that "the social life of the Old South," far from having been anomalous or anachronistic, had instead "largely contributed to produce this nation." In terms similar to those George Cary Eggleston would employ a decade later, Page argued that the Old South had given birth to the men who had "established this government," "led its armies and its navies," "opened up the great West . . . and more than trebled our territory," "christianized the negro race," and, in what seemed to Page their most lasting accomplishment, "maintained the supremacy of the Caucasian race, upon which all civilization seems now to depend."[5]

The plantation had become, in a word, *national* by the turn of the century. It provided numerous writers new ways of imagining the nation's founding and development; and, for an institution whose allure was connected to its supposed pastness—its symbolizing what would later famously be called "a civilization gone with the wind"—it figured conspicuously in visions of the nation's future, too. As James Battle Avirett of North Carolina would write in 1901, "The old plantation home life is dead. . . . But it is struggling back from the hollow bosom that once bled for it, and will ascend the heights of government at the hands of a reunited and strengthened people, with no sectional triumph upon it." Imagining that Americans would someday derive their images of the South more from such writings as his than from *Uncle Tom's Cabin* ("Mrs. Stowe's *ex parte*, and therefore unfair, statement," he called it), Avirett foresaw a time "when the faithful historian shall descend into the vaults of the dead past in quest of traditions of liberty . . . [and] discover to whom the world is indebted for the perpetuation of the republic."[6]

In texts focused more on the present, meanwhile—which is to say, on the sixty eventful years that stretched from the end of Reconstruction to the middle of the Great Depression and that compose the period of focus for this book—the plantation came to seem, to many, a miniature version of present-day "America." Its sense of dividedness and unsettledness, its possessing a sense of tradition alongside a troubled history, its needing to accommodate itself to an industrial modernity, and above all its racial complexity and the ways in which *this* gave rise to anxieties involving gender, class, and nationality—these were widespread concerns during the late nineteenth and early twentieth centuries. They were not isolated to the South nor even to the United States, and a number of texts about plantations drew parallels between the problems of the postbellum South and those of the rest of the nation and the world. Some even represented the southern plantation as synecdochic—as a space, not unlike the western "frontier," that, though localized, nevertheless offered readers glimpses into much larger historical forces. Yet what made the plantation South especially worthy of attention, its proponents contended, were the ways in which it, almost alone among the world's societies, could be seen as having succeeded in overcoming the problem of multiraciality. "Wherever whites and blacks have met, in any age or country, save in the South, there have been collision and violence—inexpressible and irreconcilable." So observed the Georgia writer and orator Henry W. Grady in the section of *The New South* (1890) devoted to "the race problem"—and in remarks that clearly ignored the "collisions" inherent in slavery and the forms of white mob violence that had been escalating during recent months. From Grady's perspective, however, the "two dissimilar races" that composed the plantation South had managed "peace and honor and prosperity" for decades because of their shared commitment to a social order in which "one [race] was in complete subjection to the other." The success of the arrangement, according to Grady and the other celebrants of southern "tradition" studied in this book, deserved the notice of the entire world: "The American Republic has achieved great things, but it will have nothing better to render into the keeping of universal history than the progress made by the two races in the South in the past twenty-five years towards the adjustment of their relations and the solution of the problem that is theirs."[7] How and why the southern plantation went from seeming a disruptive space in U.S. culture to one that appeared actually to present solutions to "universal" problems, hence to illuminate a new way forward for the entire nation—this is the central subject of *Romances of the White Man's Burden*.

My title highlights one way in which national fantasy and southern mythology merged in discussions of white male responsibility and the new dimensions it was assuming during this, "the age of empire," as the historian Eric Hobsbawm has termed the late nineteenth and early twentieth centuries. In the texts around which I have constructed this book, the figure of a white man burdened by modernity and saddled with the task of uplifting, or at least managing, "Africans" and other nonwhite races proves conspicuous. He appears often enough to make clear that he proved compelling to the culture, surfacing in nonfictional as well as fictional texts and finding his way into "serious" as well as popular literature. In the writings of Joel Chandler Harris, the Georgia author whose "Uncle Remus" stories I explore in Chapter 1, he takes the form of the patient planter who knows "that the duty of looking after the irresponsible blacks . . . involved the upbuilding and upholding of a patriarchal institution out of which grew new and grave responsibilities."[8] In the speeches of Henry Grady, one of the writers I consider in Chapter 2, he passes these responsibilities on to his sons, the young men of Grady's "New South" who shoulder a "burden no other people bears to-day" and who, "set by this problem apart from all other peoples of the earth," have the opportunity therefore of saving the world by saving the South.[9] In Henry Adams's *Democracy* (1880), a novel published just as Harris and Grady were beginning to make national names for themselves, he appears less dramatically but still significantly as the scion of a ruined Virginia family who, like a "true man, carr[ies] his burden calmly, quietly, [and] without complaint," thus reminding his associates of the kind of man capable of founding a country, a "General Washington restored to us in his prime."[10] And in William Faulkner's *Light in August* (1932), one of the novels I discuss in Chapter 4, he is transformed into a kind of roving spirit that takes possession of the souls of multiple characters, among them a northern carpetbagger actually named Burden who views black advancement as his personal cross to bear as well as a Mississippi national guardsman who discovers in militant white supremacy a "burden" that he happily "assume[s] and carrie[s]" because it seems "weightless," a way of laying claim to a lofty destiny simply by recognizing the color of his own skin.[11]

The precise function of the figure of burdened white manhood thus varies from text to text. His purpose in most, however, is to make southern history appear providential by making slavery and its corollary, the postbellum "race problem," seem like affairs that, however regrettable, had nevertheless prepared the white men of the South to act as leaders in the new century. The argument was made to play out in multiple forms and contexts—in texts about the Spanish-American and Philippine-American wars of the turn of the century, for example, several of which upheld white southern men as natural experts on the question of what to do with the "barbaric" Filipinos who came under U.S. colonial control in 1899.[12] Closer to home, white southern writers occasionally invoked the authority they supposed inherent in the figure of the planter in order to offer advice to the white citizens of northern cities who, because of black migration from the South as well as immigration from overseas, were thought to be facing growing race problems of their own. The figure thus mediated between the categories of "at home" and abroad while solidifying the supposed link between the South's past and the nation's future. By transforming the complex issues surrounding race worldwide into a single "white man's burden" and asserting that only one group had shown evidence historically of being able to bear it, the texts at the center of this study made modernity and its foremost sign, multiraciality, seem like problems that only white southern men were capable of solving.

The case is made forcefully in the novel that provides my study its title. Thomas Dixon Jr.'s *The Leopard's Spots: A Romance of the White Man's Burden, 1865–1900* (1902) was published toward the middle of the period surveyed here and demonstrates as well as any of the texts I consider in this book the linkages between plantation nostalgia, U.S. imperialism, and the new nationalism emergent during these decades. I explore these connections at length in Chapter 3. Suffice it to say here that *The Leopard's Spots* begins with the end of the Old South, ends with the old regime's virtual restoration at the turn of the century, and in its middle chapters manages to represent the rise of the Ku Klux Klan, the overthrow of the Reconstruction governments, the disenfranchisement of "the negro," and the dawn of the age of U.S. overseas imperialism as interlinked episodes in the long and triumphal history of "Anglo-Saxon civilisation."[13] Dixon's "romance of the white man's burden" thus shows that, within a single novel, the figure of burdened white manhood could assume multiple roles, from ruined but resilient planter to robed Klansman to white supremacist soldier and statesman.

Yet Dixon's title was borrowed, too. The work from which he adapted it, Rudyard Kipling's 1899 poem "The White Man's Burden," deserves some attention here, for Dixon was far from the only white southern writer to find in its extrapolations of white manhood ideas that seemed not just compelling but indeed familiar. The poem first appeared in the February 1899 issue of the U.S. magazine *McClure's*. It was republished in numerous additional venues within weeks, prompting a headline writer for the May issue of the *Dial* to dub the poem the source of "The Kipling Hysteria."[14] Kipling was already among the more celebrated living British writers in the United States when it appeared, his two *Jungle Book*s (1894 and 1895) and several additional works of fiction and poetry having sold well and won the praise of critics. "The White Man's Burden" elevated him to new levels of literary heroism, however, with one American reviewer arguing that it had propelled him "way above Browning and the rest" and another asserting that readers might find "in these lines . . . the quality which made the best literature of the age of Elizabeth so powerful and so contagious":

He stands for some of the highest qualities of the English race; for its virility, its readiness to accept responsibilities, its tremendous energy, its faith in itself. In an age when pessimism has so widely prevailed, and has sapped the vitality of so many gifted men, Mr. Kipling has seen the dark facts of life with a vision as clear as that of any of his contemporaries. But he has not succumbed to the modern mood; he has risen above it, as the really great artist must always rise above it, to express the creative, original, and aggressive temper of a great race.[15]

The poem was not expressly about "the English race," however. It was instead occasioned by the United States' having invaded the Philippines a few months earlier and, having ousted a decrepit colonial power in Spain, joined those mature but still vigorous European nations that had been captaining the grand campaign of empire for the past century. Its tone was thus world-wise, its speaker not unlike a veteran figure in some professional or even athletic field who, sizing up a newcomer, is conditionally impressed but still wishes to seem skeptical, in part to remind the upstart that, at the moment, he is still in charge, but also to challenge his young rival to accomplish more in the future than he and his generation had managed in the past.

"Take up the White Man's burden— / Send forth the best ye breed— / Go, bind your sons to exile / To serve your captives' need," the poem begins. The presumption to be able to command young America to do anything reflects the gap in experience that the speaker supposes distinguishes him, the grizzled imperialist, from his fresh-faced American companions. By the fourth line, however, when the image of colonial "captives" appears, the poem makes clear its larger perspective: that, when one factors in race and the distance that was understood to separate civilized from savage communities, the speaker and his addressees are really much more alike than different (hence the American reviewer's seeming to identify with Kipling as a member of "the English race"). This idea is reinforced by the language Kipling uses throughout the poem to refer to the subjects of colonialism: the "fluttered folk and wild" who, "new-caught" and still prone to "sloth and heathen folly," need to be conducted "slowly . . . toward the light" and are expected routinely to slide backward despite the colonizer's best efforts. The final stanza underscores Kipling's intent to challenge his American readers to continue the process their predecessors had begun of making white manhood, in effect, meaningful, a sign of some metaphysical responsibility rather than simply an inert physical fact:

Take up the White Man's burden!
　　Have done with childish days—
The lightly-proffered laurel,

The easy ungrudged praise:
  Comes now, to search your manhood
    Through all the thankless years,
  Cold, edged with dear-bought wisdom,
    The judgment of your peers.

Americans got it and, by and large, liked it. Theodore Roosevelt thought it "very poor poetry but made good sense from the expansion point of view."[16] The anonymous reviewer who wrote about it in the *New York Evangelist* was more enthusiastic on both fronts, calling it "a stirring appeal to American manhood which places principles and duty and honor above money." What the *Evangelist's* reviewer and others valued in particular was the poem's theme of the difficulty of empire: how it "does not picture it as an easy task" or "tell us it will increase our trade" but represents it instead as "a duty . . . laid upon us of governing them until they are able to govern themselves."[17] By highlighting this, however, the *Evangelist* was calling attention to what made the poem especially popular among white southerners, many of whom saw images of themselves in both its addressee—the young American being urged to get into the game of empire—and its speaker—the elder statesman who spoke full well knowing how "thankless" the task would be, how "dear-bought" would be the "wisdom" that resulted when a nobler race took it upon itself to civilize an inferior one.

"The White Man's Burden" was in fact only a few days old when, on February 7, 1899, Senator Benjamin Tillman of South Carolina took to the floor of the Senate chamber to praise Kipling as "the greatest poet of England at this time" and to call attention to how the poem, though "in some places too deep for me," nevertheless seemed to illuminate perfectly the conditions of the plantation and postplantation South: "We of the South have borne this white man's burden of a colored race in our midst since their emancipation and before."[18] By the end of May a former governor of Georgia, William J. Northen, was making similar remarks before an audience in Boston, suggesting that "the white man's burden" was simply the latest name by which Americans were referring to a set of issues that had occupied white southerners for decades: "Whatever may be its present title—the negro problem; the race question; the white man's burden; the South's shame; or the Nation's sin—call it what you may, the thing is here, full of peril and danger to the whole people."[19]

The phrase continued to resonate during the years that followed, making "The White Man's Burden" perhaps the most frequently mentioned poem in the United States at the turn of the century. It was in 1902, the same year that Dixon incorporated the phrase into the subtitle of *The Leopard's Spots*, that William Garrott Brown, a lecturer in history at Harvard University, titled the final chapter of his study *The Lower South in American History* "Shifting the White Man's Burden." In it he argued that the resources currently being appropriated for the education of black southerners might better be spent on whites.[20] Two years later Thomas Nelson Page wondered similarly about the nation's solicitousness toward ex-slaves and their descendants in *The Negro: The Southerner's Problem* (1904), a work whose title at least implies the idea of a "white man's burden." Page may well have had Kipling in mind when lamenting late in the text that white southerners "carr[ied] perpetually the burden of a vast and densely ignorant population" in their midst.[21] Six years after Page, and in a work whose connection to Kipling was much more explicit, Benjamin Franklin Riley, the president of what would later become Samford University in Birmingham, Alabama, titled his 1910 study of "the colossal race question of the South" *The White Man's Burden: A Discussion of the Interracial Question with Special Reference to the Responsibility of the White Race to the Negro Problem*. Riley wrote the book to dispute the negative outlooks toward "negro" development proposed by such writers as Page and Grady. Like them, however, he saw in the racial challenges that faced the U.S. South opportunities to "mark a new era in the progress of Anglo-Saxonism" and to develop a set of practical solutions that "would be far reaching in its effects over the world."[22]

Riley believed that black contributions to U.S. society had actually been undervalued and that "the destinies of both races [were] inseparably bound together."[23] Benjamin Tillman, by contrast, openly hated "negroes" and could only imagine them a part of America so long as they were politically powerless; he would have preferred, in fact, to have seen them emigrate or be forcibly relocated elsewhere. The fact that both could imagine black southerners a "white man's burden" thus gives some sense of just how powerfully Kipling's phrase resonated with white southern men—how it perhaps even crystallized for them something that they had been feeling about themselves, their region's past, and their relationship to their paternity for some time but had not yet found the words to describe. The fact that they and so many others laid claim to the phrase could be construed almost as a response to Kipling—an instance of something remotely like postcolonial "writing back," with, of course, the enormous qualification that those who were appropriating Kipling to describe the South were doing so with no intentions whatsoever of objecting to his representations of the colonized.[24] Rather, they were asserting that they, too, knew what it meant to be *colonizers* and were actually willing to invite "the judgment of [their] peers" *now*, based on what they and their forefathers had already accomplished.

Kipling's poem of course elicited a different response, too—one more recognizably "postcolonial" or in any event more straightforwardly opposed to the ideas presented in "The White Man's Burden." One such response, a poem titled "Charity Begins at Home," was published in the *Colored American* in March 1899, one month after the appearance of Kipling's original. Its author identified him- or herself simply as "X-Ray," a pseudonym intended perhaps to suggest the poet's ability to see beyond skin color and the racialized body, or perhaps simply to see through Kipling's arguments:

> To h—with the "White Man's Burden!"
> To h—with Kipling's verse!
> The Black Man demands our attention:
> His condition is growing worse.
> Why lose sleep over his burden?
> All mortals have their share,
> The black man's growing hardships
> Are more than he can bear. (ll. 1–8)[25]

Another parody appeared in the black press one month later. Written by Henry Theodore Johnson, an African American theologian, writer, and newspaper editor from South Carolina, it is not as confrontational initially as the poem by "X-Ray." By its middle section, however, it makes clear that it perceives the overseas adventures of the 1890s as but the latest in a long series of travesties perpetuated by white Americans against peoples of color. Its first and third quatrains read as follows:

> Pile on the Black Man's Burden.
>   'Tis nearest at your door;
> Why heed long bleeding Cuba,
>   or dark Hawaii's shore?
> . . . .
> Pile on the Black Man's Burden
>   His wail with laughter drown
> You've sealed the Red Man's problem,
>   And will take up the Brown. (ll. 1–4, 9–12)[26]

Such poems engaged in obvious dialogue with Kipling, offering in opposition to his image of nonwhite peoples as "fluttered folk and wild" evidence of black and brown advancement. Indeed, to be able to parody such
a text (such a master text, even) as "The White Man's Burden" implies at the
very least a concept of oneself as equal. Yet such poems were also involved in
dialogue with the white southern writers mentioned above who were appropriating Kipling to celebrate the plantation South as a space where the "white
man's burden" had been borne for decades. These response poems thus seem
even more powerful when viewed as reactions against such adaptations as one
authored by the white Tennessean Rufus McClain Fields and published in the
Southern Cultivator in 1904. Titled simply "The White Man's Burden," the
poem represents in dialect a black southern family's attempts to steal chickens
and watermelons from a white man—a "Marsa Kiplin," no less:

> "Take up dat white man's budden dah,
>   En strop hit on yo' backs
> Yo, po' wil' savage chillens yo'—
>   John Henry, whar dem sacks?
> . . . .
> Step light dah, Jake, en nimble lak
>   Han' dat wortermilyn heah!
> De white man's budden big en fine
>   En juicy lak did yeah!
> Fill up dem sacks, yo' niggah yo'
>   Kaze trou de longtrwl da[y],
> Dese white fo'ks mus' be tended to
>   Des lak Marsa Kiplin say." (ll. 1–4, 9–16)[27]

The appropriations here are manifold. Fields borrows from Kipling for his
title, meter, and rhyme scheme. He appropriates Joel Chandler Harris and
Thomas Nelson Page for his dialect (which of course represents a double or
triple appropriation, since Harris and Page were "borrowing" from black
southerners themselves and from earlier attempts to represent black speech
in writing). And he borrows from the minstrel stage what Houston Baker has
identified as the trope of the "chicken-stealing darky." To have seen so much
synthesized by Kipling's phrase must have seemed galling to African American
readers and writers working to contest Jim Crow and the reductive racial logic
upon which it was based. To appropriate Kipling themselves—and thus to engage in something similar to what Baker attributes to Booker T. Washington,

namely a "stepping inside the white world's nonsense syllables with oratorical mastery"—must therefore have seemed all the more urgent.[28]

This urgency would explain why, more than a decade after the initial appearance of Kipling's poem, black writers were still engaged in rewriting it, turning it inside out, upside down, and (in Robin D. G. Kelley's memorable phrase) "b(l)ackward."[29] Among the later parodies was "The Black Man's Burden (A Reply to Rudyard Kipling)," an adaptation published in 1915 by Hubert H. Harrison, the West Indian–born writer who by the 1910s had assumed the radical lead of a new Harlem-based black intellectual movement. Harris's poem follows the original especially closely, containing the same number of stanzas, seven, and turning such lines of Kipling's as "Go, bind your sons to exile / To serve your captives' need" into "And bind our sons in shackles / To serve your selfish greed." Its final stanza best conveys its message:

Take up the Black Man's burden—
    Until the tale is told,
Until the balances of hate
    Bear down the beam of gold.
And while ye wait remember
    That Justice, though delayed
Will hold you as her debtor, till
    The Black Man's debt is paid. (ll. 49–56)[30]

In an earlier essay Harrison actually begins to calculate this debt, noting, for example, that in South Carolina in 1910, state appropriations for public education amounted to $10.34 for each white child and $1.70 for each black child. "In the face of these facts," Harrison concludes the essay, "the phrase, 'the white man's burden,' seems to me like a horrid mockery."[31]

Kipling's poem drew replies from several additional African American prose writers. It drew multiple responses from W. E. B. Du Bois alone. Harrison's images of black southerners' "work[ing] the white man's grain" while "beam[s] of gold" shine upon those who own the land and capitalize the mills, not those who pick the cotton, are repeated in Du Bois's 1911 novel, *The Quest of the Silver Fleece*, most notably in the passage that opens chapter 18:

All over the land the cotton had foamed in great white flakes under the winter sun. The Silver Fleece lay like a mighty mantle across the earth. Black men and mules had staggered beneath its burden, while deep songs welled in the hearts of men; for the Fleece was goodly and gleaming and soft, and men dreamed of the gold that it would buy. All the roads in the country had been lined with wagons—a million wagons speeding to and fro with straining mules and laughing black men, bearing bubbling masses of piled white Fleece. The gins were still roaring and spitting flames and smoke—fifty thousand of them in town and vale. Then hoarse iron throats were filled with fifteen billion pounds of white-fleeced, black-specked cotton, for the whirling saws to tear out the seed and fling five thousand million pounds of the silken fibre to the press.[32]

Imagining agriculture alongside industry, technology alongside manual labor, white profit alongside black penury, and (perhaps most strikingly) beauty alongside violence, the passage is indicative of Du Bois's novel as a whole.[33] More relevant to the present discussion, it suggests how almost inevitable the word "burden" had become in representations of the South and its race and labor relations by the early twentieth century (though of course in Du Bois's prose, as in the response poems, it is "black men and mules" who "stagge[r] beneath" a "burden," not the white men who own the land, buy and sell the cotton, and regard black laborers as a cost—hence a people—to be kept down).[34]

To make this point, one might cite from those moments in *The Souls of Black Folk* (1903) when notions of a "black man's burden" surface in Du Bois's writing. In the chapter on Alexander Crummell, for example, he describes the minister's coming to realize his life's mission of antiracism not as a moment of illumination but rather as a crushing blow: "Then the full weight of his burden fell upon him."[35] In the chapter on Booker T. Washington (whom Du Bois describes in "The Forethought" as "the leader who bears the chief burden of his race to-day") he alleges that Washington's "doctrine has tended to make the whites, North and South, shift the burden of the Negro problem to the Negro's shoulders . . . when in fact the burden belongs to the nation" (41, 94). The first and most famous chapter ("Of Our Spiritual Strivings") concludes by recharacterizing "the spiritual striving of the freedmen's sons" as "the travail of souls whose burden is almost beyond the measure of their strength, but who bear it in the name of an historic race, in the name of this the land of their fathers' fathers, and in the name of human opportunity" (53).

Perhaps most interesting, though, is a passage that occurs earlier in the first chapter, one devoted entirely to images of black burden, female as well as male. Discussing Reconstruction, Du Bois argues that its sudden abortion

changed the child of Emancipation to the youth with dawning self-consciousness, self-realization, self-respect. . . . For the first time he sought to analyze the burden he bore upon his back, that dead-weight of social deg-radation partially masked behind a halfnamed Negro problem. He felt his poverty. . . . He felt the weight of his ignorance,—not simply of letters, but of life, of business, of the humanities. . . . Nor was his burden all poverty and ignorance. The red stain of bastardy, which two centuries of systematic legal defilement of Negro women had stamped upon his race, meant not only the loss of ancient African chastity, but also the hereditary weight of a mass of corruption from white adulterers, threatening almost the obliteration of the Negro home. (49–50)

If the passage imagines the heaviness of black southern subjectivity as it is felt by a man ("*he* sought to analyze the burden"; "*he* felt the weight of his igno-rance"), it begins at least to recognize what the sociologist Nicole Rousseau has recently termed "the black woman's burden": a "story," Rousseau calls it, that "begins with her role in a forced labor pool" and unfolds against a backdrop of "ever-intensifying regulation of Black women's reproduction," commodifi-cation of their bodies, and legislation of their morality.[36] What Du Bois de-scribes as "the hereditary weight of . . . corruption from white adulterers" may thus come as close as any image can to negating "the white man's burden," for while it involves a similar metaphorics of weight, by involving black women it impugns white, male motivations as anything but selfless. It does so more-over while recognizing that "legal defilement," "the loss of . . . chastity," the perpetuation of "bastardy," and the fact of rape represent impositions upon *her* body more onerous even than the awful "burden[s] . . . bor[n]e upon *his* back."

The passage thus repeats uncannily what Harriet Jacobs writes in *Incidents in the Life of a Slave Girl* (1861) when she describes finding out that "my new-born babe was a girl": "my heart was heavier than it had ever been before. Slavery is terrible for men; but it is far more terrible for women. Superadded to the burden common to all, they have wrongs, and sufferings, and mortifi-cations peculiarly their own."[37] The passage also anticipates a poem Du Bois would publish in the *Horizon* in 1907. Titled "The Burden of Black Women," the poem represents a more indirect response to Kipling than the parodies discussed earlier. Its meter and rhyme scheme vary from stanza to stanza, and it possesses nothing like the refrain that structures "The White Man's Burden" and its many responses. Seven stanzas long, however, the poem contains much that makes it clear that it, too, constitutes a reply to Kipling and his white southern interpreters. Indeed it may represent the most imaginative response of all. The poem deforms Kipling's phrase in multiple ways, referring to "the

White Man's Burden / Of Liquor and Lust and Lies" at one point and to "the burden of white men [who] bore her back" at another—an image suggestive of rape, given that it follows the woman's hearing a voice that compels her to "arise," only to find herself forced back down, her voice "stifled":

> But out of the past of the Past's grey past, it yelled from the top of the sky;
> Crying: Awake, O ancient race! Wailing: O woman arise!
> And crying and sighing and crying again as a voice in the midnight cries;
> But the burden of white men bore her back, and the white world stifled her
>   sighs. (ll. 7–10)[38]

The poem's penultimate stanza refers to a burden once again, though it is a burden of an entirely different sort: one the *Oxford English Dictionary* defines as "the refrain or chorus of a song; a set of words recurring at the end of each verse." Imagining a time after the birth of a "Black Christ," the poem foretells an era when "the burden of manhood / Be it yellow or black or white / . . . Shall sing with the Sons of Morning / And Daughters of Evensong" (ll. 55–60). Calling to mind the transnationalism of the most famous sentence from *Souls*—"The problem of the twentieth century is the problem of the color-line,—the relation of the darker to the lighter races of men in Asia and Africa, in America and the islands of the sea"—"The Burden of Black Women" thus builds toward a postnational, postracial revelation (54). It moves outward in space as well as backward in time in order to discover this vision, one in which "black men of Egypt and Ind" stand alongside "Chaldeans and Yellow Chinese, / The Hebrew children of the Morning / And Mongrels of Rome and Greece" in opposition to the sort of white colonial dominion envisaged by Kipling (ll. 34–38).

Yet what proves most compelling about Du Bois's poem is its recognition of the double meaning of "burden." Derived from the Old English verb *beran* (to bear, to carry, to bring forth), "burden" may also refer to "that which is borne in the womb; a child," according to the *Oxford English Dictionary*. In fact the word is linked etymologically to "birth," a word that may denote either "the bearing of offspring" or "lineage, extraction, descent . . . position inherited from parents."[39] This latter meaning of "birth," meanwhile, resembles the earlier meaning of "race" ("a group of people belonging to the same family and descended from a common ancestor") from which derives the more modern meaning ("any of the major groupings of mankind, having in common distinct physical features or having a similar ethnic background").[40] Viewed in this light, "the white man's burden" becomes something of an etymological tautology, a sign of what a man must *bear* because of how he was *born(e)*, an index of his *birth* in a double sense of the word.

In "The Burden of Black Women," however, the word functions differently as a double sign. It signifies paradoxically both the forms of suffering black women have had to endure as well as the forms of hope to which they have given life: the fact that historically their bodies have been degraded and their reproductive capacities exploited, and yet they have given birth to what Du Bois depicts throughout the poem as forms of salvation. Thus the vile imagery that opens the poem's third stanza:

> The White World's vermin and filth:
> All the dirt of London,
> All the scum of New York;
> Valiant spoilers of women
> And conquerors of unarmed men;
> Shameless breeders of bastards
> Drunk with the greed of gold. (ll. 11–17)

Yet thus also the messianic image that concludes the sixth stanza:

> Till the Devil's strength be shorn,
> Till some dim, darker David a-hoeing of his corn,
> And married maiden, Mother of God,
> Bid the Black Christ be born! (ll. 51–54).

The poem ends with a four-line stanza that, much like the passage from *The Quest of the Silver Fleece*, combines violent with beautiful imagery. The lines echo even more loudly the "After-Thought" that concludes *The Souls of Black Folk* and in which Du Bois, addressing an exalted "O God the Reader," makes a final plea for his text: "vouchsafe that this my book fall not still-born into the world-wilderness. . . . In Thy good time may infinite reason turn the tangle straight, and these crooked marks on a fragile leaf be not indeed THE END" (278). "The Burden of Black Women" concludes by depicting a much more disturbing set of "marks," however, namely the wounds on the "Black mother['s] . . . bosom": perhaps signs of abuse or, in keeping with the religious imagery of her poem, of her having rent her breast to feed her children.[41] Whatever the case, the poem is in its conclusion rather more insistent than *Souls* on imagining a new beginning *itself*, not leaving this up to the reader:

Black mother of the iron hills that guard the blazing sea,
Wild spirit of a storm-swept soul a-struggling to be free,
Where 'neath the bloody finger marks, thy riven bosom quakes,
Thicken the thunders of God's voice, and lo! A world awakes! (ll. 61–64)

If Kipling's "The White Man's Burden" had inspired white southern writers to imagine their native region as coextensive with the world and a model for its domination, it also provoked such responses as these: poems and prose works in which a different South—perhaps even a differently inflected "global South"—gives rise to new forms of resistance and new concepts of culture. While the present study focuses on the new southern imaginaries of Grady, Dixon, and others—writers who sought to see the South greatly expanded, and in more ways than one—it remains mindful of the new "world[s] awake[ned]" by Du Bois and others, and how profoundly limited these make the white men's visions seem.

To see such "Souths" in the literature of this period is to regard the region rather differently than it has figured in much scholarship. Until comparatively recently studies of the South have tended to explore the region in terms of a North-South dialectic and to regard it as the nation's "other"—"an American problem," "a mythic land apart," a "separate country," or a space of "aberration," to paraphrase the titles of four studies of the region published over the past two decades.[42] It is among the central claims of *Romances of the White Man's Burden* that the South must also be seen as a crucible of narratives of national identity, a space that, whatever its pretensions toward difference and exclusivity, has simultaneously generated ways of conceptualizing "America" and indeed the world in which it has seemed central.

To say this is not to deny southern peculiarity, then or now, nor is it to try to extend backward a debate that has been going on since at least the 1970s over whether "Dixie" is becoming "Americanized" or "America" "southernized." As recent scholarship on literary regionalism has shown, the dialectic between region and nation involves more than a simple contest in which one force recedes as the other advances. The relationship can seem conflicted but actually be mutually constitutive. It can involve cooptation just as easily as it can reflect genuine differences and disputes between distinct localities and an expansive state. And it can shift depending upon the region and nation one is discussing and the moment in history upon which one is focused. The case of the plantation South is illustrative. In antebellum texts it was most often represented as exotic, a space outside or at the margins of U.S. nationhood, yet even its eccentricity was differently interpreted, with some seeing it as vex-ing and proposing measures for its reform and others defending it as in need of preservation or even extension.[43] In early postbellum texts a version of this dispute continued. Hinged though it was upon a shared idea of the plantation South's distinctiveness, the argument between reformists and preservationists in some ways intensified, for it no longer focused on the legality of the institu-tion of slavery that had made more or less unquestionable the notion of the South as peculiar. Instead it took the form of whether the region constituted a barbaric space that needed to be reconstructed so that it might once again belong to "America" or whether, as one Virginia writer put it in 1866, it did not in fact already possess a "well-known superiourity in civilization . . . over the people of the North" and need therefore to be protected from would-be reconstructionists.[44]

This contest over whether the South embodied or contradicted the idea of "civilization" continued throughout the late nineteenth and early twentieth centuries. During the period I study here, in other words, there was never a universal consensus on what the South signified. Yet the frequency with which the plantation South was depicted as representative of "America" during these years confounds any model of region-nation relations that assumes a straight-forward contest between the two spaces. Whereas the centrality of the planta-tion to the southern economy had once inspired visions of a separate nation-hood, by 1900 it was animating celebrations of an expanding "America." To recognize the ways in which the spaces of region, nation, and empire converge in representations of the southern plantation is thus to add something to the recent vibrant scholarship on local color, literary regionalism, and cultural na-tionalism, a body of criticism from which the present study benefits greatly.[45]

Romances of the White Man's Burden is indebted to three additional bodies of scholarship. The first of these may have the longest pedigree. Represented by such early studies as Willard B. Gatewood's *Black Americans and the White Man's Burden, 1898–1903* (1975), it is a tradition of historical inquiry that recognizes that race and racism are by no means American inventions and consequently probes such questions as how epistemologies of race travel across national and colonial boundaries, how black subjects at home are interpellated by racial discourses generated abroad (and vice versa: how colonized subjects throughout the world are made to seem like "negroes" or, worse, "niggers" by those versed in the vocabularies of Jim Crow), and how forms of anticolonial resistance beyond the United States' borders mirror forms of antiracism gener-ated by U.S. writers, especially black writers born in or connected to the U.S. South. That Gatewood's book also borrows from Kipling for its title suggests an affinity with the present study, which focuses on white southern rather than African-American responses to late nineteenth-century U.S. imperialism yet, like *Black Americans and the White Man's Burden*, attends to the "vacillation and ambiguity" that characterizes this response.[46] More recent studies that follow in this tradition and uncover the historical complexities that make possible my rereadings of literature and culture include Nina Silber's *The Romance of Reunion* (1993), Kristin Hogansen's *Fighting for American Manhood* (2000), Vincent Rafael's *White Love* (2000), Matthew Frye Jacobson's *Barbarian Virtues* (2000), Michele Mitchell's *Righteous Propagation* (2004), Edward J. Blum's *Reforging the White Republic* (2005), Paul A. Kramer's *The Blood of Government* (2006), and Gerald Horne's *White Pacific* (2007).[47] Horne's examination of how former slaveholders beheld in the South Pacific opportunities to expand plantation agriculture and implement the forms of labor management they and their forefathers had long practiced resonates especially powerfully with the literature I study here.

A closely related body of scholarship whose influence may be detected in the chapters that follow is more recent in its development. Dating from the early 1990s, it is a body of literary and cultural criticism that insists on rereading U.S. culture in light of U.S. imperialism. As Amy Kaplan argues in an essay identifying what was once "the absence of empire from the study of American culture," imperialism is "not only about foreign diplomacy or international relations . . . [but] also about consolidating domestic cultures and negotiating intranational relations."[48] Since that essay appeared as an introduction to *Cultures of United States Imperialism* (1993), a volume edited by Kaplan and Donald Pease, the subjects of empire, colonialism, and postcoloniality have been central to numerous studies of U.S. literature and culture. Some reexamine the ways in which U.S. writers and artists have responded to the nation's imperial wars and expansionist foreign policies. Others reconsider how writers have contributed to a "culture of imperialism" even when writing about "domestic" issues or issues that seem on the surface far removed from discussions of empire. Of particular note are studies that do both: for example, Gail Bederman's *Manliness and Civilization* (1995), John Carlos Rowe's *Literary Culture and U.S. Imperialism* (2000), Laura Wexler's *Tender Violence* (2000), Shelley Streeby's *American Sensations* (2002), and Kaplan's *The Anarchy of Empire in the Making of U.S. Culture* (2002). Such studies reveal what Rowe terms "an imperial heritage—a repertoire of methods for domination—on which the United States drew in the nineteenth century" and afterward.[49] The present study (perhaps in turn) draws heavily on these studies and the methodologies they develop for uncovering what Kaplan calls "the inextricable connections between national identity and imperial expansion" that characterize U.S. culture.[50] By focusing on the southern plantation, however, *Romances of the White Man's Burden* examines a space that figures only occasionally (and certainly never centrally) in the studies just named. It thus addresses what might be considered a conspicuous oversight in the scholarly conversation, given the fact that, Streeby excepted, each of these studies pays considerable attention to the late nineteenth and early twentieth centuries yet none examines how central the plantation had become in the culture of the period.[51] The space deserves more attention, for in the plantation South we may perceive a locality in which regional distinctiveness, national centrality, and imperial expansiveness are being imagined simultaneously. To paraphrase Kaplan, it constitutes an outpost of "domestic culture" in which "international relations" are being worked out *intra*nationally as writers imagine the plantation's denizens as embodiments of "Africa" and "America" and their relationships as virtual forms of "foreign diplomacy" being conducted in a localized context.

The plantation does figure prominently in the third body of scholarship to which the present study is indebted, one that may be considered a direct descendant of both historical studies of race and empire and cultural studies of empire and U.S. literature. Called by many the "new southern studies," it seeks to relocate the South "beyond traditional boundaries and into often neglected territories of the Americas," as Houston Baker and Dana Nelson urge in an important issue of the journal *American Literature* ("Violence, the Body, and 'The South'") in 2001.[52] Because it links the U.S. South with the Caribbean, portions of South and Central America, islands in the South Pacific, and other spaces bound together by slavery and postslavery, the plantation serves logically to invite postcolonial and transnational inquiries and to disrupt what Stuart Hall has called "earlier, nation-centered imperial grand narratives."[53] Several recent studies do exactly this. They explore what Jessica Adams terms "the lingering anxious relationship between the South and the Caribbean" by performing comparative studies of the plantation literatures produced in both regions.[54] These include George Handley's *Postslavery Literatures in the Americas* (2000), Nathalie Dessens's *Myths of the Plantation Society* (2003), Valérie Loichot's *Orphan Narratives* (2007), Hosam M. Aboul-Ela's *Other South* (2007), and Elizabeth Christine Russ's *The Plantation in the Postslavery Imagination* (2009), as well as several of the essays collected in Jon Smith and Deborah Cohn's *Look Away!* (2004) and all of the essays included in Adams, Michael Bibler, and Cécile Accilien's *Just Below South* (2007). Many of these studies, in turn, build upon the theories about plantation culture generated by writers focused more on the Caribbean, especially Édouard Glissant, who writes in *Poetics of Relation* (1990) that "the ruins of the Plantation have affected American cultures all around," and Antonio Benítez-Rojo, who observes similarly in *The Repeating Island* (1989) that "the Atlantic is today the Atlantic" because of the plantation, the institution born as a result of "the copulation of Europe . . . with the Caribbean archipelago."[55]

Though the present study focuses exclusively on U.S. texts, it benefits greatly from the ideas generated by these more comparative approaches. Especially helpful are the discussions of genealogy central to Handley's and Loichot's studies. As Handley rightly notes, genealogy is "the central theme of postslavery novels" since, on the one hand, novels that celebrate the plantation do so by glorifying white father–white son lineages while of course denying the lines of descent that connect slaves to masters. On the other hand, novels that deromanticize the plantation do so by recognizing the fact of miscegenation, often staging scenes in which a planter's nonwhite heirs demand acknowledgment. Loichot extends this line of thought, identifying orphanhood as a defining condition for slaves and their descendants yet also exploring how, through narrative, "slaves or subjects in a subordinate position imagine fictive kinships not imposed by the master or master-text."[56] *Romances of the White Man's Burden* concentrates on what Handley terms "the story of the slave owner's aspiration to a clear and exclusionary line of descent and of inheritance from white father to white son," which is to say, on the plantation's licit rather than illicit relations.[57] The latter of these has received more attention in the scholarship on plantation literatures, perhaps because the former—the dream of pure patrilineal descent that characterizes much postbellum plantation fiction (and will later be recharacterized by Faulkner in *Absalom, Absalom!* as the "design")—seems not only idealistic but simplistic. It is the half of the story that seems too easy to know, the illusion too readily dispelled. As each of these chapters will show, however, the dream of a white father–white son transmission of authority and reproduction of culture generates its own set of complexities. For the fatherless Joel Chandler Harris it serves as a sign of what he lacks utterly and thus may help to explain his paradoxical veneration of both the authoritative planter-father and the ex-slave "uncle" capable of signifying on him. For Henry W. Grady, Thomas Nelson Page, Thomas Dixon Jr., and (as we have seen already) George Cary Eggleston it provides the model for a very different kind of "fictive kinship," namely one in which the nation's founders—its virtual "fathers"—are remembered for having also been planters (making the nation something like a grand plantation, its white citizens rather like planters' legitimate heirs, and its black citizens very much like perpetual slaves). For Faulkner, by contrast, the idea of planter patrilineality proves easy enough to expose as a national fantasy yet difficult to dislodge as a social reality and even more difficult to relinquish in favor of alternative models of fictive kinship and imagined community.

Given this selection of authors, *Romances of the White Man's Burden* is thus closer in methodology to those examples of a "new southern studies" oriented less toward comparative cultural criticism and more toward rereading the U.S. South via the tools provided by postcolonial theory and historicist inquiry. I am thinking especially of Leigh Anne Duck's *The Nation's Region* (2006), Jessica Adams's *Wounds of Returning* (2007), Harilaos Stecopoulos's *Reconstructing the World* (2008), Melanie Benson's *Disturbing Calculations* (2008), Peter Schmidt's *Sitting in Darkness* (2008), and (again) several of the essays collected in Smith and Cohn's *Look Away!*[58] Adams's discussion of how the plantation generates property relations that long outlive the institution itself (and how it may therefore be said still to "haunt" U.S. culture) is among the insights that guide the present study. Likewise, Stecopoulos's revisionary image of the South ("this supposedly alien region") as "a third term that unsettles the binary thinking so often used to theorize the racial politics of nation and empire" describes perfectly the regional space discussed in the chapters that follow.[59] *Romances of the White Man's Burden* differs from these studies in that most of them focus on the twentieth-century South.[60] My study focuses instead on the late nineteenth and early twentieth centuries, discovering in this period (and in particular the years 1887–1902) a turning point in how the South was written about locally by white southern writers and received nationally by white U.S. audiences. Related to this—and perhaps more significant—most studies of the South, its "postcoloniality," and its relationships to U.S. imperialism are interested in the region's resemblances to colonized spaces elsewhere in the world. Stecopoulos is especially persuasive on this point, discussing "depictions of the region [that] have both illustrated the longstanding federal failure to foster democracy in the U.S. southeast, and, at the same time, highlighted surprising connections among poor and usually black southerners and people of color in the developing world."[61] My study, by contrast, focuses on the hitherto underexamined claim that the plantation South had "largely produced this nation," to cite Thomas Nelson Page again, and continued to stand for it even (and especially) as alternative visions of national and global community were being produced by its subaltern subjects (by "X-Ray" in "Charity Begins at Home," for example, or by Du Bois in "The Burden of Black Women"). In my conclusion I argue further that the legendarily "backward" South written about by southern modernists (and by such critics as H. L. Mencken, who

Figure 1. "Love Is the Sum of It All": original sheet music included in Eggleston's novel (1907).

hoped to goad a new generation of southern cultural workers into proving him wrong) had in a sense to be invented. The prevailing literary image of the region during the preceding half-century—the imperial plantation South studied in the chapters that follow—was its diametric opposite. It posited white southern advancement, trumpeted white southern tradition, and imagined that white America, if only it could rediscover its plantation roots, would conquer the world.

To reread turn-of-the-century U.S. culture with these considerations in mind is to be able to see in a novel as undeniably minor—and almost as undeniably bad—as George Cary Eggleston's *Love Is the Sum of It All,* a text that nevertheless illuminates the period in which it was produced. The novel

did not earn the admiration of many of its original reviewers. One noted that, in general, Eggleston possessed "no special gift" for "long, involved plot-making": "His novels are simple love-stories which march straight along with just a modicum of obstacle here and there to block temporarily the course of true love."[62] Another reviewer, writing specifically about *Love Is the Sum of It All*, was even less generous, calling its protagonist's speech "for the most part twaddle" and observing that its author's command of the language failed to impress, too: "As a social critic, Mr. Eggleston has nothing new or important to say. He does not even say what he has to say well."[63] The book's title comes from a love song its protagonist, a young Virginia gentleman named Warren Rhett, had penned and published in a magazine years before the novel commences. When he first meets the young woman with whom he will fall in love and eventually be married, she is, of course, singing his song. The chapter in which this happens even includes lyrics and sheet music, should readers have wished to recreate the scene for themselves (Fig. 1). In conversations between the two lovers over the remainder of the novel, the song's refrain serves almost as a form of punctuation:

> "If I must die, as I think I must, I want your arms about me at the last, so that I may feel that the wrong I did you is forgiven."
> When he handed the letter hack to Hazel after reading it, Rhett said: "You are right. Go!"
> "Yes," she answered. " 'Love is the sum of it all.' " (379)

What *is* actually noteworthy about *Love Is the Sum of It All* is its scope. Set on a failing Virginia plantation during the early 1890s, the novel draws comparisons between it and the relatively obvious—the old plantations of the Old Dominion's antebellum heyday—as well as the far less predictable—large-scale construction sites in Mexico, Argentina, and the Zambezi River region of southern Africa, for example. Here is how. Its protagonist, Rhett, is summoned back to Virginia at the beginning of the novel to take possession of the family's vast, two-hundred-year-old plantation. His father has just died. The plantation actually constitutes an unwelcomed responsibility for him, however, for while he had grown up on it and retains a filial affection for it, he himself is a civil engineer and businessman—a graduate from one of the North's "great schools of engineering" who had gone on to establish a contracting firm in New York and now does business around the world (31). He is stunningly successful, having designed and supervised the construction of bridges, tunnels, irrigation schemes, and other projects in the Arizona and New Mexico territories, Mexico, and Central and South America. (It is in his spare time that he writes love songs. Novels, too: he published two plus a volume of poetry during his twenties. For a time he also busted broncos in Texas.) Toward the end of the novel his firm is successful in its bid to build a series of bridges over the Zambezi River, and in its final pages he and his new wife set sail for Africa, both for their honeymoon—the summation of Eggleston's love story—and for the commencement of the new construction project—the continuation of Rhett's Promethean career as a bringer of modernity to faraway places.

The fortune he has amassed on his own far eclipses the value of the plantation that devolves to him at the beginning of the novel. Rhett thus has no financial need of "Mannamac" and would likely sell it, in fact, were it not for his beloved stepmother who still resides on the plantation and lives as if it secures her credit enough to finance "the only style of living that she kn[ows] anything about," one characterized by "a lavishness of hospitality" and "a generously open house, with four or five times as many servants as were needed" (30, 39). It does not. Besieged by creditors and tenanted by former slaves willing to labor enough to subsist but not so much that the surplus value might fund their mistress's parties, the Rhett plantation is thus an encumbrance: an "utterly uneconomic" institution, he thinks to himself upon inheriting it, that now shelters dozens of "shiftless" hangers-on and is presided over by a mistress of an "inconsequent" turn of mind, hence a burden, quite literally, upon a white man, him (11, 32).

He determines to try to revive it, however, and for reasons that may be said actually to accumulate over the course of the novel. At first they involve only his stepmother and his unwillingness to see her "compelled to give up all that remains of" the dream-life of the old plantation "and lapse into some more wisely economic way of living . . . that must rob life—so far as she is concerned—of all its desirability" (12). Soon afterward it becomes a personal challenge: a question of whether he, the man of industry and business, can reform the plantation system and solve the "negro problem" in the process by applying principles of modern agricultural science and rational economics. (He succeeds on the first count by importing Italian gardeners from New York and transforming Mannamac into an enormous truck farm that serves the growing food markets of the urban Northeast. The "negro problem," he decides, is best solved simply by allowing them to sink or swim as wage earners in a postplantation economy.)

What becomes his paramount reason for wanting to restore the plantation, however, is what it has done for *him*—how it has made possible, he comes to believe, his successful careers as an engineer, international businessman, part-time artist, and occasional buckaroo. While the North had provided him his engineering degree and allowed him to start his business, it was the plantation South that had inculcated in him a set of leadership skills that none of his fellow contractors possessed. Seen from this vantage, a plantation upbringing even becomes a form of capitalist competitive advantage, a mode of training that ought to be preserved because of what it enables within a global industrial economy rather than a set of social practices that ought to be regarded as outmoded and simply sung about in Stephen Foster–like ballads. This begins to become clear to Rhett one-fourth of the way into the novel when, in response to his lover's observation that he possesses "a peculiarly commanding manner," he explains how he "ha[d] had as many as two thousand Chinese coolies under my command" while supervising the construction of a railroad in Peru (117). He recounts how he had served similarly elsewhere, each time overseeing the construction of some state-of-the-art structure yet each time having to manage a crew of "coolies, Mexican peons, convicts . . . the offscourings, the refuse, of civilization and semicivilization" (95). He recognizes this finally as his destiny—this being charged with bringing about modernity while superintending "semicivilization"—when he receives the Zambezi River contract. Though he had once sought to leave the plantation and pursue a career that emphasized innovation over tradition, he comes in the end to believe that what has made him so successful is what the old plantation has imparted to him "naturally": "In the conduct of my business, I must not only be master—I must be masterful. I am set to command men in large numbers, and they are mostly inferior men" (117) (Fig. 2).

It is while being served breakfast by a former family slave, in fact, that Rhett commences the reverie from which I cited at the beginning of this introduction: the musings about "this old Southern life" and how it had once nurtured the nation's Founding Fathers, permitting them to "do the thinking that created this republic and its institutions." By the end of the novel he sees himself as having followed in their footsteps, bringing the marvels of modern thought to the world's less advanced places and thus, like "Washington and Jefferson and Madison and the rest" before him, emerging from the old plantation with forms of enlightenment to spread "in other lands." Rhett's intellectual journey, such as it is, thus involves coming to believe something Henry W. Grady had argued in one of his essays in *The New South*: that "the new South is simply the old South under new conditions" and that its "sons," seeking "unhindered comradeship with the world," were now impelled to "fight under new conditions, for greater ends, in broader fields" (146, 161–62). What "empire" in its various forms will provide them, both Grady and Eggleston imagine, are new opportunities in which to remain masterful.

R ead out of context, Eggleston's "plantation romance" and its story of civil engineering superheroism is absurd. Read in context it is merely laughable. It is far from the purpose of *Romances of the White Man's Burden* to recover a literary and cultural context that might make *Love Is the Sum of It All* seem less than preposterous, but it is, in a sense, the point of this study to explain why such a novel as Eggleston's might have seemed unremarkable when it was first published—why one reviewer would observe that "as a social critic Mr. Eggleston has nothing new or important to say." To take seriously Albion W. Tourgée's claim that the South had come to seem "the seat of intellectual

Figure 2. "I am set to command men in large numbers": illustration from *Love Is the Sum of It All* (1907).

empire in America" by 1888 is to reconfigure our sense of the imaginative geographies of the late nineteenth- and early twentieth-century United States. It is to begin to understand why Joel Chandler Harris's *Uncle Remus* (1880) was celebrated not only as a great work of local color fiction but also as a national contribution to world literature; why Dixon's *The Leopard's Spots* sold more than one hundred thousand copies in 1902 and its successor, *The Clansman,* more than half a million in 1905; why Eggleston would attempt his own story of a planter's son becoming a world-beater in 1907; and why, in 1913, when Thomas Nelson Page was appointed U.S. ambassador to Italy, the *New York Times* would applaud him as a "thoroughly representative citizen . . . a man of exactly the quality that most [Americans] like to see accredited by the Washington government to European courts."[64] Knowing how national the plantation South and its "representative citizens" had come to seem by the early 1900s also allows us to understand better the alternate visions of the region being produced during the period by writers ranging from Charles Chesnutt and Mark Twain to Anna Julia Cooper and W. E. B. Du Bois to Ellen Glasgow and Margaret Mitchell. Du Bois's assertion in *The Souls of Black Folk* that "arguing with Mr. Thomas Nelson Page" is "the imperative duty of thinking black men" seems all the more urgent when one considers that Page presumed to speak not just for the white South but for "America," and in a conclusion to this study I discuss how such texts as *Souls* might be reread as texts that seek actually to reposition the plantation within the national imaginary and to incorporate black folk into a new narrative of American coming-into-being.[65]

The four chapters that follow focus on the writings of white southern men. I have chosen this path because, although the writings of others, Du Bois especially, shape everything I have to say in this book, recent scholarship has actually had more to say about the counternarratives evoked by plantation fiction than about the more official, more celebratory narratives to which Du Bois and others were responding.[66] This study proceeds from the belief that the more celebratory narratives are worthy of close consideration, too. Chapter 1 does this by examining Harris's "Uncle Remus" books and other writings about the plantation, paying particular attention to their reception: how, despite their tendency toward ambivalence and irony, they became positioned culturally as portraits of a social system worth imitating. Chapter 2 explores two writers for whom the plantation was more straightforwardly exemplary: Grady, who was actually close friends with Harris and set forth in his "New South" writings and speeches a program for how white southern men could continue their fathers' legacies by seeking "broader fields" of conquest; and Page, who in effect translated Grady's political vision into several works of popular fiction and whose various careers, culminating in his 1913–1919 ambassadorship, represent a kind of fulfillment of the "New South" ideal. Chapter 3 focuses on Dixon, the U.S. writer who went the furthest in imagining the old plantations of the antebellum period and the new American empire of the turn of the century as spaces historically distinct but racially contiguous. Chapter 4 leaps from Dixon to William Faulkner, the Mississippi writer who, deservedly, has been seen as moving southern literature into new conceptual territories but who nevertheless wrote with a fascination and even sympathy toward the figure of the burdened white man, placing him in line, in surprising ways, with some of the earlier writers considered here. While it is right to assert, as Eric Sundquist has, that much of the power of Faulkner's fiction results from its insistence that "the sins of the Southern fathers and the sins of the American fathers" were and are "inextricably entangled," it is necessary also to recognize that Faulkner was not the first to behold "America" when he set out to "tell about the South."[67] His preoccupation with the South as a locus of national sin represents less a revelation than a *revision*—a rewriting of the story of the South-as-national that had been going on for more than half a century by the time Faulkner, too, turned toward the South as a field for fiction.

CHAPTER 1

Uncle Remus's Empire

The first academic study of the image of the plantation in American literature was published in 1924. Titled *The Southern Plantation: A Study of the Development and Accuracy of a Tradition*, it was written by Francis Pendleton Gaines, a native of South Carolina who had grown up and gone to college in Virginia but then, like some of the other white southern men whose writings and careers I examine in this book, had needed to travel northward before discovering in the South the subject he most wanted to explore in writing.[1] In Gaines's case this meant enrolling in Columbia University's doctoral program in English and pursuing a thesis on plantation fiction under the direction of Carl Van Doren. He published it under the university's imprint soon after having completed it. Its title gives a fair indication of what it sought to accomplish, which, as Gaines elaborates in the first chapter, was both to document and explain "the penetration of the plantation concept, as the romances have interpreted it, into the popular consciousness."[2] The book opens in a decidedly nondocumentarian manner, however, offering instead a description of a recent magazine advertisement and constructing by way of it an elaborate metaphor meant to convey the place the plantation had assumed in U.S. culture by the middle 1920s. Here is how *The Southern Plantation* begins:

> A few years ago the leading periodicals of the country carried a handsomely illustrated advertisement of a phonograph company. The scene represented an old negro who sat on a little eminence and gazed wistfully across a valley. On the opposite hill the world of actuality merged into a cloud-like vision, the semblance of the ex-slave's dream: the old plantation; a great mansion; exquisitely gowned ladies and courtly gentlemen moving with easy grace upon the broad veranda behind stalwart columns; surrounding the yard an almost illimitable stretch of white cotton; darkies singingly at work in the fields; negro quarters, off on one side, around which little pickaninnies tumbled in glad frolic. It is not a far-fetched analogy to consider the gray-haired darkey, with longing in his eyes, symbolic of the American public. On the plain of

reality, as it were, we gaze across a vale of desire to the heights of illusion, to the delectable hill—and see thereon the Southern plantation. (1)

Gaines does not name the company whose advertisement he was remembering nor the venues or years in which it ran. It may have been from the Victor Talking Machine Company, which used plantation imagery in several product promotions during the early twentieth century (Fig. 3, for example). It may also have been based on Gaines's recall of multiple advertisements, so common was plantation iconography in the material culture of the time. Whatever its source, the image that Gaines himself reconstructs at the outset of *The Southern Plantation* might be seen as remarkable only in terms of how thoroughly it mines the clichés. Its individual elements could have been borrowed from any of the hundreds of literary, musical, stage, and pictorial representations of the plantation that had been paraded before an eager U.S. public during the previous half century. Minus a steamboat, in fact, they correspond almost perfectly to the list of markers later identified by the poet Sterling Brown as characteristic of "proslavery fiction": "the grown-up slaves were contented, the pickaninnies were frolicking, the steamboat was hooting around the bend, God was in his heaven, and all was right with the world."[3] The ad's composition was similarly conventional, calling to mind the nineteenth-century plantation paintings studied recently by the anthropologist and art historian John Michael Vlach and the ways in which such works typically violated "the most common compositional rule of landscape painting" by representing their subject matter from below rather than above, "render[ing] images as seen by an upturned face, one that implicitly signaled submission and respect."[4] Its motif of an ex-slave lost in reverie, meanwhile, may have been its most derivative element. The stuff of countless dialect stories, poems, and songs, it had become by that point hackneyed even as a visual sign, having been adapted by illustrators since at least the 1870s (Figs. 4 and 5) to represent the old plantation as a dreamlike space defined by "human relations that were romantic and picturesque," as the subject of the present chapter, Joel Chandler Harris, expressed the image in words in 1904: "I know that in some of its aspects it was far more beautiful and inspiring than any of the relations that we have between employers and the employed in this day and time. . . . Slavery itself is so far in the past that it feels like a dream."[5]

While the advertisement Gaines describes, which shows that African Americans were still being made to dream the dream of the old plantation well into the twentieth century, was thus in itself unremarkable, Gaines's sense of its symbolism was much more noteworthy. By locating the plantation atop a

Figure 3. The Dream of the Old Plantation I: advertisement for Victor Talking Machines (1906). Harvard College, Widener Library.

Figure 4. The Dream of the Old Plantation II: illustration accompanying "Way Down upon the Swanee Ribber" (lyrics from Stephen Foster's 1851 song "Old Folks at Home") in *Harper's Weekly* (June 28, 1873).

Figure 5. The Dream of the Old Plantation III: cover illustration for *Two Plantation Melodies! Standard and Popular!* (1878).

"delectable hill" and imagining it as a site of virtual national pilgrimage across "a vale of desire to the heights of illusion," he was making an argument that, in its broadest contours, is not unlike the one I have thus far sought to establish: that the plantation had come to assume the status of national monument by the turn of the century. John Lowe has made a similar observation recently, seeing in some of the early twentieth century's literary and filmic celebrations of the Old South—Thomas Dixon's *The Clansman* (1905), D. W. Griffith's *The Birth of a Nation* (1915), Harry Stillwell Edwards's *Aeneas Africanus* (1919), and Margaret Mitchell's *Gone with the Wind* (1936, with David O. Selznick's film version appearing in 1939)—"the triumphant culmination of the Plantation Tradition as America's favorite mythology."[6] Grace Elizabeth Hale has argued similarly that "the white South" in effect "won the peace" during these decades by popularizing its narrative of history (a "regional autobiography fixed in a plantation romance," she calls it) and modeling how a form of local pride, predicated though it may have been upon myth, could be elaborated into national fantasy.[7] Gaines might be said to have anticipated all of these arguments—and by more than seventy years—if only in his recognition of the *nationality* of the old plantation. He saw the irony in this, too, remarking that "however violent may be our profession of political equality . . . our romantic hunger is satisfied by some allegory of aristocracy." "The plantation romance," he concludes, "remains our chief social idyl of the past" (2–4).

Prescient though he was in his analysis of the place of the plantation within an early twentieth-century symbolic economy of U.S. nationhood, however, Gaines seems much more a man of his time when writing about the "old negro" perched on the hill. Indeed, the metaphor that opens Gaines's study deserves further scrutiny. Its suggestion that "the gray-haired darkey, with longing in his eyes" was somehow "symbolic of the American public" (and that this "analogy," moreover, was not at all "far-fetched") raises questions about the ways in which "the American public" was being conceptualized racially during the period. As a number of historians, Hale especially, have argued recently, it was during the late nineteenth and early twentieth centuries that the United States became "white." To flesh this out somewhat: during these decades what had long likely been assumed to be the color of the country became a matter of explicit assertion, the claims being made in forms of public discourse ranging from legal documents and political speeches to scientific papers, literary texts, and films. The shift followed the ratifications of the Fourteenth and Fifteenth Amendments (in 1868 and 1870), which removed race as a means of disqualifying persons from U.S. citizenship or denying them suffrage, and it took place in conjunction with various other historical developments perceived by many at the time to represent threats to white hegemony: increases in foreign immigration, escalations of conflicts with indigenous groups in the Great Plains and southwestern territories, an anti-U.S. insurgency in the Philippines, and so on. In light of such crises, each of which involved intensifications of anxieties surrounding race, class, and cultural diversity, it is hardly surprising that the plantation would be idealized as a space defined by the "beautiful and inspiring . . . relations" envisioned by Harris as well as by the "delectable" spatial and racial hierarchies perceived by Gaines.

Yet there is something to be made of the nonchalance with which Gaines conflates white and black in the opening paragraph of *The Southern Plantation*—how he makes practically interchangeable "the American public" and "the gray-haired darkey" in his revelation of a national "wistful[ness]" toward the old plantation. Why, I wish to ask, did it seem to him such an uncomplicated thing to do—to make analogous the two entities, the one corporate and white, the other individual and black? Why was it not "far-fetched" thus to paint a white citizenry in virtual blackface or, more radically, to imply that, at its heart, the nation might be "negro"? In other words, why, toward the end of a period marked by so many determined efforts to make "Americanness" synonymous with whiteness, would Gaines, and with such facility, equate it with blackness as well? Why make "our" desires toward the plantation identical to his, the "old negro's"?

I want to propose a two-word answer to these questions now—Uncle Remus—and devote the remainder of this chapter to explaining what I mean. My reasons for offering so brief an answer to so lengthy a series of questions are several. They begin with Uncle Remus's pervasiveness within U.S. popular culture, a sense of which I seek to convey early in the chapter. They extend much further, however, and encompass the facts that Remus was celebrated also as a great *literary* achievement and Harris, his creator, as a "genius," a term used to describe him by figures as illustrious themselves as Theodore Roosevelt and Mark Twain. Roosevelt in fact would call Harris's writings "among the most striking and powerful permanent contributions to literature that have been produced on this side of the ocean," a statement that sounds like hyperbole now yet, during its day, was not at all uncommon.[8] Translated into multiple languages and published in dozens of countries, the Uncle Remus books were among the most successful U.S. literary exports of the Gilded Age. They captivated tens of thousands of readers both at home and abroad, conveying a sense of the "genuine flavor of the old plantation," as Harris described the purpose of the original collection of Remus tales, yet doing so in a form that was intended also to be somewhat disorienting, involving as it did "the local allusions . . . the shrewd observations, the curious retorts, the homely thrusts, the quaint comments, and the humorous philosophy of the race of which Uncle Remus is a type."[9] Indeed, it was his translation of "negro" subjectivity into terms that seemed both understandable and out of reach that made Harris himself appear so compelling a figure to his contemporaries. He seemed to some, in fact, American literature's first white man genuinely capable of black thought, and he invented a new way of defending the old plantation in the process, namely as the lone space in U.S. culture that enabled the comprehension of "negroes." Recognizing this sheds additional light on Gaines, for by the time he equated "the American public" with a "gray-haired darkey" in 1924, American readers had come to know the old plantation as more than just an assemblage of clichés; they had been exposed to it also as a *point of view* and were fascinated by the possibility that it had imparted to at least one of its white sons an ability to see the world through black eyes. It explains furthermore why Harris serves as the first figure I explore at length in this study, for it was with Uncle Remus—a term that during Harris's lifetime referred both to the writer himself and to the "venerable old darkey" he had invented—that a post-Reconstruction plantation fiction tradition began to aspire to represent more than regional difference. It began in fact to formulate the idea that the plantation South might have something to teach the world.[10]

First, however: who was Uncle Remus? The elderly ex-slave who served as his author's alter ego and figured so prominently in U.S. popular culture until the middle twentieth century is no longer exactly a household name. He is certainly no longer mentioned alongside Cooper's Natty Bumppo, Irving's Diedrich Knickerbocker, Hawthorne's Hester Prynne, Stowe's Uncle Tom, Alcott's Jo March, Twain's Tom, Huck, and Jim, or any of the other characters one might expect to encounter now in discussions of how U.S. fiction developed during the nineteenth century. Less than a century ago, however, this was exactly the sort of company Uncle Remus kept. He was ranked "one of the best characters in American literature" by no less a judge than Sterling Brown in 1937.[11] Forty years earlier, he was called "one of the very few creations of American writers worthy of a place in the gallery of the immortals" by William Malone Baskervill, an early historian of southern literature.[12] Baskervill thought Uncle Remus's place among U.S. literary icons was "not very far from Rip Van Winkle['s]." According to a 1926 survey of college and high-school English teachers intended to determine which works of American fiction deserved "a permanent place" among the world's great books, Remus actually outranked Rip Van Winkle: *The Sketch Book* came in at number thirteen, *Uncle Remus* at number five. Only Poe's collected short stories, *The Scarlet Letter*, *The Adventures of Huckleberry Finn*, and *The Last of the Mohicans* ranked higher. *Moby-Dick* came in at number six, one place below Harris's debut collection, while the work of American literature to which *Uncle Remus* was most often compared initially, *Uncle Tom's Cabin*, barely cracked the top ten (Fig. 6).[13]

The magazine that conducted the survey admitted that its methods were far from scientific and its results offered more in a spirit of prompting further debate. It did note, however, that "as to the first six" books to make it on to the list "there was little difference of judgment." *Uncle Remus*, in short, once seemed to belong as surely within a canon of great American works of fiction as did *The Adventures of Huckleberry Finn* and *The Last of the Mohicans*.[14] The question of why it does no longer is not difficult to answer. Having returned to the plantation on which he had once labored as a slave to work for his deceased master's sister and her family, Uncle Remus embodies the popular postbellum idea that plantation life and work were more preferable for black southerners than the alternatives, namely city life in an industrializing "New South" or emigration to an industrialized North.[15] He thus serves as a symbol of continuity and seems to prove, by virtue of his having stayed put, that slave life had never really been all that bad, even in Georgia. He suggests furthermore that Reconstruction had achieved very little and that efforts to advance black southerners' civil rights and material well-being had only interfered with a social system whose adherents knew best how to accommodate each other. Acknowledging that there had been a "practical reconstruction which has been going on to some extent since the war in spite of the politicians," Harris, like most white southerners, objected vehemently to the idea that someone from outside of the region knew better than its own white citizens how to rebuild the plantation South (12).

To many recent readers Uncle Remus has thus seemed little more than instrumental—a propagandistic device invented at the end of Reconstruction in order to oppose the social and political remaking of the former slave states. He has been called "an image reminiscent of pro-slavery plantation novels," "a kind of literary minstrelsy," an embodiment "of the plantation myth of the lovable, happy darky," and even "a docile, contented slave," this last one involving an error of fact—Remus is an *ex*-slave in most of what Harris wrote about him—that is nevertheless illustrative.[16] The character seems so content to remain on the plantation and serve its white owners, after all, that, in the eyes of some, he might as well have remained a slave. Even Brown, the African American poet and critic who saw in Uncle Remus much more than a minstrel

"Million" Books and "Best" Books

A Glance Towards the Top of the Fiction America has Read and Produced in Three Hundred Years

By H. W. L.

 IT IS easy to agree with the superior attitude which proclaims that all lists of "best" books are futile. "Supreme Art," thundered out Victor Hugo, "is the region of Equals. There is no primacy among masterpieces." And then, be it noted, he goes on, in the very next pages of his most stimulating and least read work,—to pick out the highest peaks of the mountain-range of genius:

> "We repeat it: to choose between these men, to prefer one to the other, to point with the finger to the first among these first, is impossible. All are the Mind. Perhaps, by the strictest measurements—and yet every objection would be legitimate,—one might mark out as the highest among these summits, Homer, Æschylus, Job, Isaiah, Dante and Shakespeare."

Whether in genius or divinity, the moment we humans admit a thing to be immeasurable, at once arises a raging necessity to measure it, by any yardstick we have handy.

Admitting all that can be said as to the lack of finality in such lists, the indefiniteness of standards, and all the rest, one point seems occasionally forgotten: we do "teach literature"—in some hundreds of colleges to half a million young men and women; in some hundreds of thousands of schools to perhaps fourteen million children; in Chautauquas, reading circles, lectures, literary clubs, correspondence courses, and the like.

And the beginning of such teaching is to select, from the millions of books the world has stored up, those which are best worth studying. Once admit the necessity and possibility of choice, and where is the line to be drawn?

Moreover, all such lists are instructive and entertaining—always remembering that they shed more light on the makers than they do on literature. Any one man picking from the World Library measures chiefly himself,—quite as a nation's god measures the spiritual level, the ideals and culture of that nation.

Anyhow, it is a more modest piece of research undertaken here.

It seemed as if it might be of interest to know just what is being taught in our colleges and high schools as regards American fiction, and its comparative rank. So we asked some thousands of these professors and teachers.

The specific point is: if some condescending international critic were to intimate that the United States had not yet produced *anything* really worthy of a place beside the acknowledged masterpieces of fiction,—which ten works by American writers could be selected that would best represent our bid for a permanent place in this section of the world's literature?

About 400 men and women engaged in teaching literature answered the questionnaire.

As to the first six, there was little difference of judgment, though the choice was practically unanimous only with Numbers 1 and 2:

			Published
1.	Tales	Edgar Allan Poe	1839–45
2.	The Scarlet Letter	Nathaniel Hawthorne	1850
3.	The Adventures of Huckleberry Finn	Mark Twain	1885
4.	The Last of the Mohicans	James Fenimore Cooper	1826
5.	Uncle Remus	Joel Chandler Harris	1881
6.	Moby Dick, or The White Whale	Herman Melville	1851

At this point expected differences of opinion became much in evidence. The seventh book, for example, was picked by less than half as many as agreed on "Moby Dick." But these were the remaining four works selected:

			Published
7.	The Rise of Silas Lapham	William Dean Howells	1885
8.	Ethan Frome	Edith Wharton	1911
9.	Tales	Bret Harte	1870 *et seq.*
10.	Uncle Tom's Cabin	Harriet Beecher Stowe	1852

382

Figure 6. Uncle Remus as Literature: Henry Wysham Lanier's "'Million' Books and 'Best' Books," *Golden Book Magazine* (September 1926).

figure, struggled with this aspect of his character. Though he believed Uncle Remus to have been the most fully realized representation of a figure from the black *folk* that any U.S. writer, white or black, had managed to produce by 1880, he also recognized that Harris's "venerable, pampered Negro" seems at times "less a man [than] a walking delegate" for Jim Crow.[17] It is this image—this side of a character who could be (and in fact has been) perceived as more complex—that has seemed salient since the middle of the twentieth century. The fact that the 1946 Walt Disney film *Song of the South* portrayed only the "happy darky" aspects of his character served to precipitate what likely would have happened anyway, namely his fall from the status of icon and his relegation to what might be thought of as the museum of American popular culture curiosities. He no longer even merits the sort of debate that surrounds Twain's Jim or Cooper's Chingachgook—the *Does he show that his author was a racist?* debate. Uncle Remus has seemed so convincingly an example of white southern racism for so long that, in the words of Robert Hemenway, he belongs not in the "gallery of immortals" envisioned by William Malone Baskervill but rather in "the gallery of racist stereotypes that includes Aunt Jemima and Uncle Ben."[18]

The character will, no doubt, never again figure as a representative of the nation's literature, certainly not in the sense that he did a century ago. Yet if the story of why Uncle Remus no longer symbolizes "America" is fairly easily told, the story of how he became so celebrated in the first place requires more space. It is more complex but in many ways more worth telling, for it reveals better than any other phenomenon of the period the new associations the southern plantation was acquiring as the nation itself was being remade in the wake of Reconstruction, transforming from "a mostly rural, fundamentally agrarian society," as Nell Irvin Painter explains it, into "one that was largely urban and industrial" and therefore in need of new ways of representing itself to itself. Some of the symbols of national modernity Americans embraced during the period are obvious. As Painter notes, "prosperity, industrial might, and colonial possessions symbolized the greatness of the United States, its coming of age, its sudden awakening to an expanding world in which it had a major role to play."[19] Yet to explain how Harris's "quaint" creation may have belonged to such a world—how indeed Uncle Remus may have belonged to an "awakening . . . expanding world" not simply as an outlet of nostalgia but rather as a sign of the plantation South's relative advancement—requires attention to the complexities that characterize Harris's books as well as their receptions among diverse audiences throughout the nation and the world. The Georgia-born ex-slave, who for all we know never journeyed farther than the eighty-or-so miles that separate rural "Putmon County," Georgia, from Atlanta, the unofficial capital of an industrializing New South, nevertheless turns out to have been quite the world traveler.

One might begin to sketch this story by noting that Remus was born into a culture that retained a special fascination for elderly black "uncles." As Sarah Meer has recently noted, *Uncle Tom's Cabin* and the stage productions based on it remained popular long after the end of the Civil War and the abolition of slavery. It became a different text, of course—Meer cites a 1934 playbill promoting *Uncle Tom's Cabin* as "a drama of our country, and the only one that is a part of our Nation's History"—"but its status as a cultural wonder or as a major national phenomenon had by no means diminished."[20] Harris could thus have counted on his readers not simply to remember Stowe's title character but quite possibly to have remained engaged with him as well. They might have reread the novel, new editions of which were still being published during the late 1870s, or they might have seen any of forty-nine "Tom Show" troupes that Linda Williams has recently identified as having toured the country in 1879.[21]

Indeed, Harris encouraged the comparison. In the introduction to *Uncle Remus, His Songs and His Sayings* (1880) (Fig. 7) he invites his readers to consider the collection "a curiously sympathetic supplement to Mrs. Stowe's wonderful defense of slavery as it existed in the South" (4). He does this in the introduction's second paragraph, suggesting that he may have expected readers already to have had Stowe's character in mind when they opened his book. Intended surely to catch them off guard (Stowe a *defender* of slavery?) and alert the warier among them of his own predilection toward irony, the statement insinuates rather than states confrontationally Harris's intent to defend the old plantation. It makes the polemical nature of his own text seem even milder by offering what was still a rarity in 1880: a word of praise for the author of *Uncle Tom's Cabin* from a white man of the South. If Stowe, after all, could be thought of as having done that which Harris alleges—"Mrs. Stowe . . . attacked the possibilities of slavery with all the eloquence of genius; but the same genius painted the portrait of the Southern slave-owner, and defended him"—then his own task became easier. He needed merely to "supplement" *Uncle Tom's Cabin* by showing what could have happened on the old Kentucky plantation had Tom's original master, the benevolent Arthur Shelby, maintained better control over his finances and not been forced to sell his prized slave down the river.[22]

UNCLE REMUS

HIS SONGS AND HIS SAYINGS

THE FOLK-LORE OF THE OLD PLANTATION

By JOEL CHANDLER HARRIS

*WITH ILLUSTRATIONS BY FREDERICK S. CHURCH AND
JAMES H. MOSER*

NEW YORK
D. APPLETON AND COMPANY
1, 3, AND 5 BOND STREET
1881

Figure 7. Introducing Uncle Remus: title page from *Uncle Remus, His Songs and His Sayings* (1881).

The comparisons go deeper. Harris describes Uncle Remus in the first collection as "towering" and "picturesque"—a "sable patron" who possesses a "simple, serious face" as well as a "strong, musical voice" that he uses for the most part to win favor with white folk (176, 136, 64). Stowe had introduced her title character thirty years earlier in a passage of physical description whose terms were notably similar:

> At this table was seated Uncle Tom, Mr. Shelby's best hand, who, as he is to be the hero of our story, we must daguerreotype for our readers. He was a large, broad-chested, powerfully-made man, of a full glossy black, and a face whose truly African features were characterized by an expression of grave and steady good sense, united with much kindliness and benevolence. There was something about his whole air self-respecting and dignified, yet united with a confiding and humble simplicity.[23]

Tom was gifted with a resonant voice, too, which he uses in some of *Uncle Tom's Cabin*'s most famous scenes to sing hymns to little Eva and teach her about the possibilities of heaven—scenes that, as Stowe's novel does so often, make the abhorrent institution of slavery seem also somehow providential. Nothing nearly so consequential hangs upon the central relationship of *Uncle Remus, His Songs and His Sayings*. Its evocation of Tom and Eva is unmistakable, however, for Harris pairs the sizable Remus with a white boy similar in age and heritage to the "fair, high-bred child" at the center of *Uncle Tom's Cabin* and constructs a relationship between the two in which Remus, like Tom, plays the role of teacher-storyteller and the little boy, like little Eva, returns daily for a new lesson. The "expression[s] of awed bewilderment" and "open-eyed wonder" the boy bestows upon Remus are not identical to "zealous . . . kind offices" with which Eva rewards Tom. They are analogous, however, for both Stowe and Harris found in the relationship between a black man and white child ways of exploring forms of cross-racial devotion that, had the white characters been adults, would have introduced complexities with which neither wished to deal.[24]

Yet the differences between the two relationships prove even more revealing. They begin, in fact, to illustrate why *Uncle Remus* invites a much greater range of receptions than do the central chapters of *Uncle Tom's Cabin*. Tom reveres Eva. In one of the novel's central chapters Stowe writes that "he loved her as something frail and earthly, yet almost worshipped her as something heavenly and divine."[25] Remus's love for the little boy may be no less genuine. It involves none of the exaltation, however, and compels him to play a rather different role with regard to the boy's welfare. He assumes "an air of affection-ate superiority as he proceeds to unfold the mysteries of plantation lore to a little child," for example. When the boy oversteps a boundary and notices an inconsistency between one story and the next, Remus lets him know that his proper role is to keep quiet and listen. The old man is also perfectly willing to scold the boy when he misbehaves, to use the lure of the second half of a story to score himself an extra piece of cake, to sing nonsense songs "calculated" simply "to puzzle the little boy," and, when his rheumatism acts up, to com-plain (12, 39–43, 119–20). One hears mules braying in the background, not choirs of angels, when Remus and the boy meet on the page.

If their relationship is more earthbound, so, too, the "mysteries" that Re-mus "unfolds" to the boy are of an entirely different nature than those Tom discloses to Eva. Tom teaches Eva about the Bible, and together they make sense of the parables of Christ and "the Revelations and the Prophecies," "the parts [of the Bible] that pleased her most."[26] Conversely, Remus teaches the little boy about Brer Rabbit, Brer Fox, and other "animils and . . . beastesses": figures from African American folktales that themselves derive substantially from African oral traditions (and that thus, as Keith Cartwright illuminates, serve as signs of "creolization," a process he defines in part as what happens when "African cultural currents [are] strong enough to cross the color line") (75).[27] Stowe may make Tom the embodiment of what she describes as a na-tive African obeisance and humility ("It is the statement of missionaries, that, of all races of the earth, none have received the Gospel with such eager do-cility as the African") (343). By representing Africa as a space to which Chris-tianity has yet to arrive, however, she makes Tom a sign of an Africa still to come ("this, o, Africa! latest called of nations"), not an African past. Remus, by contrast, calls himself "Affikin" in the original collection's final paragraph, associating "Africa" with combativeness rather than docility ("Well, you des oughter see me git my Affikin up. . . . Hit's proned inter me") and identifying in himself a violent streak not unlike those that characterize Brer Rabbit and the other "creeturs" that populate the folktales (Stowe 354, Harris 231).

The figures' origins are thus, strictly speaking, pagan and their messages prove in a very real sense profane. In "Uncle Remus Initiates the Little Boy," the first chapter of the folktales section of *Uncle Remus, His Songs and His Say-ings*, Brer Fox offers to "make frens and live naberly" with Brer Rabbit only to try twice over the next two pages to eat him (20). In "The Sad Fate of Mr. Fox," the final chapter of the section, Brer Rabbit fingers his rival after a joint raid on the innards of a cow, causing Brer Fox to be killed by Mr. Man, the cow's owner. Brer Rabbit then delivers the fox's severed head to Mrs. Fox, who, having been told that it is a piece of stew meat, puts it in a pot to boil. In one of the final scenes in the section, young Tobe Fox grows "mighty hongry" and peers inside the pot to see what is for dinner:

> Dar he see his daddy head, and wid dat he sot up a howl and tole his mammy. Miss Fox, she get mighty mad w'en she fine she cookin' her ole man head, en she call up de dogs, she did, and sickt em on Brer Rabbit; en ole Miss Fox en Tobe en de dogs, dey push Brer Rabbit so close dat he hatter take a holler tree. (146)

He escapes, of course, as he does again and again in the tales collected in the six additional Uncle Remus books Harris published during his lifetime.[28] In only a handful of the tales is his victory as complete as it is in "The Sad Fate of Mr. Fox." In none of them, however, does it occur to Brer Rabbit to turn the other cheek.

Reviewers of *Uncle Remus, His Songs and His Sayings* accepted almost immediately Harris's invitation to consider the book a "supplement" to *Uncle Tom's Cabin*. Their understandings of the relationship between the two books varied, however, suggesting that, from the beginning, Harris's text was easier to enjoy than to classify. The *New York Evening Post* noted simply that Harris had "added Uncle Remus to the gallery of popular negro types to which belong Topsy and Uncle Tom." The *Eclectic Magazine* drew a clearer distinction, finding in Uncle Tom evidence of Stowe's "depths of . . . consciousness" and "creative power" but celebrating Uncle Remus as the real thing, proof of Harris's insight into "the actual, living, typical plantation negro." Another admirer observed in 1887 that "the reality of Uncle Remus" contrasted with "the sublimity of Uncle Tom," though both characters seemed equally "loveable." Yet another, the Kentucky novelist Nancy Huston Banks, commented in 1890 that Uncle Remus had actually "supplanted Uncle Tom":

> His name is known where the name of the author is not. It has become a household word in other countries than ours; but Uncle Remus himself is distinctively American, justifying in every characteristic his national acceptance. He is the unique African product of the Anglo-Saxon new world. His fun is the peculiar outcome of African humour grafted upon American wit. And the creatures grouped about him are no less distinctively American than himself.[29]

Perhaps the most interesting comparison of the two characters came in 1896, by which point Uncle Remus had become an institution: three follow-up collections had been published during the previous decade and a half while the original had recently been reissued in a lavishly illustrated new edition. In an essay published that year in the *Bookman* yet another Kentucky writer, the novelist James Lane Allen, wondered why black characters from the lower orders had lately arrested so much more of the public's attention than had their white, upper-class counterparts. Arguing that American literature needed to pay more attention to the figure of the gentleman ("the top of our civilization," "this imperial type," "this most real and sovereign being," and so on, he called him), Allen noted ruefully that "the only two names in all the range of our fiction that have attained anything like universality of acceptance . . . are the two negroes, Uncle Tom and Uncle Remus."[30]

Such comments convey once again how major a figure Uncle Remus had come to seem by the turn of the century. These last two in particular show that he factored even into discussions of U.S. literary nationalism; he seemed an appropriate figure to mention in answer to questions about whether the nation's fiction was properly conveying the character of its people. In the opinion of Nancy Huston Banks, he showed that it was: *Uncle Remus* seemed the "unique . . . product" of the collision between African and American narrative forms and comedic voices, the sort of text that could only have come about in the United States. In the view of James Lane Allen, Remus furnished evidence that American literature needed to elevate itself. Uncle Remus and Uncle Tom may have been admirable enough as representatives of their race, yet as emblems of "America" they fell short. The attention given them had thus come at the expense of the nation's nobler beings, its "masculine types of most highly developed powers."[31] Allen therefore urged his fellow writers to produce more of the sort of text I will be discussing in the next two chapters—texts devoted above all else to the grandeur and capability of a white southern planter class and its male descendants.

Of greater relevance to the present discussion, these early comparisons between Remus and Tom suggest the range of responses Harris's character began generating from the moment he entered U.S. mass culture. As a "supplement" to Uncle Tom, Uncle Remus could seem both like and unlike his antebellum predecessor—both Tom's analogue, in the sense that he possessed many of the same attachments and character traits, and his opposite, in the sense that he spoke in a different voice about different subjects. And indeed he did inspire a range of reactions, with some seeing in him an "old darkey" whose type seemed familiar and others a veritable "new negro" whose like they had not encountered before. To readers who wished to see in Remus a portrait of black simplicity and slavelike devotedness, he acquiesced. To those who desired someone more realistic—an earthier and more human figure whose decision to remain on the plantation was a sign of his being old and set in his ways—he seemed accommodating, too. To those who wished to perceive in him someone more subversive—an ex-slave who exploits white notions of how a "negro" should conduct himself, all the while telling folktales in which the dominant animals come across as dim-witted and doomed to failure—he seemed especially rewarding. In short, Harris addressed a readership that he imagined to be "not familiar with plantation life" and promised them a portrait of "an old negro . . . who has nothing but pleasant memories of the discipline of slavery" (12). That figure then goes on to tell stories in which the oppressed class routinely outwits and occasionally wreaks violent revenge upon its oppressors. Whether readers took Harris at his word when he suggested that slavery had furnished Remus nothing but "pleasant memories"—or whether, in fact, they took this as an early sign that the book might traffic in paradox and irony—was up to them. Whatever they wished a "venerable old darkey" to be, Uncle Remus seemed happy to oblige.

R ecent critics have disagreed much more intensely over what the character symbolizes, with some seeing by way of him the persistence of age-old forms of white paternalism, others the emergence after the Civil War of new and more pernicious forms of racism, and still others various developments that can be construed now as more positive—an increased appreciation for black folk creativity and a mature recognition of southern cultural hybridity, for example. One critic has even seen by way of Harris's "darkey" a repudiation of the concept of race.[32] My point in alluding to these debates is not to resolve them. It is instead, in the context of what I have been arguing thus far about Harris, to say that the Uncle Remus books actually invite them—that they encourage a range of interpretations in which they may be seen as either reactionary or subversive, nostalgic or progressive, quaint or provocative, self-evident or ironic, racist or antiracist, and so on. They manage the *either/or* by being *both/and*—an assemblage of "songs and sayings" that tend both toward the poetic and the prosaic. Read one way, they idealize the old plantation. Read another, they show signs of greater realism. They thus accommodate readings that incline sharply toward either side of these debates as well as readings that insist upon the Remus books as paradoxical and inconclusive. As Remus himself tells the little boy when he seeks to know what happens to Brer Rabbit after the conclusion of a particular story, the tale can vary depending on who tells it as well as the circumstances in which it is told: "Some tells one tale en some tells nudder; some say dat fum dat time forrer'd de Rabbits en de Foxes make frien's en stay so; some say dey kep on quollin'. Hit look like it mixt" (147).

The books are "mixt" in other ways as well. They can be considered both children's fiction and adult's fiction, for Harris aimed deliberately to reach both audiences and was pleased when parents wrote to him thanking him for having made the effort.[33] They can be seen as both personal recollection and semiprofessional ethnography, for though Harris claimed repeatedly not to be an ethnographer himself, he was happy to reproduce his correspondence with several men who were thus employed and to intimate that, in these exchanges, it was *he* who was viewed as the authority figure when it came to the southern "negro." They can be seen as both fiction and nonfiction, for while Harris did not know an actual "Uncle Remus," he based the character on two slave folktale-tellers he had known as a child. And they can be considered both lighthearted and earnest. The very first thing Harris says in his introduction to *Uncle Remus, His Songs and His Sayings,* in fact, is that, though the book was being promoted by the D. Appleton Company as among its "humorous publications . . . its intention is perfectly serious": "it seems to me that a volume written wholly in dialect must have its solemn, not to say melancholy, features" (3).

Finally, of course, the books may be considered both "black" and "white." Harris insisted throughout his life that he had acted merely as a compiler of black folktales and that his use of dialect was intended to underscore their authenticity—their having derived from oral traditions whose idioms, rhythms, structures, and forms of signification had not been eradicated or subsumed by the dominant culture. As he writes in the introduction to the first collection, "if the language of Uncle Remus fails to give vivid hints of the really poetic imagination of the negro . . . if it does not suggest a certain picturesque sensitiveness—a curious exaltation of mind and temperament not to be defined by words—then I have reproduced the form of the dialect merely, and not the essence, and my attempt may be accounted a failure" (4). Though he had been dead for two decades by the time Sterling Brown praised him for having "kept close to the people"—"No author before Harris had recorded Negro speech with anything like his skill"—he received ample feedback during his lifetime to convince him that, in his effort to sound "black," at least, he had been successful.[34] Yet he could also write in a voice belonging conspicuously to a white man, as he does in the passage just cited. Its "exaltation" of Remus's subtlety of thought, after all, is coupled with a celebration of his race's "picturesque sensitiveness," a description as reductive as some of the more patronizing things said about African Americans in *Uncle Tom's Cabin* ("In Tom's external situation, at this time, there was, as the world says, nothing to complain of. . . . Then, too, he was in a beautiful place, a consideration to which his sensitive race was never indifferent.").[35] The passage also implies the colonialist fantasy that, though Harris cannot exactly translate "negro" oral culture and convey the full measure of what it has to say, *he gets it*. He is both inside and outside of its semiotic structures, sharing with his readers a sense of the folktales' strangeness yet also communicating a sense of familiarity that comes only when one is directly exposed to something since childhood. Michelle Birnbaum has argued insightfully that the Uncle Remus books use dialect in order to make the difference between black and white seem unmistakable, to make "race appea[r] unproblematic and, most importantly, legible."[36] They do. Yet however much Harris wished thereby to manifest racial difference, he wanted also to withhold something vital from his reader—to claim access to a black folk "essence" that even he, the talented orthographer whose ability to reproduce speech impressed such masters of dialect as Twain and James Whitcomb Riley, could not express in words. Thus his concession that, at best, his writings will "give vivid *hints* of the really poetic imagination of the negro": Harris's promise is to try very hard yet fail to convey fully how well he comprehends black culture.

Thus also his defense of the plantation. What I have argued thus far about the Remus books' amplitude—their lending themselves to being pored over by English teachers, scrutinized by ethnologists, invoked by journalists and other public figures in discussions of the South's "negro problem," and read as bedtime stories to the children of these and other adults—has been offered in order to explain why they were so popular and so critically esteemed during the late nineteenth and early twentieth centuries. It has been offered, in other words, to complete the account begun several pages ago of how and why Uncle Remus managed to seem so representatively "American" at the turn of the century. Yet I have also sought to illustrate the books' complexities with an eye toward Harris's project as he conceptualized it, which may have involved attaining international literary fame but which no doubt involved defending the plantation. His vow to "supplement" Harriet Beecher Stowe, by several measures the most successful U.S. fiction writer of the nineteenth century, suggests that his sense of ambition may have been considerable. His selectively rereading her as having "defended" "the Southern slave-owner" makes clear his more fundamental purpose, however, for it shows that, whatever literary or commercial successes Harris hoped to achieve, he was committed from almost the opening words of his debut collection to writing in vindication of his home region.

He was committed to defending it, moreover, in a way that had not been tried before, insinuating that the plantation had, in a very particular sense of the term, blackened the culture of the South and held now the same promise for the rest of the nation. This is worth pausing to consider. Harris was by no means the first white southern writer to defend the plantation. Respondents to *Uncle Tom's Cabin* had been doing so since the early 1850s, after all, and the argument that southern slave labor was more humane than northern wage labor was as old as the abolitionist contention that slavery dehumanized both the slave and the slave owner. The idea that black southerners had provided *social* enrichment to white southerners—an idea that transformed questions of property relations into questions of cultural relations and refigured slavery as a symbolic rather than a political economy—was by contrast new. When I say that Harris believed the plantation had "blackened" southern culture, I thus mean something very specific. Harris by no means advocated race-mixing in a sexual or even social sense; like most white southern men of his day he abhorred the former and thought the latter unwelcomed (and also unlikely: in a 1904 essay he called it "simply a bugaboo; for there is not now, and never has been, since the dawn of civilization, such a thing as social equality"). He also imagined plantation violence and cruelty as far more anomalous than did George Washington Cable, for example, or certainly William Wells Brown (both of whom are worth mentioning because of the important books they published—Cable's *The Grandissimes* and Brown's *My Southern Home*—in 1880, the year of Harris's debut).[37] Much more so than most of his white contemporaries, however, he was willing to regard black southerners as having contributed forms of genius to what he would refer to elsewhere as "Southern civilization." He did not regard them as "co-workers in the kingdom of culture" in the same way that W. E. B. Du Bois would later envision in his own discussions of black folk, but he did see them as having shaped southern culture in ways that were profound.

Imagining the folktales and field songs as part of a tradition that could only have developed as it did as a result of the plantation system, Harris thus constructed a defense based as much on irony as nostalgia. The nostalgia is undeniable: the books are replete with moments in which Remus and other slaves lament the fact that their old masters and mistresses are dead, for example. Yet the irony is finally what distinguishes Harris's writings from most other white male southern writers of the late nineteenth century, for his books construct a parallel argument that acknowledges that slavery may have been lamentable yet, ironically enough, the plantation had still produced much that was worth celebrating. In Harris's mind these encompassed a tradition of slave songs and stories that might be regarded as authentically American; a set of relations between white and black Americans that tended toward the positive; a cultural hybridity that was undeniable (and indeed registered itself in print when one recorded something so simple as a conversation between a black man and a white boy); and, above all, himself—a person who, despite being white, had been initiated into black folk culture (just as "Uncle Remus Initiates the Little Boy" in the first collection), had profited thereby, and was now willing to acknowledge publicly his debt to his former mentors. Harris claimed only to have been an "accidental author," but he was very deliberately a medium: a figure who wished to publicize black folk expressivity, hence to celebrate what the plantation had made possible both in spite of slavery (which had limited African Americans' access to writing, for example) and because of it (since even slavery's hardships had provoked meaningful responses in story and song).

The argument was complicated, in other words.[38] It was not one of the two much more simplistic arguments in defense of the plantation that circulated within U.S. culture at the time. First, it was not the argument that the social order of the plantation reflected the natural hierarchy of the races—an argument that proved foundational to the public careers of such figures as Henry W. Grady and Thomas Dixon Jr. and will feature abundantly in upcoming chapters. Harris was no radical egalitarian or even antiracist, but he was insistent in several essays published during his lifetime that African Americans had not yet been given the chance to show whether they could contribute to U.S. civil society and that they deserved the opportunity. Second, it was not the argument that old times on the old plantation had been joyous for all involved. Uncle Remus himself may have had "nothing but pleasant memories of the discipline of slavery"—or he may not have, if one is supposed to take this statement as impossibly positive, hence ironic—yet even if one takes Harris at his word, Remus's memories are not being offered as typical of all ex-slaves'. Indeed, when, in his allusion to Stowe, Harris praises her for having "attacked the possibilities of slavery with all the eloquence of genius," he is acknowledging a structural problem of slavery: that among its "possibilities" are the forms of abuse Tom experiences at the hands of Simon Legree as well as forms of affection he receives from Arthur Shelby and Eva St. Clare.[39]

Harris made it clear in other writings, several of which focus on runaway slaves, that he recognized that black life on the old plantation could also be unbearably unhappy. There are hints of this in the Remus books, too—in the patterns of oppression and retribution that characterize the folktales, most evidently, but also in such stories as "Death and the Negro Man" from *Uncle Remus and His Friends* (1892), in which Remus tells the story of a slave who grows so "tired er work . . . dat he say he hope ole Gran'sir Death 'll come take him off, en take his marster en de overseer 'long wid 'im."[40] For the most part, though, Harris works in the Remus books to convey his comprehension of "negro" culture in other ways. He dutifully transcribes the dialect, for example, paying more careful attention to its sounds and figures of speech than had any white writer before him. He acknowledges that the folktales were "artistically dramatic" by themselves and could be presented "without embellishment and without exaggeration" from him. And he allows Uncle Remus to seem capable of irony, which, when the character is read in this way, makes him seem always elusive and Harris seem all the more attuned to black discursive nuance and intellectual gamesmanship.

Or, as the writer and later publisher Walter Hines Page would observe in 1881, "I have Mr. Harris's own word for it that he can *think* in the Negro dialect. He could translate even Emerson, perhaps Bronson Alcott, in it, as well as he can tell the adventures of Brer Rabbit."[41] Harris's reputation for having transcended the barriers of subjectivity widely supposed to separate black from white was thus being established within a year of the publication of his first book. Recognizing this—and understanding that this fantasy of intersubjectivity lay at the heart of Harris's defense of the plantation—I wish now to return to a consideration of how the Remus books manage to proximate Harris to black culture by withholding as well as disclosing information, a gesture they perform repeatedly. In each case Harris pays tribute to "negro" genius by admitting that, no matter how painstaking he might be in his transcription of dialect, he cannot properly translate what his speakers are saying. Yet in each case he also implies that it is *print* that fails to capture the meanings, subtleties, inflections, and innuendos of black folk discourse, not *him*. He possesses forms of cognition and appreciation that reflect the fact that he grew up amid slaves and retains a familiarity—a sense of at-home-ness, even—among black southerners that his nonsouthern readers may only guess at.

Some of the moments in which this happens are trivial, as when in *Uncle Remus, His Songs and His Sayings* Harris attempts to reproduce the sounds Remus makes to indicate "Tarrypin talk," the noises turtles make when they talk to each other (and that, in keeping with the books' theme of translation, the old man of course claims to be able to understand). After providing an impressive phonogram ("I-doom-er-ker-kum-mer-ker!") Harris informs his readers that he has failed: "No explanation could convey an adequate idea of the intonation and pronunciation which Uncle Remus brought to bear upon this wonderful word. . . . It can not be reproduced in print" (68). In *Uncle Remus and His Friends* (1892) he calls attention to the inadequacy of print in an even more pointed fashion. When the little boy wonders why a bull makes the sound it does, Remus informs the child that he has come to the right source and should not waste time trying to find the answer elsewhere: "You may spit on yo' thumb en turn over de leaves er all de books up dar en Mars John's liberry, yit you won't fin' out in um."[42]

Other moments of withholding are of much greater significance to Harris's authorial project. Two in particular are worth exploring at length, for they convey especially well how Harris manages to venerate black culture by failing to reproduce it, yet, in so doing, also manages to express how deeply involved with the culture he considers himself. In one of these moments, which appears in the introduction to *Nights with Uncle Remus* (1883), Harris claims once to have met "one or two" black storytellers who, "if their language and their gestures could have been taken down, would have put Uncle Remus to shame." He does this in the context of explaining how *Night with Uncle Remus* differs from its predecessor. The second of the collections, the book incorporates several folktales written down and sent to Harris by enthusiastic readers who wanted to share with him the memories that had been stirred by reading *Uncle Remus, His Songs and His Sayings*. They were thus stories Harris had read but not necessarily heard, having arrived to him mediated by white interlocution and, more simply, by writing. He therefore set out to "verify" as many as he could by talking to black southerners and trying to discern which tales seemed to be the most widely known:

One of these opportunities occurred in the summer of 1882, at Norcross, a little railroad station, twenty miles northeast of Atlanta. The writer was waiting to take the train to Atlanta, and this train, as it fortunately happened, was delayed. At the station were a number of negroes, who had been engaged in working on the railroad. . . . They seemed to be in great good-humor, and cracked jokes at each other's expense in the midst of boisterous shouts of laughter. The writer sat next to one of the liveliest talkers in the party; and, after listening and laughing awhile, told the "Tar Baby" story by way of a feeler, the excuse being that some one in the crowd mentioned "Ole Molly

Har." The story was told in a low tone, as if to avoid attracting attention; but the comments of the negro, who was a little past middle age, were loud and frequent. "Dar now!" he would ex claim, or, "He's a honey, mon!" or, "Gentermens! git out de way, an gin im room!"

These comments, and the peals of unrestrained and unrestrainable laughter that accompanied them, drew the attention of the other negroes, and before the climax of the story had been reached, where Brother Rabbit is cruelly thrown into the brier-patch, they had all gathered around and made themselves comfortable. Without waiting to see what the effect of the "Tar Baby" legend would be, the writer told the story of "Brother Rabbit and the Mosquitoes," and this had the effect of convulsing them. Two or three could hardly wait for the conclusion, so anxious were they to tell stories of their own. The result was that, for almost two hours, a crowd of thirty or more negroes vied with each other to see which could tell the most and the best stories.[43]

"Thirty or more negroes" . . . and one white man! Harris literally loses sight of himself in his rehearsal of the tale-telling scene, and not because he is playing the role of the objective observer. It is he ("a honey, mon!") who gets the contest started, after all. Rather, it is because, in the universe created within the Remus books, to be possessed of black folk knowledge and to be intimate with black folk culture is to belong to the old plantation, to possess an almost natal familiarity with the spaces "back of the big house," as John Michael Vlach has termed them, where, as Harris presents it, an authentic American culture was produced both in spite of and because of slavery. One retains one's affiliation with the plantation, moreover, even after one has left, since a scene reminiscent of old times in the Old South could be recreated within, of all places, a railroad station north of Atlanta: spaces that symbolized mobility, modernity, and the fact that an old southern society was giving way to a new one not centered around the plantation.

The second moment worth exploring in this context is closely related; in fact, it might even be thought of as representing the "theory" that lay behind the form of "practice" later implemented in such places as the train station in Norcross. It comes from the introduction to *Uncle Remus, His Songs and His Sayings*, and it conveys better than anything else Harris ever wrote both the peculiarity of his own authorial position and the value of folk literacy in multiracial society:

Curiously enough, I have found few negroes who will acknowledge to a
stranger that they know anything of these legends; and yet to relate one of the
stories is the surest road to their confidence and esteem. In this way, and in
this way only, I have been enabled to collect and verify the folk-lore included
in this volume. There is an anecdote about the Irishman and the rabbit which
a number of negroes have told to me with great unction, and which is both
funny and characteristic, though I will not undertake to say that it has its
origin with the blacks. One day an Irishman who had heard people talking about "mares' nests" was going along the big road—it is always the big
road in contradistinction to neighborhood paths and bypaths, called in the
vernacular "nigh-cuts"—when he came to a pumpkin-patch. The Irishman
had never seen any of this fruit before, and he at once concluded that he had
discovered a veritable mare's nest. Making the most of his opportunity, he
gathered one of the pumpkins in his arms and went on his way. A pumpkin
is an exceedingly awkward thing to carry, and the Irishman had not gone far
before he made a misstep, and stumbled. The pumpkin fell to the ground,
rolled down the hill into a "brush-heap," and, striking against a stump, was
broken. The story continues in the dialect: "W'en de punkin roll in de bresh-
heap, out jump a rabbit; on soon's de I'shmuns see dat, he take atter de rabbit
en holler: 'Kworp, colty! kworp, colty!' but de rabbit, he des flew." The point
of this is obvious. (10–11)

One might begin to unpack this passage by noting that its point is *not* obvious. To get it, one would need to know first what a "mare's nest" is ("an illu-
sory discovery" or "untidy or confused mess," according to the *Oxford English
Dictionary*). One would need then to be able to decipher the "negro" dialect
that appears suddenly near the end of the passage (suddenly and, one should
add, rather unnecessarily: Harris translates the first part of the story into standard English and could have done so for the remainder as well). One must
finally be able to understand the Irish dialect (the "negro" rendition of the
Irish dialect, no less) and make sense of the word "kworp" (a variation upon
"cope," which, according to the *Dictionary of American Regional English*, can
mean "come!" when "used to call horses and sometimes other farm animals")
to feel fully possessed of the meaning of the passage—to be in on the joke, as
it were, and recognize that the Irishman thinks that a mare's nest is a pumpkin
and the rabbit that runs out of the brush heap into which the pumpkin happens to roll is a horse.[44]
   An untidy or confused mess, indeed. Yet even if one manages to get (or at

least guess at) what is humorous about the passage, one likely does not feel incorporated into it. One can grasp its import, that is, and still feel as if Harris is writing from a distance. The effect is reinforced by his use of the local expressions "brush-heap," "big road," and especially "nigh-cuts," a word that does not figure into the story of the Irishman yet Harris sees fit to include anyway. The effect is created, however, by the passage's opening statement, in which Harris signals to his readers his ability to cross over from the world that includes both him and them (and whose common language includes such words as "unction" and "contradistinction") and into a world from which his readers would likely have felt excluded, one whose codes and communal narratives were supposed to have seemed alien: "I have found few negroes who will acknowledge to a stranger that they know anything of these legends; and yet to relate one of the stories is the surest road to their confidence and esteem." In so saying Harris explains his method for "verify[ing]" each folktale. More than this, however, the statement locates Harris with respect to black southern culture, conveying how at home he feels in its presence and how pleased he seems to be to earn the "confidence and esteem" of those who might otherwise distrust him because of his skin color. The folktales function for him almost like shibboleths, for his ability to retell them gains him admittance into groups who would otherwise likely distrust him and regard him simply as white—one of the "w'ite fokes" about whom Remus speaks categorically throughout the collections or, better yet, one of the foxes whom the rabbits know better than to invite into the warren.

When he included such scenes as these in his books Harris was taking advantage of the fact that the things he did best as a writer—recording dialect, recollecting folktales, and recreating a sense of the local and everyday—were in demand during the period in which he wrote. The Remus books might therefore be thought of as having adapted the logic of local color fiction for the purpose of exhibiting what Harris believed to be his uniquely interracial subjectivity. Local color texts frequently deployed the trope of the insider versus the outsider in order to instruct metropolitan audiences that the forms of knowledge they possessed might prove inadequate were they to leave behind the centers of capital and high culture and visit the nation's hinterlands and folk districts. Harris's books embody this same logic but also the additional idea that what separates him from his readers is the ability to cross barriers of racial consciousness: "I" can do this, his books imply, because of what the plantation has enabled, ironically enough; "you" cannot, for while fortune may have placed you on the winning side of the Civil War and the struggle over slavery, it did not afford you the same opportunities to come to know "negroes."

Yet when he included such scenes and delineated such relationships in his books he was drawing upon something else as well—something of greater significance than his abilities as a local color fiction writer and greater also than his simple good fortune of having been born a white male in the plantation South. Harris did know the plantation unusually well. The emphasis in this last sentence should fall upon the word "unusually," however, for unlike most of those who would become identified with the postbellum plantation fiction movement, Harris was not the descendant of plantation royalty. Far from it. He was instead born illegitimate and relatively poor in a small town in the middle of Georgia, in the mid-to-late 1840s, the precise date being a matter of dispute.[45] His father, rumored to be an Irish laborer with whom Mary Harris had begun a relationship a few months before, skipped town soon after the boy's birth, never to return. If family lore is to be believed, the man was never even identified to his son: " 'Miss Mary' . . . discarded his father's name and gave her family name to Joel, and no one ever heard her mention his father again."[46] As to the matter of a plantation birthright, Harris was born near several plantations but on none of them, a fact that did not stop him from titling the closest thing to an autobiography he ever published *On the Plantation* (1892). It was not until 1862, which is to say, not until his early teenage years and not until the Civil War was well underway, that he finally took up residence on a plantation, Joseph Addington Turner's "Turnwold," located nine miles from his home. He went there to work as a typesetter for Turner's *The Countryman*, "the only plantation newspaper that has ever been published," as the adult Harris would proudly remember it in *On the Plantation*.[47] The experience set in motion his ambition to become a journalist, the career that would sustain him from 1866 until 1880. Of greater note, it provided him the contact with black folk culture that made most of what he wrote (hence most of what I have had to say about him as the originary figure of the postbellum plantation fiction movement) possible.

The writer whose complex professional defense of the plantation I have outlined thus far in this chapter therefore possessed an equally complex personal relationship with the institution. The particular plantation that most directly shaped his views was, as he himself acknowledged, unique: it was the "only plantation" he knew of devoted not only to the cultivation of cotton but also to the production of print, which in itself made Harris's experience of the plantation atypical. In fact it may have made him the only person in the long history of the institution whose labor on a plantation led *directly* to his becoming a writer (rather than indirectly and ironically, the paths by which former slaves became authors during the eighteenth and nineteenth centuries). The relationship was unusual at a more fundamental level, however, for perhaps only someone of Harris's background could have experienced the plantation as he did. White, male, and a native of the South's cotton belt, he had grown up idolizing the region's planter class. Poor, illegitimate, uncertain about his paternity, and unsure perhaps even of his date of birth, however, he possessed a background unlike that of any planters yet in these key respects remarkably like that of many slaves.

What I have emphasized thus far in my discussion of Harris are those aspects of his defense of the plantation that emanated surely from this second set of considerations—the fact that Harris had reasons beyond his merely having been exposed to slave culture to think himself unusually connected to black southerners. He never acknowledges these explicitly in his autobiographical writings, never mentioning that he lacked knowledge of his father and that the basic circumstances of his birth were also shrouded in mystery. If he had, he might have sounded like Frederick Douglass, whose *Narrative of the Life* (1845) begins by affirming that he possesses "no accurate knowledge of my age" or of his father, either: "My father was a white man. . . . The opinion was also whispered that my master was my father; but of the correctness of this opinion, I know nothing; the means of knowing was withheld from me."[48] Given Harris's capacity to seem both humorous and melancholy at the same time, he might have sounded even more like Booker T. Washington, whose *Up from Slavery* (1901) opens by admitting that he has never known his father ("I do not even know his name") nor known with any precision where and when he was born: "I am not quite sure of the exact place or exact date of my birth, but at any rate I suspect that I must have been born somewhere and at some time."[49]

Yet it is also worth noting that Harris was capable of defending the plantation in terms involving far less irony, which is to say, in ways that were far more expressive of his desire to be understood as white. It was very likely a sense of shame that kept him from writing more openly about his origins. It may also have been that there were clear limits beyond which he did not wish to seem "black." Yet it was surely a wish that he had been descended differently that led him to venerate the South's planter class and the culture it had created in terms that we have seen before in this book and will see again. In an 1883 essay titled "Observations from New England" he comes close to representing planters as bearers of the white man's burden, describing how "the duty of looking after the irresponsible blacks . . . involved the upbuilding and upholding of a patriarchal institution out of which grew new and grave responsibilities."[50] In an earlier essay titled simply "The Old Plantation" (1877) he discusses how "the problem of slavery" had "even before the desperate cast of the die in 1861 . . . begun to perplex the more thoughtful of the Southern people."[51] Both essays represent planters as tragic heroes and the Civil War and Reconstruction as forms of unjust punishment for a class of men doing its best to deal with problems it had inherited rather than created.

Harris's recognition of the burdens borne by the plantation's black inhabitants kept him from making these arguments the sole and central messages of his fiction. He never would have achieved the recognition he did had it not been for his books' greater complexities and his understanding that the relationship between "the negro" and the plantation, however one conceptualized it, was not simple. He was no George Cary Eggleston, in other words. Yet Eggleston, whom I discussed in my introduction because of his argument that the old plantation had benefited "the whole world" by giving birth to the thinkers who "created this republic and its institutions," might in fact have borrowed the idea from Harris. In "The Old Plantation," an essay published almost simultaneously with his earliest conceptions of Uncle Remus, Harris wrote this:

> Nourished into life by slavery, [the plantation] soon became one of the features of Southern civilization—a peculiar feature, indeed, and one which for many years exerted a powerful influence throughout the world. The genius of such men as Washington, Jefferson, Patrick Henry, Taney, Marshall, Calhoun, Stephens, Toombs, and all the greatest leaders of political thought and opinion from the days of the Revolution to the beginning of the Civil War, was the result and outgrowth of the civilization made possible by the old plantation.

Harris's own literary career was of course "the result and outgrowth" of the same "civilization made possible by the old plantation," which he mourns at the end of the essay as having "passed away, but the hand of time, inexorable, yet tender, has woven about it the sweet suggestions of poetry and romance, memorials that neither death nor decay can destroy."[52] The fact that he could write about it in terms so uncomplicated as these shows that Harris could romance the plantation as seemingly sincerely as anyone.

The fact that his more complex vision of the plantation also "exerted a powerful influence throughout the world" provides me a means of bringing this chapter to a close. When Theodore Roosevelt observed in 1917 that Harris's writings were "among the most striking and powerful permanent contributions to literature that have been produced on this side of the ocean," and when the *Golden Book Magazine* reported nine years later that *Uncle Remus* ranked among the "masterpieces of fiction" that proved that American writers deserved "a permanent place in this section of the world's literature," they were voicing opinions that at the time might have seemed almost factual. Uncle Remus was an international phenomenon. A London edition of the first collection was published early in 1881 and praised later that year in the London *Spectator* as "one of the happiest literary conceptions of the day" (Fig. 8).[53] A later observer would remark of the book's English reception that "it has been read by something like enthusiasm by people not given to enthusiasm." For proof, he offered a story that *Uncle Remus* had "so delighted one of the most cultivated and brilliant women of England . . . that she no sooner turned the last page than she hurried the book off by express to Mr. Tennyson, to whom it may possibly supply enough material for fresher verse than he has lately chosen to give us."[54]

The earliest London editions of the texts reproduced most of Harris's original collection in full, including the dialect. In recognition that the strange orthography posed difficulties for some readers, William T. Stead's Review of Reviews Office published a version titled *The Wonderful Adventures of Old Brer Rabbit* in 1896 as part of its new "Books for the Bairns" children's series. Omitting both the dialect and the Remus-boy frame narrative, the volume concentrated instead on the folktales and illustrations, which, as Stead wrote in a new introduction, "the little folks like better." Stead did instruct their parents of the roles played by Uncle Remus and the little boy in the original edition, however, and he delighted that Harris had made available a culture that, without his intervention, might have remained unrecorded:

These tales were written down by an American named Harris. He puts them in the mouth of an old negro, called Uncle Remus, who tells them one by one to a little white boy, the son of his master. . . . There is something very pleasant to think of in the telling to our children of to-day of tales which have been tested by the telling to other children thousands of miles away. Millions of little darkies have laughed till they cried over the amusing adventures of Brer Rabbit; they have grown up, and they have told the same stories to their children, and these again to their little ones, until at last there came a white man with pen and with ink who wrote the tales all out in black and white. Before then there had been no written stories. They were only told over and over again by the negroes to each other. But when they were written down, they became part of the riches of the children of the whole world. And so it came to pass that we are indebted for all the pleasure and fun we get out of these Rabbit stories to curly-headed, woolly-pated blackies, far away over the sea, who, by telling these stories, have done more to give pleasure to you and to me than all the rich white men who used to own them as slaves.[55]

Stead does not go so far as to say explicitly that the plantation had been therefore "worth it," the question raised in all of Harris's writings when they intimate that slavery had been regrettable but the plantation so culturally productive in spite of the misfortune. Stead's perception of black folk culture as having enriched white audiences, however, makes clear that Harris's message about the cultural value of the plantation to white folk had found at least one receptive auditor and found him "far away over the sea."

Stead's simplified version of *Uncle Remus* became the basis of several foreign-language translations, including French and Dutch versions both published during the early 1910s (Figs. 9 and 10). By 1913 the Virginia writer Myrta Lockett Avary had learned that a new German translation was being well received in that country and that English-language editions were circulating in Australia, Egypt, and other portions of "Anglicized Africa, the Negro's native habitat."[56] By 1918 Robert Lemuel Wiggins, Harris's first academic biographer, could add to this list Japan (where "recently a guest in a Japanese home found 'Uncle Remus' the only book in English") as well as India (where the stories had been translated into Bengali by a missionary and published in a magazine aimed at Indian boys).[57] By the late 1960s—and not counting the translations published in conjunction with international distribution of *Song of the South*—foreign-language editions of the Uncle Remus stories had been published in several additional countries, among them Norway, Finland, Czechoslovakia, and Argentina.[58]

Translations of the 1896 abridged edition continued to be produced during the very early twentieth century. As the decades progressed, however, a

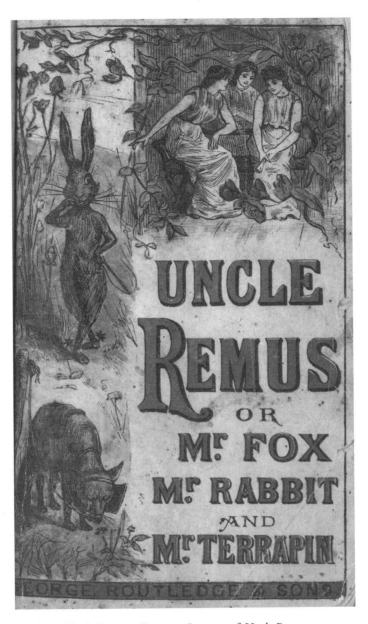

Figure 8. Uncle Remus Overseas I: cover of *Uncle Remus; or, Mr. Fox, Mr. Rabbit, and Mr. Terrapin*. Published by George Routledge and Sons (London, 1881). Emory University, Robert W. Woodruff Library Special Collections.

Figure 9. Uncle Remus Overseas II: cover of *Les Merveilleuses Aventures du Vieux Frère Lapin*, French translation of W. T. Stead's *The Wonderful Adventures of Old Brother Rabbit* (1896). Translated by M. B.-H. Gausseron. Published by Librairie Larousse (Paris, c. 1910). Emory University, Robert W. Woodruff Library Special Collections.

VREEMDE AVONTUREN

VAN

EEN OUD KONIJN.

GEILLUSTREERD.

Figure 10. Uncle Remus Overseas III: cover of *Vreemde Avonturen van een oud Konijn,* Dutch translation of Stead's adaptation. Translator unidentified. Published by Uitgevers-Mij Hepkema (Herenveen, the Netherlands, no publication date). Emory University, Robert W. Woodruff Library Special Collections.

majority of international editions of *Uncle Remus, His Songs and His Sayings* returned to something much closer to Harris's original text. Most of those translated into languages other than English made no attempt to recreate the dialect—and who knows whether such phrases as "bimeby," "w'atsumever," and "monstus full er fleas" could have been rendered effectively into the Norwegian in any event. Yet several retained Harris's introduction, which makes clear that the folktales were representative of a particular time and place, while most preserved the Remus-boy frame narrative, which, as I have argued in this chapter, Harris intended as a sign of the unique interracial relations made possible by the southern plantation.

The suggestion one takes away from examining the various international editions is that the figure of Uncle Remus proved essential to the texts' enthusiastic reception both nationwide and worldwide. Harris could have counted on the folktales themselves seeming universal, for he knew even before he had published the first collection that some of the stories he was including bore resemblance to tales ethnologists had recently collected while studying tribal societies in North and South America, Africa, and elsewhere. The figure of Remus and his relationship with the little boy proved similarly compelling, however, for while it represented something less universal (and indeed drew directly from Harris's own background, which was unique), it made white comprehension of "negro" culture and even subjectivity seem possible. Thus, when William T. Stead made the text his own by omitting the figure of Remus and referring to its author simply as "an American named Harris," he celebrated what *Uncle Remus* had accomplished in terms that Harris might have understood as legitimating his project: "Before then there had been no written stories. . . . But when they were written down, they became part of the riches of the children of the whole world."

Whether Alfred Lord Tennyson found in *Uncle Remus* a similar form of enrichment is unclear. The book did find its way into the hands of another giant of Victorian British literature, however, and he was more than happy to acknowledge his indebtedness to Harris. Rudyard Kipling, the writer whose 1899 poem "The White Man's Burden" proved so resonant in the turn-of-the-century United States and provides me an indirect source for the title of this book, read *Uncle Remus* while attending boarding school in Devon during the early 1880s. When, a decade and a half later, Kipling read a positive review written by Harris of his second *Jungle-Book*, he was delighted to strike up a correspondence:

I am taking the liberty of sending you with this a copy of the "Second Jungle-Book"—which I see with delight you have been good enough to praise in the Christmas "Book-Buyer." This makes me feel some inches taller in my boots: for my debt to you is of long standing.

I wonder if you could realize how "Uncle Remus," his sayings, and the sayings of the noble beasties ran like wild fire through an English public school when I was about fifteen. We used to go to battle (with boots and bolsters and such-like) against those whom we did not love, to the tune of Ty-yi-tungalee: I eat um pea, I pick um pea, etc., and I remember the bodily bearing into a furze-bush of a young fag solely because his nickname had been "Rabbit" before the tales invaded the school and—well, we assumed that he ought to have been "bawn an' bred in a briar-patch," and gorse was the most efficient substitute. And six years ago in India, meeting an old schoolmate of those days, we found ourselves quoting whole pages of "Uncle Remus" that had got mixed in with the fabric of the old school life.[59]

It is beyond the scope of this book to consider the extent to which Harris may have actually influenced Kipling's fiction. It is worth noting, however, that *The Jungle-Books* (1894–1895) involved interactions between humans and talking animals; that the *Just So Stories* (1902), which include such fables as "How the Camel Got His Hump" and "How the Rhinoceros Got His Skin," resemble such Remus tales as "How Mr. Rabbit Lost His Fine Bushy Tail" and "Why the Hawk Catches Chickens"; and that *Kim* (1901) revolves around a young boy of Irish descent capable of passing as Indian and his relationship with an elderly Tibetan lama—no little boy–Uncle Remus relationship, to be sure, since it is Kim who is more the trickster figure, yet one whose cross-cultural and cross-generational nature makes *Uncle Remus* potentially at least a distant source of inspiration. It is also worth noting that in one of the chapters of *The Complete Stalky & Co.* (1929), a novel based on Kipling's schoolboy days in England, the boys divide into two factions, one of which adopts Brer Terrapin as its mascot, the other, the Tar Baby. The boys sing Remus's songs and challenge each other in dialect ("Here I come a-bulgin' and a-bilin'") as they try to steal each other's idols (Fig. 11). "In a short time," Kipling writes, "the College was . . . severely infected with *Uncle Remus*."[60]

That the writer dubbed often the poet laureate of British imperialism might have found so much that was compelling in Harris suggests the need to think further about the Remus books and sensations that surrounded them

Figure 11. Uncle Remus Overseas IV: illustration from Rudyard Kipling, *The Complete Stalky & Co.* (1929).

during the late nineteenth and early twentieth centuries. The debut collection was among the most successful works of local color fiction published during the movement's heyday, making Harris perhaps the most widely celebrated southern writer to appear since Edgar Allan Poe and the first ever from the lower southern states to win such broad recognition. Not until William Faulkner emerged two decades after Harris's death would another writer from the Deep South be praised by so many for what he had accomplished in fiction. Yet using such words as "local" and "southern" to measure Harris's influence belies what his works achieved, for in addition to launching the postbellum plantation fiction movement I write about more in the upcoming chapter, they made the plantation itself seem a more significant space in U.S. culture by promoting a fantasy of cross-racial comprehension as one of the effects of white-black geographical proximity. They thus made the old plantation seem ahead of rather than behind the rest of world, and they did so as the world itself seemed to grow smaller as a result of new technological developments and new U.S. and European imperial expansions into regions inhabited mainly by nonwhite subjects. Harris's fiction does not rival Poe's or Faulkner's in terms of its complexity, nor was it quite the transatlantic phenomenon that the novel it proposed to "supplement," *Uncle Tom's Cabin*, had been during the 1850s and 1860s. Yet it might have been almost as effective as Stowe's novel in directing readers' attentions to the southern plantation and inviting them to see the space anew (though without requiring them to behold a single vision, certainly not the "cloud-like" one described in 1925 by Francis Pendleton Gaines). Though it may no longer outrank *Uncle Tom's Cabin*, it deserves at least to be considered similarly controversial.

CHAPTER 2

"The Old South under New Conditions"

Henry W. Grady, Thomas Nelson Page, and New Southern Manhood

The previous chapter made a great deal of the idea of proximity and the fact that Joel Chandler Harris's celebration of the old plantation was based primarily on his belief that close contact with black southerners had afforded white southern men forms of comprehension and even culture that few others could claim legitimately to possess. Given the emphasis thus placed upon propinquity, it is worth noting at the outset of this chapter that one of its two principal subjects, the Atlanta newspaper editor Henry W. Grady, once shared a desk with Harris (Fig. 12). The two worked together at the *Atlanta Constitution* from 1876 until 1889, which is to say, during the period in which Harris went from being a journalist little known outside of Georgia to an internationally celebrated author whose writings were transforming the ways readers worldwide understood the plantation South. Grady's fame was not as far-reaching as Harris's, but it was considerable. As the preeminent spokesman for the "New South" movement, a term he did not invent but did more than anyone else to popularize, Grady achieved a national reputation second only to Harris's among writers from Georgia during the pivotal 1880s.[1] He was beseeched throughout the decade by northerners as well as southerners to run for national office, so great was his popularity. Following his sudden death from pneumonia at age thirty-nine, the *New York Times* bemoaned the loss of a man it felt "would, we are confident, have been a greater figure in the South than any other that has risen since the war."[2] Harris interpreted the event similarly, observing in the memorial collection of Grady's writings he edited that the death of his close associate had represented a loss to the entire nation: "He died the best beloved and most deeply lamented man that Georgia has

Figure 12. Plantation Proximities I: photograph of the desk used by both Harris (seated, right) and Grady (represented in the framed picture atop the desk; Grady had died in 1889) (ca. 1890). Emory University, Robert W. Woodruff Library Special Collections.

ever produced . . . sacrificing his life in behalf of a purpose that was neither personal nor sectional, but grandly national in its aims."[3]

Harris was not as close personally with the other writer discussed in this chapter, Thomas Nelson Page, yet the two have been positioned alongside one another in discussions of postbellum plantation fiction since both rose to fame during the 1880s. Page's *In Ole Virginia*, his first book, and Harris's *Free Joe and Other Georgian Sketches*, his fourth, were both published by Charles Scribner's Sons in 1887. First editions of each text featured full-page advertisements for the other in its back pages (Figs. 13 and 14). An early review of *In Ole Virginia* praised Page for having followed Harris's example in daring to compose artistic narratives out of the base material of black southern oral culture: "When 'Uncle Remus' and 'Tom' Page are reproached with an itching for the out of the way, they are easily exonerated when we remember how the great poets and artists have wrought [their best works] using the tools God gave them."[4] Meanwhile an 1895 primer on English literature published by the American Book Company devoted a portion of one of its two chapters on "American Literature, from 1647–1895" to "Negro Folklore—its Peculiarities Illustrated by Page and Harris." Only 220 pages long, the book's first chapter surveys all of English literature prior to the Norman Conquest while its section on Shakespeare spans fewer than seven pages. That it devotes two full pages to Harris and Page—more than it gives to Nathaniel Hawthorne, Harriet Beecher Stowe, Edgar Allan Poe, and James Fenimore Cooper combined—suggests once again how significant a development plantation fiction once seemed to many Americans because of the unprecedented glimpses it appeared to provide into "negro" thought and culture.

Close though they thus were in different ways to Harris, Grady and Page were even closer to each other in terms of how they understood the South's plantation past. Both built upon an image of the plantation developed in Harris's writings in order to defend it against allegations that it had been culturally unproductive. Both went much further, however, imagining that it had been the plantation South that had in many ways built "America" and that it would be the region's white, male descendants who would assume leadership roles as the United States continued its historic mission on an even greater global scale. Embracing all of the romance but few of the ironies of Harris's plantation writings, Grady and Page envisioned an antebellum southern society whose superiority as a "civilization" seemed manifest when seen in light of the problems of the post-Reconstruction period. They then developed visions of a "New South" emerging from the old, and though they acknowledged that its rise would represent several profound shifts—the region would need to industrialize with the help of northern capital and accede to at least some forms of expansion of federal power, most notably—they argued that beneath these transitions lay deeper *continuities* and that what in fact white southern men had been granted after Reconstruction were opportunities to restore the region built by their fathers to its rightful place within an expanding nation. By exploring this image of the plantation South—one less "provincial" and more nationalistic than any ever pictured by Harris—this chapter aims thus to distance Grady and Page from the author of the Uncle Remus books and position them instead as the architects of another new vision of the old plantation.[6] It was with Grady and Page that the space reimagined by Harris as having been productive in ways beyond the economic became reinvented also as the birthplace of a nation. The fantasy of cross-racial comprehension that, in Harris, had inspired a complex portrait of the South's cultural hybridity produced something else in the writings of his two most proximate succes-

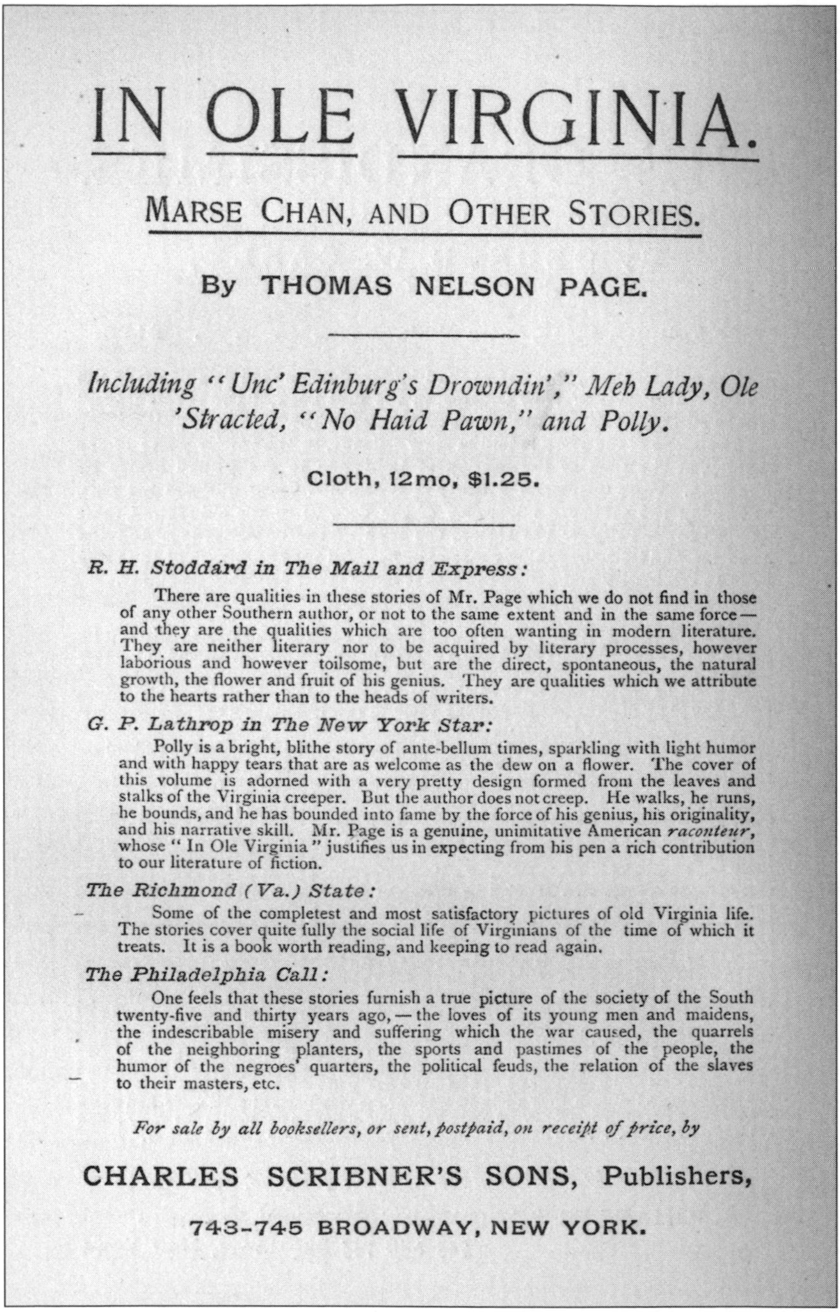

IN OLE VIRGINIA.

MARSE CHAN, AND OTHER STORIES.

By THOMAS NELSON PAGE.

Including "Unc' Edinburg's Drowndin'," Meh Lady, Ole 'Stracted, "No Haid Pawn," and Polly.

Cloth, 12mo, $1.25.

R. H. Stoddard in The Mail and Express:

There are qualities in these stories of Mr. Page which we do not find in those of any other Southern author, or not to the same extent and in the same force—and they are the qualities which are too often wanting in modern literature. They are neither literary nor to be acquired by literary processes, however laborious and however toilsome, but are the direct, spontaneous, the natural growth, the flower and fruit of his genius. They are qualities which we attribute to the hearts rather than to the heads of writers.

G. P. Lathrop in The New York Star:

Polly is a bright, blithe story of ante-bellum times, sparkling with light humor and with happy tears that are as welcome as the dew on a flower. The cover of this volume is adorned with a very pretty design formed from the leaves and stalks of the Virginia creeper. But the author does not creep. He walks, he runs, he bounds, and he has bounded into fame by the force of his genius, his originality, and his narrative skill. Mr. Page is a genuine, unimitative American *raconteur*, whose "In Ole Virginia" justifies us in expecting from his pen a rich contribution to our literature of fiction.

The Richmond (Va.) State:

Some of the completest and most satisfactory pictures of old Virginia life. The stories cover quite fully the social life of Virginians of the time of which it treats. It is a book worth reading, and keeping to read again.

The Philadelphia Call:

One feels that these stories furnish a true picture of the society of the South twenty-five and thirty years ago,—the loves of its young men and maidens, the indescribable misery and suffering which the war caused, the quarrels of the neighboring planters, the sports and pastimes of the people, the humor of the negroes' quarters, the political feuds, the relation of the slaves to their masters, etc.

For sale by all booksellers, or sent, postpaid, on receipt of price, by

CHARLES SCRIBNER'S SONS, Publishers,

743-745 BROADWAY, NEW YORK.

Figure 13. Plantation Proximities II: advertisement for Page's *In Ole Virginia* that appeared in Harris's *Free Joe and Other Georgian Sketches* (1887).

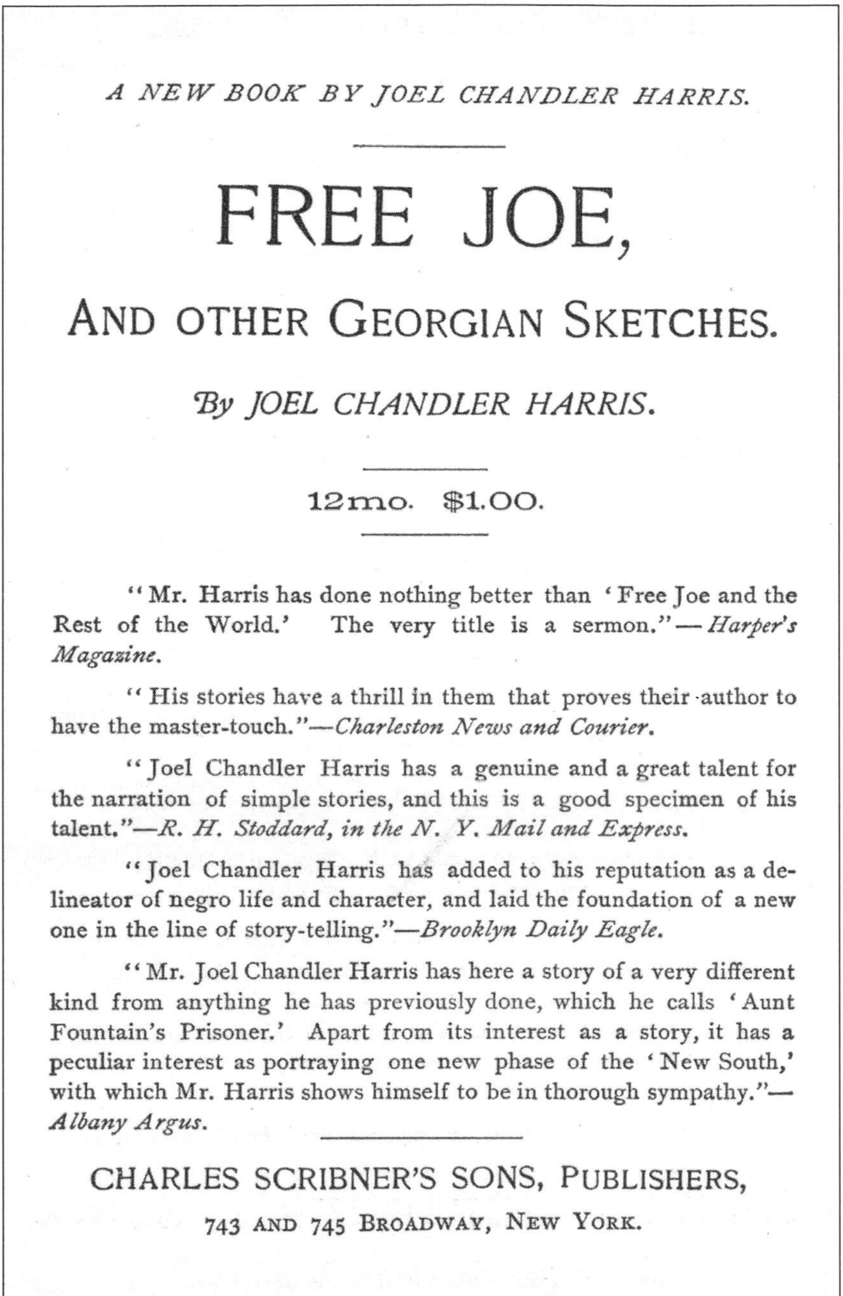

A NEW BOOK BY JOEL CHANDLER HARRIS.

FREE JOE,

AND OTHER GEORGIAN SKETCHES.

By JOEL CHANDLER HARRIS.

12mo. $1.00.

"Mr. Harris has done nothing better than 'Free Joe and the Rest of the World.' The very title is a sermon."—*Harper's Magazine.*

"His stories have a thrill in them that proves their author to have the master-touch."—*Charleston News and Courier.*

"Joel Chandler Harris has a genuine and a great talent for the narration of simple stories, and this is a good specimen of his talent."—*R. H. Stoddard, in the N. Y. Mail and Express.*

"Joel Chandler Harris has added to his reputation as a delineator of negro life and character, and laid the foundation of a new one in the line of story-telling."—*Brooklyn Daily Eagle.*

"Mr. Joel Chandler Harris has here a story of a very different kind from anything he has previously done, which he calls 'Aunt Fountain's Prisoner.' Apart from its interest as a story, it has a peculiar interest as portraying one new phase of the 'New South,' with which Mr. Harris shows himself to be in thorough sympathy."—*Albany Argus.*

CHARLES SCRIBNER'S SONS, PUBLISHERS,

743 AND 745 BROADWAY, NEW YORK.

Figure 14. Plantation Proximities III: advertisement for Harris's *Free Joe and Other Georgian Sketches* that appeared in Page's *In Ole Virginia* (1887).

sors; it became the basis of a new narrative of U.S. nationhood in which white southern men might be seen once again as founding fathers.

The fact that Grady and Page were so much more invested than Harris in the idea of a plantation patriarchy as foundational to the nation can be attributed, at least in part, to differences among the three writers' backgrounds. Unlike Harris, Grady and Page knew and admired their fathers, both of whom owned land and slaves and served as officers in the Confederate army. Grady was born first, in Athens, Georgia, in 1850, the son of William S. Grady, a successful storekeeper and real estate investor, and Ann Gartrell Grady, a descendant of at least two plantation-owning families from Georgia.[7] The owners of five slaves at the time of Henry's birth, they purchased a sizable mansion and farm in 1863 and might have become much more prosperous during the years that followed (they would have been proprietors of an unusually diversified set of southern enterprises) had not William died in 1864 from wounds sustained at the Battle of Petersburg. Though the family's prospects were diminished as a result, they were still able to support Grady as he completed his education, which he did by attending the University of Georgia from 1865 to 1868 followed by the University of Virginia from 1868 to 1869. He concentrated on oratory at both, having become interested in politics and in careers that might involve him in public speaking and political commentary. What attracted him to Virginia, in addition to its having produced several of the South's most prominent public men, was that it had been founded by Thomas Jefferson, the public figure whom Grady regarded as "the greatest this country has ever produced."[8] That Jefferson had also been a planter only contributed to Grady's belief that southern "civilization" lay at the foundation of American social and political genius.

Page was born within three years of Grady, and his connections to the nation's Founding Fathers were even closer. The son of John Page and Elizabeth Burwell Nelson Page, he was descended from two of the First Families of Virginia. On his mother's side, the Nelsons, he was related to two former Virginia governors, one of whom, Thomas Nelson Jr., had been among the signers of the Declaration of Independence. On the Page side he was descended from one additional former governor, John Page, who had been among Jefferson's closest friends and may even have housed the future president as he drafted the Declaration. An earlier ancestor also bearing the name John Page had been among the founders of Williamsburg and most successful planters of the early Virginia colony. The fortunes of both families had diminished by the time Thomas Nelson Page was born in 1853. They owned considerably more slaves than the Gradys, however—as many as sixty during most of Page's boyhood—as well as a plantation, Oakland, that Page would later describe as "one of the best . . . in all that region."[9] Page studied at Washington College from 1869 to 1872, the first year of which his college president was Robert E. Lee. Like Grady, he then went to the University of Virginia, graduating with a degree in law in 1874. Also like Grady, he revered Jefferson, writing at one point that Jefferson's career "had been crowded [with] almost as many services of world-benefit as ever fell to one man's lot."[10]

The idea that founding a nation was part of a white southern man's paternity was thus, for Page, at least, not entirely fanciful. Having grown up hearing stories of the Revolution in which his ancestors played conspicuous parts, he perhaps sensed from an early age that he was the product not only of two distinguished families but also of American history itself. In an 1892 essay on his ancestry, in fact, he noted that the earliest Page plantations had been located near Jamestown, site of the first permanent English settlement in the New World, while the first Nelsons had established themselves in Yorktown, site of Cornwallis's surrender to Washington. "As York, the territory of the Nelsons, witnessed the last act in Virginia's colonial drama, so Rosewell, the seat of the Pages, saw the first act."[11] A young Henry Grady could not have imagined his family's history so closely aligned with the history of the United States. He might well have seen it as linked to the story of an emergent southern nation, however, for his father's greatest business successes occurred during the run-up to the Civil War and the purchase of the plantation home took place at a moment when Confederates still entertained thoughts of final victory. The fact that Grady's father died in battle only increased his sense of patriotism, and when later he would refer to his father in his speeches, as he did once in an address delivered near the battlefield where his father had been wounded, it was in terms befitting a national hero: "Beyond is Petersburg, where he, whose name I bear, and who was prince to me among men, dropped his stainless sword and yielded up his stainless life. . . . Sacred to me, sir, [is] the soil that drank his precious blood."[12]

Descended though they were from planters of minor and even major historical significance, however, neither man wrote excessively about his particular paternal lineage. Instead, both chose to imagine an antebellum planter class as the father figures of a region and nation. That is, they sought to make universal among the white men of the New South, then to extend to sympathetic white men from outside of the region, connections to a planter patriarchy that would transcend ties of blood, specificities of place, and limitations of social class. Their project was to replace literal ties of kinship with metaphorical ones built around claims of racial responsibility and destiny; and, as direct descendants of the planter class whose virtues they were thus seeking to universalize, they could claim both to know the plantation far better than most and to possess an inherent power to "give it away," to transform a literal inheritance into a figurative one and then to bestow it upon the rest of the nation.

Thus, when Grady spoke to students at the University of Virginia twenty years after his own graduation, he addressed them first in terms of their shared paternity: "It was on these hills that our fathers gave new and deeper meaning to heroism and advanced the world in honor!" Within a few paragraphs, however, he was referring to his audience less as a distinct breed than as the beneficiaries of a unique history. Their responsibility now, he told them, was to impart to their fellow citizens those qualities they had inherited from their heroic planter forefathers. Noting for example that he himself had begun to "teach my son to love Georgia; to love the soil that he stands on"—and in so doing making clear the importance of the father-son exchange to his overall message—he went on to identify patriotism as one of the virtues that white southern men were unusually well qualified to contribute to national culture:

> We note the barracks of our standing army with its rolling drum and its fluttering flag as points of strength and protection. But the citizen standing in the door-way of his home, contented on his threshold, his family gathered about his hearthstone, while the evening of a well-spent day closes in scenes and sounds that are dearest—he shall save the republic when the drum tap is futile and the barracks are exhausted.
>
> This love should not be pent up or provincial. The home should be consecrated to humanity, and from its roof tree should fly the flag of the republic. Every simple fruit gathered there; every sacrifice endured, and every victory won, should bring better joy and inspiration in the knowledge that it will deepen the glory of our republic and widen the harvest of humanity![13]

Or, as Page would later observe in comments similarly nativist yet also expansionist, the Old South's "tendency toward exclusiveness and conservatism" and its "admit[ing] the jurisdiction of no other tribunal than itself" had in effect given Americans reasons to expand their homeland. Writing in celebration of what the nation had achieved since the end of Reconstruction, Page argued that "the sudden supremacy of the American people today is largely due to the Old South, and to its . . . civilization."[14]

If the partnership at the heart of Harris's plantation fiction had been be-

tween an elderly black man and a young white boy, then, and if it had func-
tioned, at least to an extent, to expand notions of southern culture by recognizing its black as well as white dimensions, the relationship at the center of
Grady's and Page's plantation writings was entirely different. It was between
planters and their white "sons"—their actual descendants as well as their metaphorical offspring, since both writers were eager to make others feel connected
to a planter patriarchy. It was expansive, moreover, not because it credited
black southerners with having shaped the region's culture but rather because it
impelled young white men to carry forward the values of an imagined planter
patriarchy into new situations and spaces, new scenarios that might require
the forms of "expertise" engendered by having grown up observing white men
own and oversee slaves. "The glory of our republic," according to such a vision, came to seem a sign that the "civilization" of the Old South had persisted
despite the end of slavery. African Americans, meanwhile, were allowed to
play one of only two roles within this new national imaginary. They could be
grateful subjects, offering praises to the powers that be for having bestowed
upon them the blessing of slavery and benevolence of white mastery. Or they
could seem ingrates, which, given the centrality of the plantation in this new
South-centered narrative of U.S. history, made them appear less than "American"; it could make them seem almost the enemies of civilization itself.

That they had become *citizens* with the ratification of the Fourteenth
Amendment in 1868 mattered little. In the terms of representation developed
by Grady and Page, African Americans came to seem more like *dependen-
cies*—more like the sometimes acquiescent, sometimes rebellious subjects of
empire over whom Rudyard Kipling would soon be urging white American
men to assume responsibility: "To wait in heavy harness, / On fluttered folk
and wild— / Your new-caught, sullen peoples, / Half-devil and half-child."

These ideas are in fact legible in the first work that either man managed
to publish in a national venue, a poem by Page titled "Uncle Gabe's
White Folks." Published in *Scribner's Monthly* in April 1877—the very month,
as it turned out, that federal troops began their withdrawal from the former
Confederate states—the poem also appeared at about the same time that Harris was inventing the figure of Uncle Remus and producing sketches from
his vantage point in the *Atlanta Constitution*. Like Harris's sketches, Page's
poem was written in dialect and represented the speech of a former slave.
Page did not yet directly draw inspiration from Harris, however, for Harris
was still three years away from becoming a national sensation. Rather, he was
following the example of Irwin Russell, a Mississippi poet whose "negro" dia-

lect poems had begun appearing regularly in *Scribner's* in 1876. Most of Russell's poems, including the later one for which he would become best known, "Christmas-Night in the Quarters" (1878), presented plantation vignettes from the perspectives of slaves and ex-slaves. "Uncle Gabe's White Folks," by contrast, attempts over its seventy-nine lines to offer a miniature epic history stretching from the Old South to the New. In it a former slave recounts the good times he and his fellow slaves had enjoyed under their former master and mistress, both now deceased. He hints at the hard times that had followed the Civil War and the South's loss of slave labor. "To pay what ole marster owe," Uncle Gabe says at one point, the family had had to sell the plantation and most of their possessions, including their "very clo's." Yet he also mentions a son, "de young marster now," who has been away from the plantation for ten years but has promised to return, buy it back, and restore it to its former glory. The poem is directly addressed to a white auditor not identified at the beginning of the poem. In the final lines, it is revealed that the poem's addressee is in fact the young master.

"SARVENT, marster," the poem begins, the capitals appearing in both the original *Scribner's* publication and in *Befo' de War*, a collection of dialect poems by Page and fellow Virginia writer Armistead C. Gordon published in 1888. The effect is to emphasize the speaker's delight at being a servant—to say, in effect, *at your service* with great enthusiasm—hence to show in only the poem's first word that Uncle Gabe remains devoted to the old social order.[15] Yet the effect of the opening words is also to transform the reader into a "marster": to elevate him or her into a position of superiority and then to provide a set of images of the old plantation that Uncle Gabe assumes the reader knows little about yet will find captivating nonetheless.

> SARVENT, marster! Yes, sah, dat's me—
> "Ole Uncle Gabe" 's my name;
>   Thankee, marster, I 'm 'bout, yo' see.
> An' d' ole ooman? she 's much de same,
>   Po'ly an' 'plainin', thank de Lord!
>   But de Marster 's gwine ter come back from 'broad. (ll. 1–6)

The speaker continues exchanging pleasantries with the reader for two additional stanzas, discussing the mansion near which they have met as a "fine ole place," mentioning how much finer it had been when "d' marster an' d' mistis lived up deyre," and insisting that their nobility had rubbed off on him, too: "'N' sah, dey wuz ob high degree, / Dis hyar nigger am quality." In the fourth stanza Uncle Gabe voices his astonishment that his auditor might not have heard of his master and mistress, godlike that they seem to him ("D' knowed all dat d' wuz to know"). He then begins describing in detail his "white folks" and the lives they had once lived, noting their immense wealth ("Gol' ober d' head an' under d' feet"), their extensive holdings in land and livestock ("de hogs mec' de hill-sides look like black"), the leisureliness of their daily lives ("Jes' t' her *kerridge*,—dat wuz fur / 'S ever [my 'l missis] walked"), and so on. As he does so he seems oblivious to the fact that he is talking to his young master, though once his auditor's identity is revealed in the final stanza, he claims to have "knowed yo' soon's I see yo' face." In the final couplet he cites from the twenty-third Psalm and imagines his young master's return as a sign of providential restoration: "De ravins shell hunger an' shell not lack, / D' marster, d' young marster's done come back!"

The form of the poem amplifies its meaning. Its first three stanzas, in which Uncle Gabe converses politely with the apparent stranger, follow a regular ABABCC rhyme scheme. Its fourth stanza, in which Gabe expresses his surprise that the stranger does not know of his old master and mistress and begins to tell their story, includes an extra line, suggesting that once Uncle Gabe begins discussing the old plantation and its owners in earnest, he cannot stop. The final two stanzas make this even clearer. Stanza five is twenty-six lines long, stanza six, twenty-eight. Unlike the earlier stanzas, they are less conversational. Stanza five in particular represents an uninterrupted series of memories, evidence that Uncle Gabe may be so absorbed in reminiscence that he has lost consciousness of his auditor. The rhyme scheme of the opening three stanzas breaks down in the second half of the poem, too, as the speaker becomes more and more lost in his reverie and the form of poem expands to allow him to toss in additional details and memories—to follow the drift of his imagination rather than formalities of conversation.[16] Nor is the poetic order of the opening stanzas fully restored at the end. The final stanza concludes with seven lines written in an irregular ABAB*B*CC rhyme scheme, which comes closer to resembling the form of Uncle Gabe's reverie than that of the opening three stanzas of conversation. The poem thus expresses formally an antebellum/postbellum divide. Its opening stanzas, in which Uncle Gabe and his auditor speak mostly about the postbellum condition of the plantation, are more predictably structured. It subsequent dream sequence, however, in which Uncle Gabe seeks to recreate for his auditor a sense of the antebellum past, is longer and more spontaneous. And even though the speaker snaps back into the present with his recognition that "d' young marster's done come back" at the end of the poem, the form of his speech maintains the dreamlike irregularity of the second half of the poem. What returns at the end of the poem is thus not only the young master. With him, Uncle Gabe believes, arrives the opportunity to continue being as carefree as he had once been when under the supervision of his old master.

What is most remarkable about the poem, however, is the relationship it seeks to develop with its reader. Transforming him or her into a "marster" in only its second word—and doing so in light of the fact that the average reader of *Scribner's* in 1877 was not likely to have been a southerner and even less likely ever to have been called "marster"—the poem seduces its reader into enjoying the form of privilege that comes simply from being the white person involved in an impromptu conversation with a black man in nineteenth-century Virginia. Though the reader is necessarily a stranger at first, he or she is positioned within a well-defined social order that has already made clear the roles that both participants in the conversation should play. Encouraged thus to inhabit this subject position, the reader is further rewarded at the end of the poem by being welcomed as the returning "young marster"—a return not of a prodigal son, since the young master has spent the past ten years amassing the capital that will allow him to repurchase the plantation, but rather of a savior:

> Dy glory, Lord! I knowed yo', chile,
>   I knowed yo' soon's I see yo' face;
> Whar hez yo' been dis bressed while?
>   "Done come back an' buy de place?"
>   Oh! Bress de Lord for all his grace!
>   De ravins shell hunger an' shell not lack,
>   D' marster, d' young marster's done come back! (ll. 73–79)

Rather than seeming alienating—the reader enters the poem a stranger to the Virginia plantation, only to exit having been identified as someone else entirely—the effect of the poem remains inviting throughout. By the end, the reader is permitted to play the role of the son of the beloved "old marster" and to imagine his return as marking the glorious second coming of the Old South.

Already in his first published work, then, Page managed to incorporate most of the elements that would sustain his writings for the next several decades. Above all there was the figure of the loyal ex-slave speaking sincerely of his love for the old plantation and its proprietors. There was also the dialect, contributing to the ex-slave's authenticity and making his devotedness seem at least marginally more plausible because it *looked* as if it emanated from a black rather than white mouth. There was the cataloging of the beautiful elements of plantation life: the slaves singing joyfully, the big house provisioned handsomely, the master's conducting himself authoritatively and the mistress elegantly, and so on. There is no mention of magnolia, but there is an allusion to moonlight when Uncle Gabe describes "de flocks ob sheep . . . so gret an' white, / Dey 'peared like clouds on a moon-shine night." And, of course, there is the central relationship involving a planter-father, his planter-son, and the fact that the return of the latter signifies a virtual return of the former. When "young marster" comes back to buy back his father's plantation, Uncle Gabe receives him with the same attitude of worship that he had once bestowed upon the young man's father ("When eber de marster got right pleased," he says at one point, "de marster's face . . . use to shine wid 'e heavenly grace"). So overwhelming is the religious imagery, therefore, that the poem cannot rightly be described as allegorical. Rather than looking forward to an afterlife—the sort of thing actual slaves had once done in order to be able to endure miserable lives spent working in the fields—Uncle Gabe regards his masters themselves as divine and the plantation as a veritable heaven-on-earth.

G rady's introduction of himself to a national audience was rather less rapturous. It involved similar images of a slave's fidelity and white southern man's return to a ruined plantation, however, and depicted the Old South as a society from which modern Americans still had much to learn. Titled "The New South," it took the form of a speech delivered before the New England Club of New York in December 1886. At the time Grady had been on the editorial staff at the *Constitution* for a decade and had built it into the leading newspaper in Georgia. He had also delivered several public addresses locally and had worked as the Atlanta correspondent for the *New York Herald* and a few additional nonsouthern newspapers. His renown was for the most part regional, however, and when he ventured to New York in late 1886, it marked the first time he would speak to an audience outside of Georgia as well as the first time the New England Club had invited a southerner to address its membership. Among the more famous men in attendance were the industrialist John Pierpont Morgan, the theologian Lyman Abbott, the lawyer Elihu Root, and the retired Union general William Tecumseh Sherman, whose reputation among Georgians Grady dared to acknowledge as part of his speech: "General Sherman . . . is considered an able man in our parts, though some people think he is a kind of careless man about fire."[17]

That joke set up remarks about Atlanta's having risen "from the ashes," which introduced the central idea of his speech: the idea that the South had emerged from the Civil War and Reconstruction a stronger society than it had been before. In remarks that he would revise in subsequent speeches, Grady actually spoke in his debut address of the limitations a plantation economy had imposed upon the culture of the antebellum South:

> The South found her jewel in the toad's head of defeat. The shackles that had held her in narrow limitations fell forever when the shackles of the negro slave were broken. . . . The old plantation, with its simple police regulations and feudal habit, was the only type possible under slavery. Thus was gathered in the hands of a splendid and chivalric oligarchy the substance that should have been diffused among the people, as the rich blood, under certain artificial conditions, is gathered at the heart, filling that with affluent rapture, but leaving the body chill and colorless. (90)[18]

Grady's primary purpose in 1886 was to convince northern capitalists to invest in the South, and he was willing at that point to speak of the plantation as an institution that the New South had largely transcended. (He would be criticized by some southerners for this one aspect of the speech upon returning, and as I discuss later in this chapter, his future writings and speeches would explain the relationship between the Old South and the New differently.) Yet even as he was depicting the old plantation as an organism by nature always on the verge of atrophy, he was working to identify those aspects of an older southern society that warranted conserving.

He did this, for example, by referring back to an even more distant "southern" ancestor, John Smith, and speaking of him as the original American entrepreneur to an audience composed largely of northeastern businessmen. His not-so-subtle point was to suggest to the New England Club of New York that their "southern" roots were in fact as deep as their Puritan ones. He did this also by likening the South's recent history to the Puritans' errand and suggesting that the birth of the New South marked a continuation of the New World saga. Arguing that secession had been less an act of rebellion than an appeal to God to determine whether the nation could remain half-slave and half-free, Grady expressed gratitude that the question had been "adjudged by a higher and fuller wisdom . . . and that human slavery was swept forever from American soil, [and] the American Union was saved from the wreck of war." Viewed in this light, the South became a "consecrated ground"; like Page, Grady was willing to exploit religious metaphors in order to depict recent southern history as providential. He was also willing to link a sense of religion with a veneration of southern patriarchy in order to reconfigure ideas of American nationalism. Noting that his hometown of Athens had erected a monument to its Confederate dead that bore among its inscriptions the name of his own father, Grady proclaimed that "not for all the glories of New England, from Plymouth Rock all the way, would I exchange the heritage he left me in his soldier's death" (91–92). Imagining the South's defeat as a reaffirmation of God's intentions for the United States, Grady could see in a statue erected in a medium-sized southern city something analogous to a national monument.

What Grady most wished to celebrate about the Old South, however, were its race relations and how far in *advance* of the rest of the nation the region had supposedly long been. Though he began his speech by rejoicing that the "South of slavery and secession . . . is dead," and though he was willing to regard the Emancipation Proclamation as the act that had assured the North of its righteous victory, "commit[ing] you to the cause of human liberty, against which the arms of man cannot prevail," he still insisted that race relations in the South had always been "close and cordial" (83, 89). He regarded as proof that the southern system provided the best arrangement of a multiracial society the fact that black and white southerners had remained "close" in spite of slavery. Scourge though slavery had been, it had not impeded what Grady felt to be the forms of natural affection that would develop when a multiracial society was structured so whites held the power to make decisions regarding the governance of society as a whole. He took as further proof of the South's social superiority the fact that slaves had remained on the plantation during and after the war: "We remember with what fidelity for four years [the negro] guarded our defenseless women and children, whose husbands and fathers were fighting against his freedom" (89). Regarding them as patriots, almost, Grady invited his audience to consider the parallels between slaves who defended their plantations and soldiers who fought for the Confederacy, both of them responding to an instinctive call to protect their "homes."

While the Civil War had thus brought slavery to its fortunate end, in Grady's view it had also jeopardized the one thing about antebellum southern life—its strict adherence in its social codes to "natural" racial hierarchies—that warranted maintaining. The fact that African Americans had for a brief period begun to acquire equal rights (especially in Athens, which was a center of Freedmen's Bureau activity from 1865 to 1868) represented the one outcome of the war that Grady could not incorporate easily into the providential history he was authoring.[19] What he could do, however, was to see in the "negro problem" a sign that God had in fact entrusted white southern men with a mission every bit as consequential as the one Union soldiers had followed while fighting to preserve the Union and liberate slaves. This he illustrated in one of the rhetorical flourishes for which Grady would become best known, the story of the anonymous "footsore Confederate soldier" returning to his devastated plantation after the surrender at Appomattox:

> Think of him as ragged, half-starved, heavy-hearted, enfeebled by want and wounds, having fought to exhaustion, he surrenders his gun, wrings the hands of his comrades in silence, and lifting his tear-stained and pallid face for the last time to the graves that dot, old Virginia hills, pulls his gray cap over his brow and begins the slow and painful journey. What does he find . . . when, having followed the battle-stained cross against overwhelming odds, dreading death not half so much as surrender, he reaches the home he left so prosperous and beautiful? He finds his house in ruins, his farm devastated, his slaves free, his stock killed, his barns empty, his trade destroyed, his money worthless, his social system, feudal in its magnificence, swept away; his people without law or legal status; his comrades slain, and the burdens of others heavy on his shoulders. Crushed by defeat, his very traditions are gone. Without money, credit, employment, material, or training; and beside all this, confronted with the gravest problem that ever met human intelligence— the establishing of a status for the vast body of his liberated slaves. (86–87)

Having already invited his audience to consider themselves linked to southerners by way of such figures as John Smith, and having also paid homage to New England if only to urge a reconsideration of Virginia and Georgia as similarly historically important, Grady suggested that southern planters were superior to other Americans in one regard: they had borne "the burdens of others heavy on [their] shoulders" for a longer period of time than had anyone else. They had therefore exhibited a greater endurance in the face of challenges posed by multiraciality than had the Union soldiers whose victorious homecomings had primarily been to *white* homesteads—to places that had remained safe not only from battle but also from the problems Grady associated with race.

Though it would be impossible to identify with any certainty the precise moment that the idea of a "white man's burden" became the white North's preferred mechanism for reconciling with the white South, one could do worse than to point to this, perhaps the climactic moment in Grady's 1886 speech. The image seemed to resonate with his audience, for he would feature it even more prominently in later speeches (as in an address delivered less than a year later in Dallas, where he would speak to an audience composed primarily of southerners of the South's "problem . . . to carry within her body politic two separate races. . . . This burden no other people bears today").[20] It also marked a turning point within the speech itself. The earlier sections of "The New South" were devoted to renouncing slavery, burying the Old South's economy, honoring the heroes of the North (including even Sherman, the most reviled of Union generals in Georgia), and revising U.S. history in such a way that the South became a copartner rather than a problem. His opening gestures, in other words, were meant to underscore the similarities between white northerners and white southerners. Following the anecdote about the "footsore Confederate soldier" and its concluding invocation of the idea of burdened white manhood, however, Grady's tone shifted slightly to something more confrontational. "Never was nobler duty confided to human hands than the uplifting and upbuilding of the prostrate and bleeding South," a task that would have been difficult enough, Grady urged, even if white southerners had not been faced with the additional difficulties represented by Emancipation. The presence of this challenge, however—"the gravest problem that ever met human intelligence"—made the story of the rise of the New South heroic, even epic. Thus, Grady was willing to end his speech by daring his audience not to admire white southerners: "Now, what answer has New England to this message? Will she permit the prejudice of war to remain in the hearts of the conquerors, when it has died in the hearts of the conquered?" (87–88, 92). According to newspaper accounts, his audience responded with an emphatic "no" after each of these questions. Yet what was also going on amid this renunciation of sectional "prejudice," of course, was the adoption of another: a prejudice against African Americans because of the "burdens" they supposedly represented to white society. Having lost the war, white southern men were being nominated to face an additional challenge over which they might be victorious. And having won the war, white northern men seemed to be responding to the idea that, if the nation were indeed going to be facing a growing race problem in the future, white southern men might prove uniquely capable of dealing with it.

Grady began his 1886 speech by apologizing to his New York audience for speaking in a "provincial voice" (83). By the end he was speaking differently, though not because he had ceased trying to sound "southern." Quite the opposite. His aim had in fact been to elevate white southernness to the point that it seemed identical to U.S. nationality. Given the enthusiasm exhibited by his audience—newspaper accounts noted that he was interrupted repeatedly with applause—he likely thought his first effort to redefine his home region for the nation had been successful:

Every foot of soil about the city in which I live is as sacred as a battle-ground of the republic. Every hill that invests it is hallowed to you by the blood of your brothers, who died for your victory, and doubly hallowed to us by the blow of those who died hopeless, but undaunted, in defeat—sacred soil to all of us—rich with memories that make us purer and stronger and better—silent but staunch witnesses in its red desolation of the matchless valor of American hearts and the deathless glory of American arms—speaking an eloquent witness in its white peace and prosperity to the indissoluble union of American States and the imperishable brotherhood of the American people. (92)

The repetition of the word "American" makes clear that by the end of his speech Grady was no longer seeking simple recognition from his audience of white northerners. Having rewritten the South into the story of early America by gently reminding his audience of Virginia's primacy in the history of England's colonization of North America, he had moved on to a bolder project. By his conclusion he was speaking confidently and even definitively about contemporary U.S. nationality, presuming to lecture an audience that included Sherman on what it meant to be "American." This was despite the fact that the subject of his address, "The New South," might have seemed by definition to have limited him to a much more local set of concerns.

It is thus worth pausing here to consider what Grady was accomplishing and what indeed might have been happening in terms of northern attitudes about the South during the decade bracketed by Page's and Grady's national debuts. The year of "Uncle Gabe's White Folks," 1877, marked the end of Reconstruction and the beginning of what white southern historiographers would soon call the "Redemption" era of southern history. That spirit is captured in Page's poem, which depicts a young southern man's repurchase of his father's plantation as a redemptive act, a fulfillment even of Uncle Gabe's prophecy in the opening stanza: "de Marster's gwine ter come back from 'broad." Yet "Uncle Gabe's White Folks" appeared at a moment when African Americans retained at least some of the rights and forms of material advancement gained during the era of "radical" Reconstruction, only recently ended. Their political status, though by no means secure, was stronger by comparison than it would be twenty years later, by which point the era of Jim Crow was underway and the U.S. Supreme Court had ruled in *Plessy v. Ferguson* (1896) that the forms of racial discrimination practiced in the South and elsewhere did not necessarily violate the Fourteenth Amendment, the cornerstone achievement of Reconstruction. Grady's "New South" speech was delivered exactly in the middle of this period, nine years after the end of Reconstruction and ten before Jim Crow would be ruled constitutional. To say that it turned a tide would be to claim too much, yet at the very least it registered a profound change that was underway. By identifying a "negro" problem as the next challenge to be overcome in the unfolding of an *American* and not simply a southern historical saga, moreover, it provided a means of constructing a national epic out of the story of the plantation South—of making the most "local" of local color fictions a narrative of nationhood, too.

It was during the two or three years after Grady delivered his December 1886 speech, in fact, that plantation fiction became the demonstrable national sensation it would remain for the next two decades. In my introduction I made reference to Albion W. Tourgée, the Ohio-born lawyer, social activist, and novelist who observed in an essay published in the *Forum* in September 1888 that the South seemed to him suddenly to have taken the lead in defining U.S. culture:

> A foreigner studying our current literature, without knowledge of our history, and judging our civilization by our fiction, would undoubtedly conclude that the South was the seat of intellectual empire in America, and the African the chief romantic element of our population. As evidence of this, it may be noted that a few months ago every one of our great popular monthlies presented a "Southern story" as one of its most prominent features; and during the past year nearly two-thirds of the stories and sketches furnished to newspapers by various syndicates have been of this character.[21]

Writing less than two years after Grady's "New South" speech, Tourgée was likely thinking about either March or April 1888, during which a slew of "Southern stories," most of them set on plantations, appeared in no fewer than seventeen national magazines. (The April *Century* alone contained three such items, including "Marse Phil," another dialect poem by Page in which an elderly ex-slave addresses the reader as a "young marster," the "ve'y spi't-an'-image" of his father.) Most of these were short stories and sketches, which, given the limitations of form, did not envision historical narratives quite as vast as the one Grady was proposing. Yet they did fixate on the figure of the freedman remaining on or returning to the plantation—"the African the chief romantic element of our population," as Tourgée calls him. And since this figure was typically loyal to his former master yet incapable of supporting himself on his own, the works that featured him managed at least to imply that slavery had been to his benefit and to depict postslavery as a development that

Figure 15. Plantation Proximities IV: illustration that accompanied Page's "Marse Phil" in the April 1888 *Century.*

would require white southern men to resume subsidizing and managing "the negro's" welfare. "Marse Phil" exemplifies this. In its last stanza the "young marster" gives the speaker of the poem a five-dollar piece to thank him for the services once rendered to his father and mother. In another item that appeared that month—Harris's "Ananias," a short story published in *Harper's*—a former slave who had traveled with Sherman's army is pictured "gwine back ter Marster" after discovering that his northern taskmasters would pay him nothing and reward him with none of the affection he had known on the plantation. Both the poem and the short story featured black men who tell their stories to white visitors who arrive on horseback. The similarities between their illustrations (Figs. 15 and 16) suggest how standardized the tropes of plantation fiction were becoming, hence why someone such as Tourgée might have felt overwhelmed by the imagery he was encountering in "our great popular monthlies."[22]

Figure 16. Plantation Proximities V: illustration that accompanied Harris's "Ananias" in the April 1888 *Harper's New Monthly Magazine*.

Within twenty years, though, the epic story envisioned by Grady in the 1886 speech would be finding more frequent literary expression. Thomas Dixon's *The Leopard's Spots* (1902), a novel I discuss at length in the next chapter, stretches from the Civil War to the turn of the century in order to present the fantasy promised in its subtitle, *A Romance of the White Man's Burden*. Harris's *Gabriel Tolliver*, published that same year, focuses more on Reconstruction yet still manages to tell a story of epic significance in which white southern men awake after Emancipation "startled and stunned . . . they opened their eyes to the situation [and] found themselves confronted by conditions that had no precedent or parallel in the history of the world."[23] Both anticipate *Gone with the Wind* (1936), Margaret Mitchell's epic novel in which a similar sequence of historical turning points—secession, war, defeat, Emancipation, Reconstruction, "Redemption"—provides Mitchell the opportunity to explore what happens when a white woman, Scarlett O'Hara, assumes what amounts to a white man's burden after her father dies and leaves her Tara, the vast plantation he had founded.

Of greatest relevance to this chapter, though, is Page's *Red Rock* (1898), a novel that preceded all of these and may have been the first to try to translate the historical vision of Grady's "New South" into literary form. The novel does not extend as far backward into history as Grady's speech, beginning as it does during the late antebellum period, not the early seventeenth century and era of John Smith. The plantation that serves as the novel's central setting and provides it its name, Red Rock, was established much earlier, however. In fact, its name derives from a "huge bowlder" located near the family cemetery and bearing a "great red stain, as big as a blanket"—by legend, a bloodstain left when, ages earlier, the founder of the plantation had slain an Indian chief in retribution for the chief's having murdered the man's wife. A violent variation upon the John Smith–Pocahontas story, the legend that Page relates in the opening paragraphs of *Red Rock* serves to highlight the fact that its eponymous plantation was erected as part of the historical processes of Indian-fighting and U.S. westward expansion. Local "color," in this case "that deep stain in the darker granite" that serves "as a perpetual memorial of the swift vengeance of the Jacquelin Grays," is thus also in *Red Rock* a sign of *national* character: a symbol analogous to the "sacred soil . . . silent but staunch witness in its red desolation of the matchless valor of American hearts" celebrated by Grady as the southern equivalent to Plymouth Rock in his "New South" address.[24]

The name referred to in the passage above, "Jacquelin Gray," belongs to the planter paterfamilias whose killing of the Indian chief provides *Red Rock* its legendary point of origin. It belongs also to the novel's present-day central character as well as to his father. Just as Page himself had inherited names from multiple men who had figured prominently in Virginia's history, Jacquelin Gray, *Red Rock*'s protagonist, represents an individual whose natal aspiration is almost to become corporate, to embody all of the men who had preceded him as Red Rock's owners and its slaves' masters. Page describes him as in some respects typical, "just what most other boys of his station, stature, and blood, living on a plantation, under similar conditions, would have been." He makes clear, however, that a "typical" planter's son is almost necessarily exceptional because of what his paternal ancestors have achieved. When Jacquelin was born, in fact, his father was away "in Mexico, winning renown in those battles which helped to establish the security of the United States" (3). A tradition of empire building thus runs deep in the Gray family—so deep that, during the run-up to the Civil War, its men oppose secession because it would mean breaking up the nation they and their fathers had fought to create. They do side with the Confederacy once the southern states have seceded, and Jacquelin, though he volunteers to fight, spends much of the war a prisoner in a Union camp. He performs nobly despite his limited capacity for heroics, at one point allowing a friend to be freed as part of a prisoner exchange when he himself is offered the opportunity. Like the young men of the New South about whom Grady would speak in 1886, however, he would have to wait until after the war to prove himself fully worthy of his paternity.

That opportunity comes, of course, as a result of Reconstruction—as Page depicts it an era in which the natural orders of U.S. society are turned upside down because "negroes" are made masters over their former owners, white northerners become cultural imperialists by transforming into "Reconstructionists," white southern scalawags betray the principles of race as well as region by collaborating with freedmen as well as carpetbaggers, and white southern planters' sons are saddled with the responsibility of recreating the society their ancestors had spent ages building and perfecting. In Page's melodramatic rendering of recent U.S. history, restoring the plantation thus means righting the world. In Jacquelin's case this involves litigating to recover the title to his father's plantation, which a corrupt former overseer turned scalawag has illegitimately acquired. He accomplishes this, though by no means quickly: the central question of the novel—whether Jacquelin can fulfill an early pledge to his father to "keep the old place"—requires more than five hundred pages to answer. (*Red Rock* thus represents an elaboration of the same plot hinted at in fewer than eighty lines of poetry in "Uncle Gabe's White Folks." Page's literary career, which spanned from 1877 until 1922, was characterized less by a desire to originate scenes and ideas than by a compulsion toward rehearsing the same ones in different levels of detail and from different perspectives, doing so always, though, with the same moral and message in mind.) In the meantime Jacquelin recovers from his war wounds, makes a journey to China, returns to find that his closest friends have joined the Ku Klux Klan to save the South from malicious carpetbaggers and insubordinate "negroes," dons the Klan robes himself in order to save a carpetbagger from a lynch mob—an act that makes the Klan appear assiduously legal rather than terroristic—and, by doing all of this, wins the hand of his childhood sweetheart. He brings her back to Red Rock in the final paragraph of the novel "to tell of his new happiness" (584).

A novel with a literal happy ending (and an almost once-upon-a-time beginning: it commences with an introduction printed entirely in italics and promising to tell the story of a place "*too far from the centres of modern progress to be laid down on any map that will be accessible*"), *Red Rock*'s plot is far less important than its political vision (vii). Page claimed actually to have rewritten the entire novel because, in its original form, it had seemed *too* political.[25] Yet whatever the original text may have looked like, the final version strives primarily to illustrate why white southern men should never have been denied power over their plantation domains and why the period between Emancipation and Redemption had thus represented a period of irregularity in the long history of white dominion in America, from the days of Indian-fighting to those of the rise of the Ku Klux Klan. His method for illustrating this political vision was largely identical to Grady's, for it involved inventing scenes in which young white men enter into a planter patriarchy both literally, in the sense that they assume control of plantations, and figuratively, in the sense that they devote themselves to the cause of white supremacy that the plantocracy had long symbolized.[26]

The scene in which Jacquelin is first recognized as a "man" involves a discussion between him and his father about Red Rock and what might happen to it should his father die during the war:

> He talked to him as if he were a man. Jacquelin suddenly felt all his old timidity of his father vanish, and a new spirit, as it were, rise up in his heart. His father told him that now that he was going away to the war, he might never come back,—but he left, he said, with the assurance that whatever happened, he would be worthily succeeded; and he said that he was proud of him, and had the fullest confidence in him. . . .
>
> Mr. Gray told Jacquelin of his will. He had left his mother everything; but it would be the same thing as if he had left it to him and [his younger

brother]. . . . "I leave it to her, and I leave her to you," he said, putting his hand on the boy's shoulder. Jacquelin listened, his mind suddenly sobered and expanded to a man's measure. (47)

This sense of expansion happens again only a few pages later when the elder Jacquelin Gray is indeed killed in battle and his son, convinced that "there ought to be one of us in the old company," declares his intention to his mother to join the Confederate army. After he does so "Mrs. Gray rose suddenly and flung herself into his arms and hugged him and clung to him, and wept on his shoulder, as though he were his father. So the change comes: the boy in little trousers suddenly stands before the mother a man; . . . the children have gone; the old has passed; and the new is here" (51). The Gray family's "New South" thus arrives even before the end of the war. Like Grady's, however, it involves a son's becoming worthy of his father—a recommitment to the past rather than an attempt to forge something new.

The most interesting moment in what is paradoxically Jacquelin's evolution toward his *ancestry* occurs later in the novel. Near its midpoint and following the death of his mother he learns that the scalawag who temporarily controls Red Rock has refused to allow her to be buried beside his father and plans eventually to have the graveyard moved. That night Jacquelin steals into the mansion and finds the scalawag, whose name is Hiram Still, asleep over some papers at what used to be his own father's desk:

Suddenly there was a step, or something like a step, near him   he was not sure about it, for he must have been dozing—and he looked up. His heart jumped into his throat. Before him in the hall stood, tall and gray, the "Indian-killer," his eyes blazing like coals of fire.

"Good God !" he gasped.

No, it was speaking—it was a man. But it was almost as bad. Still had not seen Jacquelin before in two years. And he had never noticed how like the "Indian-killer" he was. What did he want?

"I have come to see you about the grave-yard," said Jacquelin. The voice was his father's. It smote Still like a voice from the dead. (261)

Page's assertion in *Red Rock*'s opening paragraphs that the stain on the boulder serves as a "perpetual memorial of the swift vengeance of the Jacquelin Grays" anticipates this moment, at which Jacquelin Gray actually becomes "Jacquelin Grays." By defending his mother, whom his father had virtually bequeathed to him during their final conversation, he becomes even more like his sire. By vindicating a white woman—the act by which the original Jacquelin Gray had staked his claim upon the New World—he becomes like the Gray primogenitor. He comes close even to embodying his ancestry, manifesting his father's voice and his more distant ancestor's appearance. In so doing he vanquishes the white southern turncoat and achieves full manhood: "it was speaking—it was a man" (Fig. 17).[27] The moment he does so represents one of two climactic scenes in the text, both of which make clear that the tide of history is turning away from the forces of Reconstruction and toward those of traditional white southern power.

The other such scene occurs fewer than thirty pages earlier. Taking place also at night, it marks the birth of the Ku Klux Klan (Fig. 18). As with the scene soon to come, Page recounts the moment in the language of a ghost story:

> In the dead of night, when the cabins and settlements were wrapped in slumber, came a visitation, passing through the county from settlement to settlement and from cabin to cabin, in silence, but with a thoroughness that showed the most perfect organization. . . . The yard had been found full of awful forms wrapped like ghosts in winding-sheets, some of whom had entered the houses, picked up the guns and ammunition, and without a word walked out and disappeared. (237)

The Klan, which under its hoods represents the South's white male citizenry from high to low, has formed to seize the guns recently distributed by a carpetbagger to create a black militia. In both virtual hauntings that take place at the center of *Red Rock*, then, those targeted are the forces of Reconstruction while those perpetrating the hauntings are the men Page considers the legitimate heirs to power in the South. These include Jacquelin Gray, the literal descendant of the most powerful planters his community has known. Yet they also include the Klansmen, some of whom are well-born but others of whom are common. The phenomenon I have been discussing thus far in this chapter—the imaginative processes by which a "New South" ideology made it possible for *non*descendants to feel connected to a planter patriarchy—is thus realized with particular efficacy in *Red Rock*. Over a span of thirty pages in the central section of the novel, a literal heir as well as an assemblage of more figurative ones becomes "possessed," as it were, by the spirits of the Old South.[28]

And when, in one of the novel's final episodes, Jacquelin teams with a less aristocratic friend and both don the Klan robes to conduct a secret mission, Page completes his vision of new southern manhood. Familial blood

Figure 17. Plantation Hauntings I: illustration from *Red Rock* (1899).

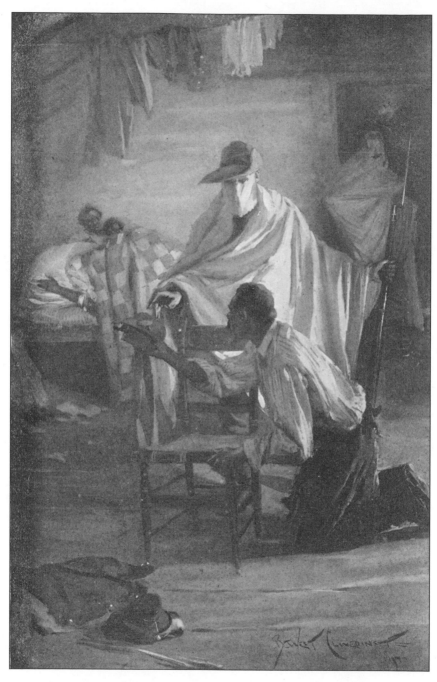

Figure 18. Plantation Hauntings II: illustration from *Red Rock* (1899).

still matters, but it matters less in the New South than "white" blood. Once he dons the robes, after all, Jacquelin is less a representative of his family—of the *Grays*, no less—than of the ideals of whiteness. Denied the opportunity to participate in the first Klan raid because he had not yet returned from China, Jacquelin leaps at the opportunity to do so later when he perceives duty calling. His and his friend's mission is, moreover, to abduct the carpetbagger for his own good and prevent him from being lynched by the more violent members of the Klan. A gesture toward realism—Page recognized in a way that Thomas Dixon would later resist that the early Klan was capable of less-than-noble acts—the scene in which the two Klansmen rescue the carpetbagger so that he may later face justice is even more purposefully a gesture toward white supremacy. The carpetbagger is white, after all: even though he is a Yankee, a corrupt politician, and an arms supplier to "negroes," he deserves to be treated, the leaders of *Red Rock*'s "New South" determine, like a U.S. citizen.

The culmination of Page's novel is therefore to uphold the Fourteenth Amendment and its assurance of equal protection in the case of a white man, hence to make the Ku Klux Klan, or at least its nobler element, a defender of the Constitution. Evaluated racially, *Red Rock* turns out to be militantly pro-American.[29] The idea that Grady had begun popularizing just over a decade earlier—that white southerners had always been the equals of white northerners in terms of their contributions to national culture but, given the challenges of postslavery, had lately taken the lead in determining whether "America" would continue to grow and prosper—thus receives its fullest nineteenth-century literary treatment in Page's 1898 novel. Thoroughly conventional as a love story, *Red Rock* is much bolder as a restatement of history and reconstitution of "America" as what Edward Blum has termed "the white republic."[30] It is bolder still in its effort to combine multiple narrative forms, from family legends to North-South romance plots to courtroom dramas to ghost stories, in order to accomplish yet again what "Uncle Gabe's White Folks" had attempted two decades earlier: namely, inviting nondescendant readers to imagines themselves the virtual heirs of a planter patriarchy.

Such efforts at redrawing the maps and reconfiguring the genealogies of American identity relied upon a particular deployment of the concept of race, one that by 1898 had become characteristic of plantation fiction. As Raymond Williams taught a number of years ago in *Keywords* (1976), the word "race" entered the English language first to indicate an actual "line of descent" only to become by the middle nineteenth century a way of indexing "broad differential groups among humans." Originally used to denote kinship, usually of the patrilineal sort (the "race and stock of Abraham" is the example of this usage provided by Williams), by the second half of the nineteenth century, which is to say, during the period studied in this book, it had become a way of imagining "blood" ties among individuals who otherwise had no familial relationships with one another.[31] Rather remarkably, however, what was being enacted in the texts discussed thus far in this chapter were fantasies in which the literal lines of descent that connected fathers to sons were being extended into metaphorical ones. The intention was that any white American be able to imagine an "ole Marster," a "footsore Confederate soldier," or even a hooded Klansman a symbol of whiteness, hence a "relative" at least by race.

Page's entire fictional output proceeds along these lines. To read *Red Rock*; the stories collected in *In Ole Virginia* (1877), his most popular book; *Two Little Confederates* (1888), a children's book based on his own childhood rec-ollections of the war; or any of the additional several works of fiction he pub-lished during his lifetime is to see again and again an image of a white southern family expanding to accommodate sympathetic Yankees, sometimes through marriage plots, sometimes by appeals to the reader's racial sensibilities. The family expands, moreover, while managing never to surrender its fundamental beliefs, above all its belief that "the negro" requires white southerners to take care of him. This belief, hence Page's white supremacy, is articulated most forcibly in *The Negro: The Southerner's Problem* (1904), a treatise on southern race relations that at first depicts white southerners as a breed apart because of their proximity to "negroes"—their having "live[d] in constant touch with the blacks . . . [and] known them in every relation of life in a way that no one who has not lived among them can know them." The book builds toward much broader gestures regarding white racial instinct, however. Addressing such top-ics as "Slavery and the Old Relation between the Southern Whites and Blacks" and "The Old Time Negro," Page develops a solution to the race problem by way of the image of the old plantation that had circulated in literary texts, his as well as others, over the previous quarter century. He regards the plantation as having developed naturally. Reconstruction, meanwhile, had involved the imposition of unnatural legal and political measures to elevate "negroes" be-yond their capacities. He thus argues that, as the South turns more toward in-dustry in the twentieth century, black southerners should be required to prove themselves within the new economy rather than depend on any governmental or philanthropic agency to elevate them. Relying on measures of external im-provement, Page argues in the final words of the text, would violate "the law of nature, universal and inexorable—that races rise or fall according to their character."[32]

In so saying—and in claiming exclusive jurisdiction over "the negro" as "the southerner's problem"—Page was once again echoing Grady, who, following the success of his 1886 speech in New York, was invited to address additional audiences throughout the country. In most of these speeches he repeated the central themes of "The New South," vowing that the region had forsworn sectionalism, promising that it was embracing industry, and insisting that the only thing hindering its development now was northern interference in the race problem, "a problem, in solving which the South must stand alone," as he said in an 1887 speech in Dallas. That speech represented one of the ways in which Grady's public stance was evolving, for it placed much greater emphasis on the magnitude of the race problem to the world, hence the importance of what white southerners were achieving by resolving the issue themselves:

> The races and tribes of earth are of Divine origin. . . . The Indian, the Malay, the Negro, the Caucasian, these types stand as markers of God's will. Those who would put the negro race in supremacy would work against infallible decree, for the white race can never submit to its domination, because the white race is the superior race. . . .
>
> The white race must dominate forever in the South, because it is the white race, and superior to that race by which its supremacy is threatened.[33]

Speaking to a southern audience, Grady may have felt moved to expand on the racial component of his message. Yet when he was invited to speak two years later in Boston—"within touch of Plymouth Rock and Bunker Hill . . . here in the cradle of American letters, and almost of American liberty," as he said at the outset of the speech—he changed his tone but little. Daring even to nominate himself a "missionary," an "apostle," and a bearer of the gospel of white supremacy seeking to "plant the standard of a Southern Democrat in Boston's banquet hall," Grady kept his message the same as it had been in Dallas:

> The resolute, clear-headed, broad-minded men of the South—the men whose genius made glorious every page of the first seventy years of American history . . . realize, as you cannot, what this problem means—what they owe to this kindly and dependent race—the measure of their debt to the world in whose despite they defended and maintained slavery. And though their feet are hindered in its undergrowth, and their march encumbered with its

burdens, they have lost neither the patience from which comes clearness, nor the faith from which comes courage.[34]

Newspaper accounts of the event suggest that it may have been even better received than the speech three years earlier in New York—and this despite the fact that he was speaking in New England and that his message by 1889 should no longer have surprised anyone in his audience. It had remained largely the same, having changed only in that it placed greater emphasis on the race problem and proved more celebratory of the old plantation, whose economic insufficiencies he no longer discussed. Rather, the old plantation of Grady's nonfiction, like the one of Page's fiction, had become a touchstone for evaluating national character. It had become less an economic than a cultural institution, which meant that industrialization could be seen as signaling its virtual rebirth, not its demise.[35]

The New South is simply the Old South under new conditions."[36] So wrote Grady in *The New South*, a series of articles written for the *New York Ledger* in 1889 and published in book form in 1890, the year after Grady's death. Grady became sick while in Boston, apparently delivering the speech cited above with a high fever and feelings of exhaustion. He died within a week of his return to Atlanta, making him seem to many who commented on his death almost a martyr to the cause of North-South racial reunion. It also contributed mightily to his already considerable national celebrity and likely earned his final speeches and writings even greater notice than they might have attracted otherwise. The *New York Times* noted in its obituary that he was almost unexampled in recent U.S. history: "Few men who have never entered the public service were more widely known throughout the country than Henry W. Grady."[37]

The New South illustrates little that has not already been commented on in this chapter. What makes it noteworthy is that, like the 1889 speech in Boston, it represents Grady speaking to what he clearly imagines as a national audience. And whereas only three years earlier he had made a rather elaborate if strategic show of his veneration for the culture of New England and the North, by 1889, when he wrote *The New South*, he seemed to think he no longer needed to ingratiate himself to his readers nor devote a great deal of space toward defending his home region. His relative silence on such issues as the problems associated with slavery and "the feudal habit[s]," as he had once termed them, of a planter "oligarchy" reluctant to modernize suggest that, during the three years that had elapsed since his initial rise to national fame, Grady sensed that the South seemed already a different space to his readers.

Thus, he would refer to the South in the opening sentence of his book as "one of the most interesting regions in the civilized world," a remark that makes clear that, in terms of its levels of cultural attainment, the South should no longer be considered laggard. He then catalogs the region's natural resources and speaks of its white citizens as "a people that in swift and amazing recuperation have discounted the miracle wrought by the French people after the Franco-Prussian war, and have given new glory to the American name, and a new meaning to energy" (141–42). Rather than comparing them initially to northerners, which had been his strategy in most of his earlier speeches, Grady here seeks a broader context to explain the significance of the South and its "people."[38] He does this elsewhere in *The New South* by claiming, for example, that it is the region's duty to "produce and enlarge the crop," cotton, "that clothes the world"; that its "combination" of natural resources, climate, and cheap labor "is not surpassed elsewhere on earth"; and that its postwar "restoration and development . . . has challenged universal admiration" (143, 145, 228). Even the problem of postslavery, which Grady calls "the only shadow that rests on the South," presents an opportunity to show the world what white southern men can achieve and why fate has left it to them to discover a solution to the problem: "The American Republic has achieved great things, but it will have nothing better to render into the keeping of universal history than the progress made by the two races in the South in the past twenty-five years towards the adjustment of their relations and the solution of the problem is theirs" (252).

The New South is neither a work of narrative history in the mold of those Page would write later ("The Old South" and "Social Life in Old Virginia before the War," both collected and published in 1892, for example), nor certainly is it a historical novel in the mold of *Red Rock*. Interestingly, however, its structure is in many ways reminiscent of a work of epic history, with its first chapter discussing the South's deep history and the outbreak of the Civil War, the second, third, and fourth chapters detailing in different ways how white southerners had overcome the challenges of defeat by committing themselves to hard work and to re-seeing their region in terms of its industrial potential, and its fourth chapter mentioning the "shadow cast" by the race problem yet asserting that this, too, represents a challenge white southerners will overcome "to tender into the keeping of universal history." Its final chapter, meanwhile, actually returns to the subject of the Old South's planter patriarchy in order to emphasize the idea that it had not been transcended. Whereas he had once spoken of them as feudal lords trapped in the past by slavery and making the best they could from a plantation system gradually becoming outmoded, by 1889 he was developing different images, speaking instead of planter-fathers and their planter-sons as having led parallel lives, "the old man, trembling and aged, but happy in the heart and home of his son—the young man, confirmed in his new life, and holding it to be, though more strenuous, yet broader and better than the old life ever could have been" (257–58).

Red Rock and, as we will see in the next chapter, the early novels of Thomas Dixon embody these ideas as well, suggesting that one might discover an essential southernness whether one was examining the past or studying the present or indeed looking toward the future, or whether one was contemplating the activities of white southerners themselves or simply beholding the natural resources they superintended. The result of any such exploration of the South produced what can only be described as an expansive vision, a sentiment best expressed when Grady engages directly with the subject of father-son relationships that has been at the heart of this chapter:

> So much for the past of the South—and only in so much as it must affect the future. . . . The old blood in its descending strains will scarcely mount higher, run more clearly or resolutely, flow more freely at duty's call or stain less where it touches, than in the turbulent and strenuous days that are gone. In devotion, in courage, in earnestness, in ability, the sons shall not surpass their fathers. Happy will it be for them and for theirs if in these cardinal virtues they equal them!
>
> But the sons fight under new conditions, for greater ends, in broader fields. The blight of slavery is lifted from above and about them. The wall that shut them in is leveled, and the South stands in unhindered comradeship with the world. . . . The promise of her great destiny, written in her fields, her quarries, her mines, her forests, and her rivers, is no longer blurred or indistinct, and the world draws near to read.
>
> How rapidly she has adapted herself to these new conditions—how she has grown to the requirements of her larger duty—how she has builded from pitiful resources a great and expanding empire, [*The New South*] shall now proceed to tell. (160–62)

Though Grady would be dead by the time these words appeared in book form, much would be published over the next twenty years to confirm his vision that the South constituted not simply a region or section of the United States but rather "a great and expanding empire" whose lead the nation should follow.

That the connections between fathers and sons emphasized by Grady and Page from the outsets of their public careers should have been part of a campaign toward white supremacy and the disenfranchisement of black southerners is not surprising. One way to resist political and social change is to imagine power in patrilineal terms, and one way to retain power in the face of change is to make arguments in favor of expanding only slightly the community of those capable of exercising civil authority—in this case, by retaining the limits based on gender and establishing new limits based on race that, prior to Reconstruction, did not require emphasizing. That these father-son connections should also have led both Grady and Page to become advocates for a kind of imperialism was far less obvious. I wish to bring this chapter to a close by considering why, in the case of these two men, the New South and its defining characteristic, new southern manhood, should have produced visions of regional and national history and destiny so undeniably expansionist and imbued with a spirit of empire.

Grady died almost a decade before the Spanish-American War (1898–1899). It is almost certain that, whether he had remained in journalism or finally made the leap into politics, he would have taken a public stance on the issue. While it is impossible to say what his stance would have been, any opposition to the war and the ideas that made it so popular—the notion that it had come time for the United States to join the community of conquering nations and "take up the white man's burden" in such places as Cuba and the Philippines—would have to be explained in light of his earlier comments, such as those just cited and those made as part of the 1889 speech in Boston, in which he proclaimed that "the uplifting force of the American idea is under every throne on earth. . . . To redeem the earth from kingcraft and oppression—this is our mission! And we shall not fail. . . . Our history . . . has been a constant and expanding miracle from Plymouth Rock and Jamestown all the way." He would have found even more challenging the prospect of denying the following comments, which came during an 1889 speech at the University of Virginia and must rank among the most determinedly imperialist made by any U.S. figure during the late nineteenth century:

> I catch a vision of this Republic, its mighty forces in balance, and its unspeakable glory falling on all its children, chief among them the federation of English-speaking people, plenty streaming from its borders and light from its mountain tops, working out its mission under God's approving eye, until the dark continents are opened and the highways of earth are established and the shadows lifted, and the jargon of the nations stilled and the perplexities of

Babel straightened—and under one language, one liberty, and one God, all the nations of the world hearkening to the American drum beat and girding up their loins, shall march amid the breaking millennial dawn into paths of righteousness and of peace![39]

These last two rhetorical flourishes came at the ends of the speeches in Boston and Virginia, making it possible to add a stage to the narrative of history discussed earlier as characteristic of Grady's speeches. Southern (and American) history began in Jamestown, he believed. It progressed then through a 250-year period of growth, during which the plantation became its defining institution. It then entered the period of secession and the Civil War, during which white southerners appealed to God to discover a way forward for themselves and the nation. And then, after defeat, it entered the era of Reconstruction, during which "the negro problem" manifested itself and provided white southern men a chance to vindicate themselves, which they had been doing since the beginning of the era of "Redemption" and the birth of the New South. What came next, such passages as these suggest, would be a veritable age of empire, in which white southern men would follow the examples of their fathers and "fight under new conditions, for greater ends, in broader fields."

Thomas Nelson Page's imperialism can be discerned with less speculation about what he thought of the Spanish-American War and the idea of U.S. overseas expansion. Forty-five years old at the time the war broke out, Page published *Red Rock* in its midst and even wrote a poem, "The Dragon of the Sea," that was published in a collection titled *Spanish-American War Songs* (1898). Daring "the Spanish ships" to "fir[e] a single shot / Upon the Spanish Main" (by which he likely intended to pun on the fact that the *U.S.S. Maine* was the battleship whose destruction provided the United States its pretext for entering the war), Page then launched into a long history in verse of Spanish naval defeats at the hand of the English. Predictably, he depicted the English victories as events that his *U.S.* readers could claim as part of *their* heritage:

God! how they sprang! And how they tore!
    The Grenvilles, Hawkins, Drake!
Remember, boy, they were your sires!
    They made the Spaniards quake. (ll. 13–16)[40]

A first cousin of Page, William Nelson Page, was a captain of a militia that fought in the war. And though Page himself never served in the military, he would later enter the U.S. diplomatic corps, becoming U.S. ambassador to

Italy from 1913 to 1919 and publishing such works based on his overseas experiences as his *North African Journal* (1912) and *Italy and the World War* (1920). Such undertakings and writings reflect the fact that, by the early twentieth century, Page had committed himself to the idea of the United States as a "redeemer nation" whose role was to involve itself in overseas affairs to a much greater extent than it had in the nineteenth century.

Yet even as early as 1892, six years before the outbreak of the war that would confirm that the nation had entered a new colonialist phase, one might have predicted that Page would have signed on. That year, as part of a collection of essays titled *The Old South*, Page published "Social Life in Old Virginia before the War," a lengthy historical essay purporting to tell once again what Page had by that point rehearsed multiple times in fiction, nonfiction, and poetry: the history of Virginia's plantation economy and society from the early nineteenth century through the present day. Its structure and motifs should by now be predictable. It began locally, with a description of the plantation household Page had known as a child, which he offers up as typical. Along the way it venerates the planter patriarchs and matriarchs that had instilled in such young men as himself the values that made them among the United States' leading citizens. It pays homage to the figure of the mammy and other slaves and ex-slaves whose loyalties to their masters and mistresses were not compromised by Emancipation. And, of course, it ends by gesturing toward the future and imagining that the plantation, though it has been radically reconfigured by history, will continue to shape U.S. culture as that culture projected itself abroad:

> The South under her new conditions will grow rich, will wax fat; nevertheless we have lost much. How much only those who knew it can estimate; to them it was inestimable.
>
> That the social life of the Old South had its faults I am far from denying. What civilization has not? But its virtues far outweighed them; its graces were never equaled. . . . It largely contributed to produce this nation; it led its armies and its navies; it established this government so firmly that not even it could overthrow it; it opened up the great West; it added Louisiana and Texas, and more than trebled our territory; it christianized the negro race in a little over two centuries, impressed upon it regard for order, and gave it the only civilization it has ever possessed since the dawn of history. It has maintained the supremacy of the Caucasian race, upon which all civilization seems now to depend. It produced a people whose heroic fight against the forces of the world has enriched the annals of the human race—a people

whose fortitude in defeat has been even more splendid than their valor in war. It made men noble, gentle, and brave, and women tender and pure and true. It may have fallen short in material development in its narrower sense, but it abounded in spiritual development; it made the domestic virtues as common as light and air, and filled homes with purity and peace.

It has passed from the earth, but it has left its benignant influence behind it to sweeten and sustain its children. The ivory palaces have been destroyed, but myrrh, aloes, and cassia still breathe amid their dismantled ruins.[41]

As we see in the upcoming chapters, such expansionist interpretations of southern history did not end with Grady and Page. For Thomas Dixon they would provide a means of regarding the Ku Klux Klan as an even greater expression of white racial destiny. And for William Faulkner they would enable an interrogation of much of U.S. history by way of a focus on a single county in Mississippi. For Grady and Page, however, they allowed a transformation that needed to take place in order to make possible much of the southern fiction of the early twentieth century. They transformed the southern plantation from an exotic locale, which it had remained even in the fiction of Joel Chandler Harris because of its emphasis on the South's cultural hybridity, and rendered it a synecdoche for an "America" imagined as much more culturally homogeneous. Its precise relationship to the nation would change in the fiction produced by later southern writers. Its synecdochic function, however, might be considered the contribution that Grady and Page made to a U.S. cultural imaginary focused around the actions of white men.

CHAPTER 3

Manifest Destinies, Invisible Empires

Thomas Dixon's Imperial Fantasies

In his unfinished, posthumously published autobiography, Thomas Dixon Jr. recounts a conversation he had had with his publisher, Walter Hines Page, shortly before Page published *The Leopard's Spots* (1902), Dixon's debut novel and the first in his trilogy celebrating the rise of the Ku Klux Klan:

> My reception had greatly expanded my self-importance. It had not occurred to me for a single moment that the book might be accepted and published by an enterprising young house and fall flat as a pancake and never make a dollar or cause a ripple of interest.
>
> So I led off with a remark that brought a roar from Page:
>
> "You can set it down as a certainty that it will sell a hundred thousand copies—"
>
> My publisher not only laughed, he put his hand on my arm as if to hold me down to realities.
>
> "Forget such nonsense! Books don't sell by the hundred thousands. . . . A sale of twenty-five thousand copies of a novel is a big success. Thomas Nelson Page has taken the wind out of your *sails*—if I may make a pun. You're about fifteen years late for a sensation on this subject."[1]

The story may or may not be true. Walter Hines Page's most recent biographer doubts its authenticity, in part because it later depicts Page returning Dixon's manuscript to him stained with the publisher's own blood.[2] According to Dixon, Page claimed to have been so captivated by the manuscript that he could not put it down even while walking to work: "I was reading the last chapter when a street car knocked me down and nearly killed me."[3] Less sensational but no less suspicious, the anecdote resembles in its broadest contours the kind of story Dixon liked to tell over and over again in his works of fiction: one in which a white man from the U.S. South, possessing a talent and vision that not everyone around him fully recognizes, becomes the motive force behind a mass movement, proving his critics wrong and his doubters shortsighted, and, in the end, achieving a form of cultural conquest.

The Leopard's Spots sold one hundred thousand copies within a few months of its appearance and more than a million before going out of print. Its successors sold similarly well, especially *The Clansman* (1905), the second novel in the trilogy, which would later provide the basis for D. W. Griffith's film *The Birth of a Nation* (1915). Looking back at the period just before his debut as a novelist, Dixon could attribute to himself something of the same assuredness that, in *The Leopard's Spots*, he assigns his main character, a "man of genius" whose "success" in politics, Dixon observes at one point, "is as sure as if it were already won." Running on a platform of white supremacy in the late 1890s, the man is elected governor of North Carolina in one of the novel's final chapters, and Dixon, ever the numbers man, insists upon quantifying the victory: "Gaston was elected Governor by the largest majority ever given a candidate for that office."[4] A similar ending characterizes *The Clansman*, whose protagonist, a Klan leader in South Carolina during Reconstruction, also wishes to see black political participation brought to an end in his state. The novel concludes with a congressional election whose outcome—"success or failure, life or death"—is a source of worry for the protagonist's bride-to-be. He responds by predicting triumph on a massive scale: "Success, not failure. . . . The Grand Dragons of six states have already wired victory. . . . [R]ange on range our signals gleam until the Fiery Cross is lost among the stars!"[5]

The story that Dixon tells repeatedly within the Klan trilogy, in other words, eventually became the story Dixon would tell *about* the Klan trilogy. The fact that the novels rehearse the same plot again and again—protagonist envisions then achieves a lopsided victory over the forces unleashed by Emancipation and Radical Reconstruction, "tradition" and "purity" team to defeat modernity and hybridity in a landslide election or a paramilitary campaign—is evidence surely of Dixon's lack of imagination as a writer. Yet it also illustrates what he was trying to do by writing novels. "I had made no effort to write literature" or "to shine as a verbal gymnast," he writes in his autobiography. "My sole purpose in writing was to reach and influence with my argument the minds of millions."[6] Thirty-eight years old when *The Leopard's Spots* first appeared, Dixon was not a young writer hoping eventually to be ranked among the major literary figures of his generation. His goal, as it turns out, was considerably more audacious: Dixon was trying to change the world. The novel struck him as potentially a more effective means of accomplishing what he had been trying to do in his earlier careers as a politician, then preacher, then circuit lecturer. It provided a way to reach an ever-wider audience with a message that, by the late 1890s, posited white supremacy as the foundation for a global political order. *The Leopard's Spots* was itself an attempt to achieve what its protagonist discusses as the "dream" of the "young South" in one of his campaign speeches: "Our old men dreamed of local supremacy. We dream of the conquest of the globe" (435).

This chapter reads Dixon's authorial ambitions in light of his professed faith in U.S. national destiny and his galloping visions of white world supremacy. It sees these, in turn, as signs of what had become imaginable about "America" as a result of the plantation fiction of the previous two decades. To the list of factors critics have tended to cite in order to explain Dixon's reasons for wanting to rehabilitate the Ku Klux Klan—revulsion at the lingering popularity of *Uncle Tom's Cabin*, devotion to an uncle who had actually been a Klan leader, a fetishizing of white womanhood as the marker of cultural coherence, a fascination with white manhood that borders on the homoerotic, a need to resolve the contradictions inherent in whiteness itself—this chapter adds yet another: a desire to move beyond even the imperialist vision of the plantation developed in the speeches of Henry W. Grady and fiction of Thomas Nelson Page (whose "sails," as it turned out, Dixon far outdistanced with the proceeds from his first book alone). By reexamining the circumstances that led to Dixon's becoming a novelist, however, this chapter argues that imperialism should be considered the paramount concern of the Klan trilogy. White female purity, the threat of black rape, and the violent and instinctive response of the white mob constitute the key narrative elements of Dixon's fiction, as Scott Romine has argued recently.[7] Yet in Dixon the story of black rape and white response, though it takes place invariably in an out-of-the-way space typical of local color fiction, points inevitably to a story whose geography is much larger: one in which black degeneracy in the Carolinas symbolizes a translocal threat marked usually as "African," and one in which white mobs prefigure white electorates, then white nations, then finally a white global-imperial ruling class that, in Dixon's grandest idealization, is not bounded by nationality. The title of his unpublished autobiography, *Southern Horizons*, perhaps gives some sense of how Dixon sought to dislocate the regional from the merely local and to claim it instead as a way of contemplating a world beyond even national boundaries. Reading the Klan novels for evidence of a similar perspective, we may recognize in Dixon an architect not just of U.S.

racial nativism but of a kind of transnational racialism as well: a writer for whom "expanded . . . self-importance" describes not only his reaction to having his first novel "accepted and published" but also the role he imagined for himself and other white southern men in the new century.

It is with a view of a "southern horizon" that Dixon actually begins the Klan trilogy. *The Leopard's Spots* opens on the battlefields of Appomattox, Virginia, at the close of the Civil War, and in the novel's opening sentence, Robert E. Lee watches from on high as his soldiers begin the journey homeward—which is to say, southward—toward a land over which now hangs "the shadow of the freed Negro," a metaphor that Dixon later revises into a "black cloud . . . already seen on the horizon" (5, 63). As Lee looks on, his vast, "once invincible army" descends into a moment's "chaos" as news of defeat circulates among them. The novel then focuses on a single brigade from North Carolina, Dixon's home state, as it resumes marching formation with "perfect discipline," an act that calls to Dixon's mind "the passion of the first days of the triumphant Confederacy" and expresses what he later imagines to be the definitive characteristic of "the white race," namely its innate orderliness and unity. Having thus recorded both a historic loss and a historic restoration of order—and having done so within the novel's first two paragraphs, no less—Dixon then focuses on a smaller group of "ragged country boys" who splinter off from the larger brigade and travel toward a small Appalachian community based on Dixon's actual hometown. The first chapter concludes by following a single ex-slave as he returns with the soldiers to his native plantation to deliver news of his master's death.

The spatial logic of the opening chapter of *The Leopard's Spots* thus involves dilation and localization. The object at the center of its field of vision shrinks from army to brigade to group to individual within the novel's first four pages. The field of vision itself contracts, too: Lee's panoramic vista, which is what the reader is provided at the beginning of the text, is reduced within a few paragraphs to the perspective of the ex-slave as he returns to the plantation: "Dars de ole home, praise de Lawd! En . . . Lordy, dars Missy watchin' at de winder!" (6–7). The significance of the space under the reader's surveillance decreases from the monumental ("the field of Appomattox") to the anonymous (a "modest cottage" in a "little village" in North Carolina's Appalachian southwest). Thus it can be said that the mode of fiction Dixon is adopting to tell his story is "shrinking" as well, from something reminiscent of historical romance to something much more like local color fiction.[8]

Yet the more that Dixon's novel focuses on the particular, the more expansive it becomes as well. When it shifts its focus from the brigade to the single group of soldiers marching toward North Carolina, it introduces them thus:

> They were the sons of the men who had first declared their independence of Great Britain in America and made the country a hornet's nest for Lord Cornwallis in the darkest days of the cause of Liberty. What tongue can tell the tragic story of their humble home coming? . . .
>
> It is little wonder that in this hour of [northern] triumph the world should forget the defeated soldiers who without a dollar in their pockets were tramping to their ruined homes. (6)

Just prior to this, *The Leopard's Spots* proclaims North Carolina "the typical American Democracy," while, earlier still, it dubs the Civil War "the bloodiest, most destructive war the world ever saw. The earth had been baptized in the blood of five hundred thousand heroic soldiers, and a new map of the world had been made" (4–5).

In the universe Dixon creates at the outset of the Klan trilogy, therefore, "little villages" typify "American Democracy," Confederate veterans embody national history, and "humble home comings" entail earth-shattering consequences. The focus of Dixon's novel is always racial—"the shadow of the free negro" is introduced before the band of "ragged" soldiers and well before the figure of the loyal ex-slave—but it is also always simultaneously local and global. By the point it has mentioned "the South" for a second time, in fact, *The Leopard's Spots* has alluded to "the world" five times and "the earth" twice. The portrait of the plantation South that Dixon creates at the outset of his first novel is thus of a small community that epitomizes a world order and is involved in a globally significant racial contest even as "the world" ignores it: "It is little wonder that . . . the world should forget the defeated soldiers." Remembering them, "the world" is encouraged to recognize itself, to imagine Dixon's country boys as kinfolk and fathom "the shadow of the free negro" as a threat that envelops white men and women everywhere. It is invited, in a sense, to assume the white man's burden by the act of reading, hence the novel's subtitle, *A Romance of the White Man's Burden*, and hence also Dixon's implication that what Rudyard Kipling had named in his poem three years earlier applied equally well whether one was thinking of Africa or Appalachia. What was true of the Philippines was true of Kipling's India was true of the North Carolina Piedmont, and so on; or, as a Klan leader propounds in one of the culminating scenes in *The Clansman*, "'*quod semper, quod ubique, quod ab omnibus*'—what always, what every-where, what by all has been held to be true" (333).[9] While the plantation South may have been the place Dixon knew best, and while his literary de-but was thus characteristically "regionalist," he wrote about the region pre-cisely because it did not seem to him exceptional. It seemed instead univer-sal, a locale that typified others—in short, a space wherein white supremacy appeared quite literally mundane.

Thomas Nelson Page, for one, was never quite so reductive. He was no stickler for particularity, to be sure: this was a writer who, in an 1892 essay, argued that "the Old South" "had largely contributed to produce this nation" and who, in *Red Rock* (1898), transformed a single boulder into a symbol of Indian-fighting during Virginia's colonial period as well as the white South's triumph over its Yankee and "negro" oppressors during Reconstruc-tion.[10] Yet Page, like Henry W. Grady, Joel Chandler Harris, and most other writers of the late nineteenth century, saw the plantation South as culturally and historically unique. Though they differed from each other in terms of what precisely they understood the plantation to mean, they agreed that its multiraciality and supposed social harmony made it a distinct community whose example the world would soon follow, a space that in some ways had arrived at a multiracial modernity before everyone else. Not so Dixon. Like his predecessors, he thought the plantation South exemplary and summoned his readers to heed the lessons learned as a result of Reconstruction. Yet he also insisted on seeing the region as "typical," a sign of what always and everywhere ("*quod semper, quod ubique*") happens when the white race comes into contact with its inferiors. It wins—a two-word sentence that could be said to provide the plot summary for both *The Leopard's Spots* and *The Clansman* as well as sev-eral additional works Dixon published during his lifetime. The situations vary from text to text, but the conflict ("the challenge of race against race to mortal combat," as he calls it in *The Clansman*) and outcome (the "confirm[ation of] the Anglo-Saxon in his title to the primacy of racial sway," as he phrases it in *The Leopard's Spots*) do not (275, 408).

David Stricklin is thus right to dub Dixon a novelist of "strange consis-tency."[11] "Strange compulsiveness" might be an apt description, too, for later in this chapter I attend to some of the odd patterns of repetition—the white supremacist novelist's nervous tics, one almost wants to call them—that char-acterize his writings. First, however, it is worth probing further the idea that Dixon was different: that even though he, like Page, was the son of a planter and could count among his ancestors heroes of the Revolutionary War, he was preoccupied less with the plantation and its history—Page's primary themes—and more with the idea that the plantation symbolized "Anglo-Saxon . . . primacy." Why were his writings so much less "attached" to places than they were to bodies and indeed bloods? Why, in short, was he so much more a racist than a regionalist?

The exchange between Dixon and his publisher, Walter Hines Page, is illustrative, for even if Dixon exaggerated its details, it still seems likely that his publisher mistook him for a second Thomas Nelson Page. That is, he read *The Leopard's Spots* with *Red Rock*, *In Ole Virginia* (1887), and other works in mind and thought Dixon's manuscript, though worth publishing, yet another example of what plantation fiction had become by the late 1890s. As I have argued thus far in this book, this was no simple or small thing, for the plantation had grown, figuratively speaking, from a space whose literary allure was its exoticness to one whose true meaning, as it had been trumpeted in text after text, was its nationality—its having remained committed to the ideals that "had largely contributed to produce this nation" and thus made the South the most "American" of U.S. localities. So when he thought that he was reading something reminiscent of Page, Dixon's publisher likely had in mind texts other than Page's earliest, most "localized" short stories and poems. He was perhaps thinking of those passages in *Red Rock* in which Page celebrates the plantation as foundational to "America" and therefore imagining Dixon as yet another of the New South's literary nationalists.

Yet Dixon was convinced he was doing something new. To his publisher's joke that "Thomas Nelson Page has taken the wind out of your *sails*," Dixon allegedly responded thus:

> "I see that you haven't read Thomas Nelson Page—or you certainly must not have read my script—"
>
> "I'll say that I *have* read your manuscript," he broke in, taking it up from his desk. "You see that dark stain on the cover? That's blood! Good red blood from your first reader's veins. . . ."
>
> "And you still think Thomas Nelson Page has anticipated me? He has never touched on my theme!"[12]

Dixon was a blood freak. The word itself and variations on it occur on average once every eight pages in *The Leopard's Spots* and once every six in *The Clansman*. Later in *Southern Horizons*, moreover, in a discussion of his publishing house's preparation of his first book, he describes the "joyous time" he had "selecting the color of the cloth for the binding. . . . I chose a blood red cloth."[13]

Of greater relevance to the present discussion, however, is how determinedly Dixon presents *The Leopard's Spots* as unlike anything ever written by Page. Given how much it has in common with *Red Rock*—the epic sense of history, the plantation settings, the depiction of Reconstruction as a violation of the South and the rise of the Klan as therefore heroic, and so on—it is not obvious which "theme" exactly Dixon thought his predecessor had "never touched on." Thus it not clear what about *The Leopard's Spots* he thought promised to make it so much more sensational than the plantation fiction of the prior two decades—fiction that, as my own study has documented, had proved plenty sensational in its own right.

To answer this question requires the reiteration of a fact mentioned earlier that Dixon had turned to novel writing at a relatively late age, having already become a public figure of some prominence during the 1890s as a lecturer and preacher. Ordained as a Baptist minister in 1886, he headed a church in Boston from 1887 to 1889 then one in New York until 1895, at which point he became convinced that church politics were limiting his ability to reach the widest audience possible. Resigning from the ministry, he formed his own nondenominational "Church of the People" and preached in an opera house that could accommodate several thousand people and was often filled to capacity. He also toured the country as a lecturer throughout these years and spoke to audiences that were often similarly large, his first biographer estimating the total number of people who saw him at five million, making him among the leading lecturers of his day.[14]

The subjects of his lectures, sermons, and occasional pamphlets varied. Among those extant are a pamphlet titled "Pagan New York," one of several pieces he wrote describing how difficult it would be to convert the entire city to Protestant Christianity; a series of responses to the leading agnostic lecturer and writer of the day, Robert Ingersoll, whom Dixon viewed for several years as his archrival; addresses touching on such social controversies as prohibition, divorce, the New Woman, labor unrest, and anarchism; and of course addresses on the race problem, all of which make clear his antipathy toward the ideas of black civil and social equality (evidence of which abounds in a speech titled "A Friendly Warning to the Negro," for example, which urges African Americans to relinquish the vote and reestablish relationships of happy dependency upon white southern men or else "be ground to powder").[15] Those that provide the greatest insight into what Dixon believed he was pioneering with his Klan novels, however, are several addresses he delivered in New York in 1898 and

1899, simultaneous with the Spanish-American War. Dixon was seized with the subject: of the twenty-nine orations published together as *Dixon's Sermons* in 1899, more than half address the war and its significance. Their titles alone give a fair sense of Dixon's views, for among the subjects he addressed were "The Destiny of America," "The New Fourth of July," "The Mightiest Navy in the World," and "Roosevelt, the Heroic Leader." He delivered some of the addresses with Cuban and American flags displayed from his pulpit, the Cuban cause having been what first compelled him to address the war. He soon advocated a prolonged military occupation of the Philippines, too, however, since long before the end of the war Dixon had come to see in it the culmination of—though it sounds grandiloquent—all of human history.[16]

To read *Dixon's Sermons* is to encounter a writer for whom *everything* seems to be falling into place, one whose every social, political, racial, and religious view seems to be being confirmed by the rapid unfolding of events. New possibilities seemed to be opening up, too. Dixon was thus writing hurriedly himself, delivering sermons every Sunday in which he made reference to current events and contextualized them by citing Scripture, recounting history, and explaining what was being revealed as a result of the nation's successes in battle. Thus, the first oration published in the *Sermons*, "The Battle Cry of Freedom," begins by citing from the book of Luke ("The spirit of the Lord is upon me because he hath sent me to proclaim release to the captives, to set at liberty them that are bruised") then announces this: "A nation has caught these words from the lips of Jesus Christ and gone forth on its divine mission." Later, after remarks about Cuba's "lying at our feet . . . starving and suffering" and beseeching the United States' help, he rehearses the events of the recent past and explains what they mean to him and his audience:

> The twenty-first day of April, 1898, was God's judgment day for Spain in Cuba. The fleet sailed. A mighty nation moved forward to execute the will of God.
>
> I am proud that I am an American citizen.
>
> For the first time in modern history, a great nation has accepted the Spirit of Jesus as the motive power of life.
>
> The old law of nations recognizes self interest as the supreme standard of life. The law of Christ is sacrificial and redemptive love. This nation has taken up its cross in Cuba. It has begun a holy war. . . . It is the sublimest incarnation of Christianity of this century. (3–4)

Dixon was delivering his message on May 1, less than two weeks after the dec-laration of war and the departure of the U.S. fleet to the Philippines. The *New York Times*'s front page that morning had featured a large map of the islands so that Americans might know the space their navy was invading. Next to it was a story headlined "A Week of Victories" whose subheadings ("Washington Authorities Think Decisive Successes at Manila and Cuba Are Near . . . No Spanish Guns on Shore Believed to Equal the Batteries on the American War-ships") help to explain why Dixon's first war sermon conveys so much elation, such a strong sense that he was living at a moment toward which history had been building for centuries.[17]

The final words of the sermon, "It is a glorious thing to be an American Citizen to-day," echo the ones from earlier: "I am proud that I am an Ameri-can citizen." By the end of his text, though, "to be an American Citizen" was in Dixon's view to be quite a lot besides. It was to be a member of a chosen people, a Christian soldier, an "Anglo-Saxon," a speaker of English ("the lan-guage that conquers the world"), a competitor to the great empires of Europe, and a member of a nation that had healed fully from the Civil War. And, not surprisingly, a giver of blood: "We have said to the Cuban people, 'Our hearts are moved with anguish and righteous wrath . . . we extend to you our hands, our treasure, our hearts, our hearts blood'" (6). Dixon reiterated these themes in his next war sermon, "The Anglo-Saxon Alliance," which he delivered two weeks later. Imagining the U.S. and British "vast empires" joining forces to rule the world, he stressed how much the two nations had in common, includ-ing their language, histories, and above all again, bloodlines: "We are of one blood. . . . I am all over an Anglo-Saxon. I count myself an average American in feelings, character and purpose" (11). In a later sermon, "The Nation's Call the Voice of God," he discourses on the nation-state as a historical entity, noting how "[a]s the nation grows it absorbs one by one the functions of the Ancient Church," a belief that compelled him to observe that "[t]he President of the United States is the highest religious dignitary in the world" (33–34). And in a later one still, "Destiny of America," he makes clear how resolutely he supports U.S. imperialism as an idea, arguing that "[p]rogress has been the watchword of the nation; expansion the law of its life." "The expansion of such a nation," he continued, "is, of course, the prime necessity of its growth. Therefore America will add territory in the future as it has added territory in the past" (79).

In these sermons Dixon makes only occasional mention of the South and then only to note that, glorious though it had been in its old civilization and heroic in defense of its social systems, it had now joined the North as part of a nation with a much higher purpose than any sectionalist one. "The nation was baptized in the blood of five hundred million heroes, and from ashes and dust rose again its new life," he contends in "Destiny of America." "To-day there is no North, no South, no East, no West; we are one people" (77). And yet as the legendarily "splendid little war" drew to a conclusion mere weeks after it had begun and the question shifted from whether the United States should invade Spain's colonies to whether, as Dixon phrases it in the title of a later sermon, "The Philippines—Can We Retreat," he began to remind Americans of their "solemn duty to the ignorant, suffering, and struggling Phillipinos [sic]" who required U.S. guidance and support, "[w]hatever their intellectual status" (55–56). Emphasizing their blind loyalty to and essential dependence on white Americans, he adapted the tropes of plantation fiction to recommend a course for U.S. foreign policy in the future.

And then, when a series of violent racial conflicts erupted across the South later in 1898, most notably in Wilmington, North Carolina, yet another piece of the puzzle Dixon was assembling in his mind seemed to fall into place. In "A Friendly Warning to the Negro," written in response to the recent conflicts, Dixon found cause to call upon his own plantation background in order to delineate a future for African Americans, whom he believed were not possessed of the same destiny as whites:

> The mission of the African is not to govern the Anglo-Saxon. It is time the negro knew this, and he is going to find it out for the first time in his life. . . .
>
> The negro should migrate from the congested districts of the South to the Northern states, the Western territories, to Porto Rico, to Cuba and the Philippines Islands. He should be encouraged and assisted in that migration. There are too many negroes in the black belts of the South. (119)

Within weeks of the United States' taking possession of its new colonial territories, then, Dixon was discovering in them a partial solution to the "negro problem" at home.[18] What underwrote his vision, which equated black citizens with colonial subjects, was how well he knew "the negro" as a category, a knowledge that, following Page, Grady, and Harris, he believed had devolved to him as a result of his regional heritage: "I know the negro in the South; I know him in the North; and I know him as he is. . . . The first face I ever looked on in this world was the face of an old negro woman. My early playmate was a coal-black negro of my own age" (113). Though he was still a few years away from writing the novel in which he would conflate the experiences of being a planter's son and soldier of empire, and though Rudyard Kipling had yet to supply him the phrase that would in turn figure into the subtitle of *The Leopard's Spots,* Dixon was already romancing the white man's burden in 1898, beginning to imagine the globe as, when properly governed, a vast version of the plantations he had known as a youth.

Walter Benn Michaels drew attention to Dixon's writings several years ago with an argument that they, along with the writings of Thomas Nelson Page, represented "the major anti-imperialist literature of the turn of the century."[19] It will be apparent from the previous chapter and the first half of this one that I read both writers differently, Dixon especially. Page may be read as having set out during the 1870s and 1880s to memorialize the plantation South and its culture of white supremacy only to discover that, by the 1890s, his views also seemed consistent with a vision of the United States as an empire (hence his writing poems in support of the Spanish-American War, essays on "Old Virginia" that conclude with encomiums to U.S. expansionism, and so forth: Page's subject matter expanded from the local to the global as his nation's primary political preoccupations shifted away from the reconstruction of the South and toward the extension of U.S. power overseas). Dixon, by contrast, determined to become a fiction writer only after the Spanish-American War. Born in 1864, he was younger than Page but still old enough to have joined the ranks of southern local colorists making their debuts during the 1880s and 1890s had the writing of regionalist fiction seemed to him his original life's purpose. It did not. What pointed him in the new direction was the war, which seemed to clarify "the Anglo-Saxon's" world mission and give meaning to U.S. history—in short, to produce the racist and nationalist euphoria that is recorded so unmistakably in *Dixon's Sermons.* Of equal importance—and this is the argument with which I conclude this chapter—the war had ended rather abruptly and seemed to Dixon to be fading too quickly into memory by 1900. The Klan novels may thus be read as attempts to recreate for his readers in fiction those feelings he himself had experienced during the early weeks of the Spanish-American War, when regions had disappeared, "Anglo-Saxons" the world over had seen their destinies revealed, and Dixon had found himself rather suddenly in possession of a worldview, a way of interpreting almost anything as an episode in the long history of the white conquest of the globe.

First, however, Michaels's argument that Dixon was an "anti-imperialist" is worth exploring, if only because, without it, students of American literature might not now be paying so much attention to Dixon. Prior to the early 1990s and Michaels's insistence that scholars take notice of the Klan novels themselves, Dixon was still by and large a figure studied only insofar as his writings illuminated *The Birth of a Nation*.[20] Focusing on the novels, Michaels observes evidence of an anti-imperialist movement that emerged in response to the Spanish-American War and sought to project race *hatred* globally. Hardly an anti-imperialism founded on concerns for the rights of the colonized, the movement discussed by Michaels was based instead on a different set of arguments. First, it understood that U.S. expansionism would eventually require the incorporation of new territories into the nation as states and their inhabitants as citizens, the Constitution containing no provision for the maintenance of permanent colonies. Second, it viewed suspiciously any effort to extend the powers of the federal government, which colonialism would necessarily require but which Reconstruction had already shown to be a bad idea. Third, and above all, it abhorred the idea of a multiracial citizenry and thought that in any event, even if colonialism were judged not to violate the Constitution, prolonged contact with nonwhites would abase white Americans, with recent U.S. history having furnished evidence that it did.[21]

And, indeed, there were U.S. anti-imperialists who thought precisely in these terms, the most famous of whom was probably South Carolina's Senator "Pitchfork" Benjamin Tillman. In a speech delivered in 1899 Tillman claimed that Americans understood "what it is to have two races side by side that cannot mix or mingle, without deterioration and injury to both and the ultimate destruction of the civilization of the higher."[22] He thus led a group of congressmen who opposed imperialism primarily on the grounds that it would mean the further contamination of the state, a voluntary expansion of something like "the negro problem" that in his view had given Americans trouble enough already. Yet Dixon understood the world differently.[23] By all means he considered Reconstruction an act of virtual colonization of the white South, a belief he makes clear in *The Clansman* when a sage Abraham Lincoln rebukes a would-be Radical Republican congressman who seeks dominion over the former Confederacy: "The Constitution grants to the National Government no power to regulate suffrage, and makes no provision for the control of 'conquered' provinces" (42). The sort of imperial conquest he saw represented by the Spanish-American War, however, Dixon understood as an extension of the racial principles that underlay the Constitution and preceded even the founding of "America." Thus in *Dixon's Sermons* he could propose an "Anglo-Saxon alliance" between the United States and the most far-flung empire the world had ever known so long as England were colonizing "dark" spaces, not "white" ones:

> When England began her course of injustice and oppression toward her Colonies, our fathers led a triumphant rebellion and founded this Republic. It was a bitter draught for the proud old mother-land, but . . . [i]t was good for the soul. . . . England changed her colonial policy and thenceforth built squarely on the principles of liberty, equality and justice. The sun does not set on her world empire to-day. And its integrity is unassailable because built on the principle of liberty and justice. (4)

So long as the empire in question seemed an expression of white supremacy, Dixon applauded it, championing it as a beacon of light, a fortress in the kingdom of Christ, an exporter of liberty and justice, a symbol of white virility, and so on. Indeed what disqualified Spain—potentially a "white" imperial power otherwise—was that it had grown old and appeared no longer in control of its colonial subjects. It seemed no better than an outpost of "barbarism and tyranny" as a result, a nation that, as England had earlier, would learn a hard but necessary lesson by being whipped by young America, whose "boys" were much better representatives of white racial energy (1).

What mattered most to Dixon, in other words—far more than whether a nation's foreign policy violated its constitution—was whether that policy confirmed his much deeper conviction that, simply stated, whites conquered. His imperialism turns out to have been as uncomplicated as it was all-encompassing. If Dixon could see in an "empire," real or imagined, clear evidence of white triumph, he was for it (thus his celebration of the British Empire as "unassailable," the rising U.S. empire as desirable, and, as we shall see, the "Invisible Empire" of the Ku Klux Klan as representative of the same racial forces expressed in these other imperial configurations). If he could not—if, for example, its underclass were primarily white or, worse, its ruling class "miscegenated" or "negro"—he objected (thus his mention of "injustice and oppression" in the thirteen colonies as well as Lincoln's remarks about "conquered provinces": both represented forms of rule that denied white subjects what Dixon believed to be a racial birthright, the right to self-determination in matters of government).

Most of what I have drawn on thus far to contest the idea that Dixon represents a voice of "anti-imperial Americanism" have been sermons published prior to the Klan novels. There is, of course, the possibility that, in the three years that separated the publication of *Dixon's Sermons* and that of *The Leopard's Spots*, Dixon's attitudes about U.S. imperialism had changed enough to warrant the thesis that he was an anti-imperialist. I now wish to return to the novels, however, in order to show that they extend rather than abandon the imperialist doctrines contained within the *Sermons* and thus represent not "the major anti-imperialist literature of the turn of the century" but rather an important defense of recent U.S. expansionism as well as a vindication, in that context, of prevailing white southern views about the impossibilities of racial cooperation in national politics.

The distance between Dixon's oratorical and literary careers begins to shrink if one accepts that, as he recounts in *Southern Horizons*, he actually wrote portions of his first novel *while* delivering his lectures:

> I finally reached the point of constructing the story while doing other work through a double personality. I could rise before an audience, start my lecture going, never missing a point of laughter or applause, and begin work on a novel with my creative faculties. But I got so excited once over a dramatic situation that my tongue suddenly stopped work on the lecture. A low murmur ran through the audience. I saw something was wrong, scratched my head, caught what the trouble was, and switched on the talk again. In a minute I was back on the novel merely keeping one eye on the audience to see that they didn't murmur again. (261–62)

Dixon's insistence that his "sole purpose in writing" *The Leopard's Spots* had been "to reach and influence with my argument the minds of millions" makes the connections between lecturing and novel-writing even more salient. Having learned already how to reach hundreds of thousands with "arguments" but having been limited by the fact that he could deliver only one lecture at a time and needed to travel great distances by train between them, he viewed the novel very much as a means of reproducing himself. He even creates two versions of himself in *The Leopard's Spots*, one the young man who ends the novel by becoming governor of North Carolina, the other an older preacher who aids the young man in his political quest. Dixon himself had been elected to the North Carolina state legislature at age twenty before determining two years later to pursue the ministry. His construction of a "double personality" was thus an aspect of the novel's composition as well as of the text itself.

What shows most vividly that he conceptualized *The Leopard's Spots* as a better vehicle for delivering the messages he had once conveyed in New York's Grand Opera House and the nation's lecture halls is that *Dixon's Sermons* is itself reproduced in the novel. Some of its passages survive almost intact while its historical vision provides the novel its overall structure. After its Appomattox beginning and its retreat from there to the Appalachian foothills, the novel follows the career of Charles Gaston as he rises from being a planter's son—the heir in fact to the plantation to which the former slave Nelse returns at the outset of the novel—to winning the governor's office. Before achieving this, he chairs the committee that effects the overthrow of the elected government in one of North Carolina's cities because it includes "negro" officials—a clear allusion to the events in Wilmington, North Carolina, of late 1898.[24] Before this he serves as the leader of a local Klan outfit. And as if these were not events enough to compose a novel, in a pair of late chapters Dixon alludes to the Spanish-American War, though not because Gaston or any other character joins the military. Rather, he invokes it because, recalling his own experiences of the war (which is to say, of the war as an *idea*), he believed the episode transformative, an event that had "flashe[d] the search light into the souls of men and nations, revealing their unknown strength and weakness, and the changes that had been silently wrought in the years of peace" (405). Gaston and his fellow white southern men are indeed affected by reports of the war, for though none of them participates directly in it, they glean from it the resolve to overthrow the local "negro" government. Gaston himself is additionally moved to try for the governor's mansion.

The chapters in which the war is mentioned are titled "The New America" and "Another Declaration of Independence," titles that bear resemblance to several of Dixon's war sermons ("Destiny of America" and "The New Fourth of July," for example). The fact that the novel stretches from Appomattox to Wilmington by way of events in Santiago and Manila Bay, moreover, realizes in narrative form one of the observations Dixon makes in the sermon titled "The Battle Cry of Freedom": "The new Constitution proclaimed in the fall of Lee's army at Appomattox found its first logical act of life in the order for our fleet to sail against Spain. We have entered our new life. We have become a new force in the history of the world. It is our destiny" (5). This idea of a "new Constitution," meanwhile, provides perhaps the clearest link between the sermons and the novel. On the eve of his election Gaston makes a speech about white racial duty and destiny that wins over his audience and assures his victory. As part of it he says this:

The Anglo-Saxon is entering the new century with the imperial crown of the ages on his brow and the sceptre of the infinite in his hands.

The Old South fought against the stars in their courses—the resistless tide of the rising consciousness of Nationality and World-Mission. The young South greets the new era and glories in its manhood. He joins his voice in the cheers of triumph which are ushering in this all-conquering Saxon. Our old men dreamed of local supremacy. We dream of the conquest of the globe. (435)

While delivering "The Battle Cry of Freedom," Dixon himself had said almost the same thing before an audience in New York in 1898:

We are in fact witnessing the birth pangs of a new giant nation. The conception of this new nation was accomplished at Appomatox [sic], in 1865, when General Lee surrendered to General Grant. The South fought for the old Constitution. The South's interpretation of that Constitution is now acknowledged to be absolutely correct. But we had outgrown the Constitution, and we had to write a new one in the blood of heroes. The South fought for the principles of State Sovereignty, Individualism, Local Government. The North fought for the greater, newer principles of Nationality, Solidarity, Unity. The South collided with the sweep of the Nineteenth Century and was crushed. (5)

The revised version of the speech, such as it is, that appears in *The Leopard's Spots* suggests that during the intervening years Dixon had reconsidered his imagery and chosen not to write about a "crushed" South but rather a superseded one, an "Old South" composed of men very much like the ones about whom Grady had written earlier ("In devotion, in courage, in earnestness, in ability, the sons shall not surpass their fathers. . . . But the sons fight under new conditions, for greater ends, in broader fields").[25] Yet Gaston's speech still makes abundantly clear that, by writing a novel, Dixon was seeking to continue his sermonic career by another means. Indeed, the fact that *The Leopard's Spots* turns on a speech—that one of its climactic moments is an act of oratory—shows how little Dixon had changed since 1898, how he still thought of himself as a prophetic figure versed in a knowledge of race, religion, and history, each of which, when "read," revealed the same story: that of the "Anglo-Saxon . . . entering the new century" with an "imperial crown" on his head and "sceptre of the infinite in his hands."

Such comments support the claim made at the outset of this chapter that the point of the Klan novels is imperialism: to read them as an extension of the *Sermons* is to recognize that Dixon was seeking to perpetuate a historical episode and all that had been revealed to him during it. He was seeking also to communicate what he and so many others had *felt* at that moment, hence to make reading a way of keeping alive a sense of nationalized racial purpose. Of course many of the millions who would read Dixon's novels would not have heard or read his earlier lectures and sermons and could not have made the connections being elucidated here. Yet there is much else about the novels that would have invited their being read as "pro-imperialist." The chapters in *The Leopard's Spots* celebrating the Spanish-American War are one further example. The fact that Dixon borrowed from Rudyard Kipling's still-popular poem to give the novel its subtitle is another. Beyond these, however, each of the Klan novels, including *The Traitor* (1907), the final novel in the "Reconstruction Trilogy," stage domestic conflicts in imperial terms by explaining postbellum politics as a contest among three more-or-less distinct, more-or-less imperial entities. The first "empire" to appear in *The Leopard's Spots*, for example, is the Radical Republican Congress, which Dixon likens to the Huns early in the text: "Congress became to the desolate South what Attila, the 'Scourge of God,' was to civilised Europe" (102). The second, which collaborates with the first but is nonetheless an independent entity, is an "African empire" composed of former slaves bent upon colonizing the South, a first step in conquering the entire United States, Dixon warns. One of its leaders delights in the political instabilities of the Johnson administration, proclaiming, "There is no President. The Supreme Court is chained. In San Domingo no white man is allowed to vote, hold office or hold a foot of land. We will make this mighty South a more glorious San Domingo" (93).

The third domestic "empire" to emerge in *The Leopard's Spots* is the Invisible Empire of the Klan itself. It makes its first appearance after this same "full-blooded Negro" magistrate demands a kiss from a white woman who had come to him seeking help for her destitute family (88). The Klan forms in direct response to the black leader's proposition. Two nights later, it captures and lynches him, suspending him from the balcony of the court house, "[h]is neck . . . broken and his body . . . hanging low," "[h]is thick lips . . . split with a sharp knife," and the following note hanging from his teeth: "*The answer of the Anglo-Saxon race to Negro lips that dare pollute with words the womanhood of the South. K. K. K.*" The scene anticipates the later, more famous lynching scene in *The Clansman*, which serves also to galvanize the Klan and permits similar fantasies of white union. The passage thus encapsulates several of the rhetorical strategies Dixon will use throughout the trilogy. The first and most obvious is its idealization of "southern womanhood" and its suggestion that black political empowerment places white women under constant threat. The second is its obsessive focus on the black male body, which contrasts with the relative abstraction and erasure of white bodies. The third is its suggestion that black speech (mere "words" in this passage) is virtually identical with black action, requiring its regulation or, better yet, its silencing. The last is its act of interpreting a "southern" event in global, historical terms, so that a black man's verbal proposition that a southern white woman kiss him becomes an occasion to stage an epic battle between the "Negro" and "the Anglo-Saxon race."

Dixon would expand upon these strategies in *The Clansman*, developing even more clearly the idea that postbellum national destiny depends on the outcome of the contest among the three "empires" vying for control of the South during Reconstruction. In a prefatory note, Dixon explains Reconstruction as a "bold attempt . . . to Africanise ten great states of the American Union," and he insists throughout the novel that black southerners are in reality simply the soldiery of an imperial "Africa." The continent takes on the trappings of a hostile nation-state, as Dixon represents it. At the same time, "Africa" is being dislocated from any physical, geographical space, becoming instead an idea that is at once nowhere and everywhere, a way of locating "the black race" and rendering it a coherent, antagonistic force. Doing so, Dixon sidesteps such vexing issues as the fact that during the period about which he was writing Africa itself was the object of the European colonial scramble, its land mass being divided into separate possessions.

In *The Clansman*, however, "Africa" is actually being consolidated on the hypermasculine, monstrous, even expansionist black male body. Thus, we see a black orator in the text being represented in terms of his "chiselled lips and massive nose, his big neck and broad shoulders . . . and projecting forehead," in which Dixon sees "pictures of the primeval forest. The head of a Caesar and the eyes of the jungle'" (93). The black rapist who appears later in the novel is depicted in similar terms. Dixon gives him the mock imperial moniker Augustus Caesar, makes him "the Captain of the African Guards," and then fixates on the enormity of his physical features: "the short, heavy-set neck of the lower order of animals," "lips so thick they curled both ways up and down," "enormous nostrils . . . in perpetual dilation," "enormous cheekbones and jaws [that] seemed to protrude beyond the ears and hide them," and so forth (216, 327). In fact, many of the black men that appear in Dixon's novels tower over their white counterparts. The first one mentioned in *The Leopard's Spots* is described as a "giant," the second one as a "towering figure of the freed

Negro" (6, 32). The black magistrate whom the Klan lynches, though not necessarily immense physically, nonetheless possesses "a tiny mustache which he tried in vain to pull out straight Napoleonic style"—yet another instance of imperial ambitions manifesting themselves in the black male physiognomy (89).

Those who are not described as physically imposing are usually possessed of firearms, which they go about discharging randomly—more instances of unrestrained black male potency that seem simultaneously to fascinate and revolt Dixon. His descriptions of white Radical Republicans in Congress, meanwhile, tend to represent them as devoid of any physical potency. In *The Leopard's Spots*, he describes Thaddeus Stevens, Charles Sumner, and Benjamin F. Butler as "a triumvirate of physical and mental deformity" (97). In *The Clansman*, he gives Stevens the alter ego Austin Stoneman and then fixates on his clubfootedness and "painful hobble." Sumner, "supposed to be the most powerful man in Congress," is in fact only Stoneman's mouthpiece, his power "a harmless fiction which pleased him, and at which Stoneman loved to laugh" (39, 91). Even the more minor figures in the Radical Republican regime feature physical abnormalities, such as the scalawag judge who appears in the first part of *The Traitor* and whom Dixon describes as overweight, "creeping," shuffling, and turtle-shaped.[26]

In short, most of Dixon's white characters who wield power as a result of Radical Reconstruction are physically unfit to rule. What power they have gained has been the result of "crack-brained theories," political conspiracies, and, most importantly of all, a willingness to collaborate with the black potentates of the "African" empire, who, quite literally, provide the able bodies they need to carry out their schemes. The white congressmen still constitute something of a separate imperial force, with Dixon saying at one point in *The Clansman* that the Radical Republicans want "to make the South a second Poland" (9). He reinforces the idea later by referring to the senators in charge of reforming the South as an "Imperial Committee with the Hon. Austin Stoneman as its chairman" (134). Last, when Abraham Lincoln is assassinated and Andrew Johnson ascends to an enfeebled presidency, Dixon muses that "the seat of Empire had moved from the White House to the little dark house on the Capitol hill, where dwelt an old club-footed man" (79). Yet Dixon is careful never to represent Congress as possessing any legitimate imperial might. It achieves what potency it has by mortgaging its future, by collaborating with black bodies.

It is this collaboration, even codependency, between the "African" and congressional empires that generates the panic that motivates Dixon's novels.

The panic derives from Dixon's belief that any sort of cooperation between the races—especially on this grand a scale—is impossible given what he supposes to be the illimitable desire "of the Negro race to rule the white man of the South, the former slave to rule his master."[27] To confer citizenship, suffrage, and the right to bear arms upon black southerners is thus to commit a kind of white racial suicide. "[S]o long as the Negro is here with a ballot in his hands," Dixon writes in *The Leopard's Spots*, "he is a menace to civilisation. The Republican party['s] . . . attempt to establish with the bayonet an African barbarism on the ruins of Southern society was a conspiracy against human progress" (196). Dixon deploys a similar conditional reasoning throughout the novels. He argues in *The Traitor* that to grant black southerners equal rights is simply to acquiesce to black dominion (87). He reasons more ominously in *The Leopard's Spots* that "one cannot seek the Negro vote without asking him to your home sooner or later. If you ask him into your house, he will break bread with you at last. And if you seat him at your table, he has the right to ask your daughter's hand in marriage" (244).

Collaboration is thus impossible: given Dixon's faith in the one-drop theory, it would mean the gradual blackening of the government, hence the nation. As he fantasizes in *The Leopard's Spots*, "One drop of Negro blood makes a Negro. It kinks the hair, flattens the nose, thickens the lip, puts out the light of intellect, and lights the fires of brutal passions. The beginning of Negro equality as a vital fact is the beginning of the end of this nation's life. There is enough blood here to make mulatto the whole Republic" (244). Dixon actually oscillates between ascribing agency to the African imperialists and regarding them as simply the dupes of white Republicans in Congress. But because their "blood" predominates whenever the two races mingle as equals, "Africans" are always, in one sense, possessed of a type of potency that whites lack. Thus the refrain that one of Dixon's alter egos repeats throughout *The Leopard's Spots*: "Shall the future American be an Anglo-Saxon or a Mulatto?" (161). Dixon in this instance deploys a binaristic view of the issues because, even though he identifies three separate centers of "empire" in his Klan novels, he believes that the congressional empire's dependence upon black votes and, more to the point, black bodies will render it nonexistent in the near future, a victim of its own misplaced, self-consuming faith in black political capability. The African empire would triumph because, as Dixon renders the equation late in *The Leopard's Spots*, "Amalgamation simply meant Africanisation" (386).

In addition to "invisible" empires, Dixon's novels thus feature "immiscible" ones, too: empires that cannot "mix" (or be "mixed") without ceasing

to be what they once represented and without relinquishing all claims of being at the vanguard of civilization. Dixon makes the point abundantly clear
in the following scene from *The Clansman*, in which Representative Austin
Stoneman, now unable to walk even with a cane, is transported into Andrew
Johnson's impeachment hearing on the shoulders of "two gigantic negroes," a
set piece Dixon plays for all it is worth.

> The negroes placed him in an arm-chair facing the semicircle of Senators,
> and crouched down beside him. . . .
>
> No sculptor ever dreamed a more sinister emblem of the corruption of
> a race of empire-builders than this group. Its black figures, wrapped in the
> night of four thousand years of barbarism, squatted there the "equal" of their
> master, grinning at his forms of Justice, the evolution of forty centuries of
> Aryan genius. To their brute strength the white fanatic in the madness of
> his hate had appealed, and for their hire he had bartered the birthright of a
> mighty race of freeman. (170–71)

Dixon's mention of sculpture is apt given the fact that his characters function much better as inert symbols of a supposedly larger racial history than
as actual dramatic personae responsible for sustaining a narrative. Here, they
symbolize the impotence and inadequacy of white Radical Republican rule,
the sinister potency of African political participation, and the idea that cooperation between the races portends doom for white Americans. Having sought
the support of black henchmen—literally, in the sense of being carried by
them, and figuratively, in the sense of the black vote—the Radical Republican
congressman is making possible a future in which they will replace him, hence
their "grin[s] at his forms of Justice." The "race of empire-builders" he has
"corrupt[ed]" is his own.

Into this milieu of race-mixing and illegitimate imperial incursion rides
Dixon's Klan, reminiscent, he records at various points, of the Christian cru-
saders of the Middle Ages, the Scottish warriors that had opposed British
rule, the Continental Army of the American Revolution, the German soldiers who had fought against Napoleon in 1812, the Polish fighters who had
kept alive hopes for an independent state in spite of Turkish invasions and
European partitions, and, less specifically, simply the defenders of "outraged
civilisation" everywhere. Dixon could be so indiscriminate in his comparisons
because his "knights," costumed from above their heads to the tops of their
shoes, served above all as "vehicle[s] for the expression of whiteness," as Judith
Jackson Fossett has argued: "It is only with the 'absoluteness of disguise' . . .

that the mission of the Klan can be effected. In other words, the rising tide of unbroken barbarism displayed by blacks can be dissipated only with a concomitant donning of white disguises." White cotton robes—which, as Fossett rightly argues, connote a certain gender ambiguity and possess a racial history that should have troubled Dixon, their "having been sown, reaped, and processed by . . . black hands"—nonetheless facilitate racial fantasizing.[28] Behind their robes, Klan members can be whiter than they ever could otherwise, and they can permit such a writer as Dixon to dislocate and disseminate whiteness across spatial and temporal boundaries in ways much more effective than actual "white" characters in their everyday garbs.

They can also represent empire in what Dixon believes to be its only legitimate form: empire as systematic, dispersed, and regulated white supremacy. In the preface to *The Clansman*, Dixon stages their entrance in what could be called—not inappropriately, given the novel's future—a cinematic fashion: "In the darkest hour of the life of the South . . . suddenly from the mists of the mountains appeared a white cloud the size of a man's hand. It grew until its mantle of mystery enfolded the stricken earth and sky. An 'Invisible Empire' had risen from the field of Death and challenged the visible to mortal combat" (2). Like the "visible," miscegenated empire they are fighting, the "Invisible Empire" emerges via an expression of embodiment: here, in the form of a "man's hand." Whereas its rival remains forever trapped within the body—inexpressible, as Dixon sees it, in terms of anything but "kinky heads, black skin, thick lips, white teeth, and flat noses"—the empire of the Klan becomes immediately an abstraction, a "mantle of mystery" that fills the sky and that will later be said to signify "the resistless movement of a race" (341).

Dixon celebrates the Klan's victories over its Reconstructionist foes in much the same language as he had commemorated U.S. naval victories over Spain in *Dixon's Sermons* and in *The Leopard's Spots*. "Within a few months this Empire overspread a territory larger than modern Europe," he writes. "In the approaching election it was reaching out its daring white hands to tear the fruits of victory from twenty million victorious conquerors" (343). Dixon thus measures the Klan's success in several forms, among them the amount of territory over which it was spreading and the number of elections it was able to tilt in favor of white Democrats and moderate Republicans. Its most important victories, however, might be what Dixon supposes to be its capacity to reform white northern attitudes about Reconstruction. Austin Stoneman's son, himself a former Union soldier, counsels his father late in the text that the Klan represents "the organised virtue of the community." Still later, when Stoneman orders federal troops into North Carolina to suppress the Klan, the troops end up cheering it, finding themselves both impressed by its regalia and sympathetic toward its racialist cause. Stoneman himself repents his racial transgressions at the end of the novel, admitting that he had fallen into a "black abyss of animalism" by adopting so severe a stance toward white southerners. He asks forgiveness for his recent past by denouncing Radical Reconstruction as misguided and fraudulent. In a final speech, he even begs to be readmitted into the racial community the Klan emblematizes by asserting, suggestively, "We all wear masks" (328, 353, 371).

Stoneman removes the "mask" of Radical Republican hatred toward white southerners in order to adopt another: a figurative "mask" that signifies membership within the white community, a "mask" to which the Ku Klux Klan had given material expression in the form of an all-white costume. Just as he represents the Klan's donning of robes as a natural rather than artificial expression of whiteness, however, Dixon depicts Stoneman's sudden change of heart as an inevitable and honest consequence of racial destiny rather than as another form of disguise. The episode signifies the end of the rival "Imperial Committee" of the Radical Republican Congress. The "African" empire had expired a few chapters earlier when the Klan, in a sign of sudden white resurgence, had lynched the black militia leader Augustus Caesar over the rape of a white woman, depositing his body "in his full uniform" on the lawn of the state's black lieutenant governor. News of the lynching had spread "in rapid succession in every newspaper not under Negro influence in the state," galvanizing its white populace, permitting them "the thrill of exultant joy," and restoring racial order to their communities (327). So, too, had the "Invisible Empire" spread quickly: "In quick succession every county followed the example of Ulster" wherein the Klan had first exerted its power in North Carolina. The result, Dixon records, was a "gale of chivalrous passion and high action, contagious and intoxicating, [which] swept though the white race. The moral, mental and physical earthquake which followed the first assault on one of their daughters revealed the unity of the racial life of their people. Within the span of a week they had lived a century."

The sense of time that pervades these episodes provides a crucial way of linking Dixon's Klan fantasies with his enthusiasm toward American empire—a link I will pursue further below. Before doing so, I want to end this discussion of the three metaphoric "empires" that clash in the Klan trilogy by examining how Dixon accounts for the Klan's triumph over its rivals. *The Clansman* ends with three episodes that are remarkable if for nothing else than for their brevity, resolving as they do more than 370 pages' worth of narrative in about a page and a half. The first of these episodes is Austin Stoneman's scene of repentance, which ends with a white southerner offering a kind of absolution by "slipp[ing] his arms around the old man's shoulder and beg[inning] a tender and reverent prayer." The second is a scene of rescue wherein the Klan saves Stoneman's son from a wrongful execution at the hands of federal troops—an episode to which Dixon devotes a paltry three sentences in spite of its seemingly dramatic potential.

The third, which comprises the novel's final paragraphs, is a scene of romantic reunion. In it, the young grand dragon of the Klan and his bride-to-be, Stoneman's daughter, discuss their future together:

> At twelve o'clock, Ben stood at the gate with Elsie.
>
> "Your fate hangs in the balance of this election tonight," she said. "I'll share it with you, success or failure, life or death."
>
> "Success, not failure," he answered firmly. "The Grand Dragons of six states have already wired victory. Look at our lights on the mountain! They are ablaze—range on range our signals gleam until the Fiery Cross is lost among the stars!"
>
> "What does it mean?" she whispered.
>
> "That I am a successful revolutionist—that Civilisation has been saved, and the South redeemed from shame." (374)

In terms of its structural composition, the scene models what art historian Angela Miller has termed "the empire of the eye": an act of surveillance wherein the viewing subject beholds the landscape, perceives in it signs of a glorious personal and national destiny, and imagines himself somehow, someday possessing it.[29] As Dixon stages it, the young Klansman is already actually well on his way to achieving possession. His fellow Klansmen have seized control of adjacent territories and report back to him news of their conquests by setting alight a series of crosses. This, the Klansman explains "firmly" to his apprehensive fiancée, makes him "a successful revolutionist," or a worthy heir to the patriots enshrined in accounts of earlier U.S. history. With dizzying rapidity, then, Dixon conjoins ideas of religion, representative government, regional control, marriage and masculine authority, national history, and racial destiny, all in a passage whose visual architecture and principal themes connote the spread of empire.

What happens at the end of *The Clansman*, in short, is the idealization and conflation of the categories of region, nation, and empire. They are idealized in that they have become, for the moment, racially and ideologically "pure," African Americans having been evacuated from the text, Radical Republican race traitors having been converted to white supremacy, white women having the assumed subordinate roles as "sharers" in their husbands' destinies, and white men having reclaimed their homeland. The categories are then conflated in the novel's final sentence. Its mention of "successful revolution" suggests more than faintly the idea of national rebirth. More to the point, its juxtaposition of "Civilisation" and "the South" comes close to collapsing the two, rendering Dixon's home region a kind of preserve for the "civilizing" ethos that, as he had argued in 1898, mandated that the United States become an imperial power.

Dixon had recorded in one of his sermons that "[t]he American nation is the incarnate genius of that democracy that is conquering the world. There may be an eddy in the stream; but the tendency of human thought, of human civilization, is steadily toward this goal" (79). As should be clear, he did not subscribe to any notion of democracy so "radical" as to permit black suffrage, but he does end *The Clansman* by celebrating the potential "election" of Klansmen to office, a fantasy intended to show that the Klan's cause could be conducive to civil government and not just to mob violence. Reconstruction represented to him "an eddy in the stream," an interruption in the progress of civilization outward from its centers of white empire. The Klan's victory reorients "the American nation," placing it once again on its rightful imperial course. Writing in 1905, then—seven years after the United States' emergence as a global imperial power—Dixon is able to devise a narrative that traces the origins of turn-of-the-century American imperialism back to the North Carolina Piedmont, the year 1870, and the Ku Klux Klan's successful defense of white civilization.

If, however, history is so foreordained for Dixon—if the United States' victory over Spain in 1899 and the Klan's triumph over its Reconstruction foes in 1870 are destined occurrences evincing an Anglo-Saxon superiority supposedly several millennia old—why do the key events in the Klan trilogy almost invariably take place suddenly? Why do such individual white characters as Austin Stoneman come to realize their racial destinies only in moments of "sudden fury," "sudden change[s] of the wind," and "sudden thunder" (370–73)? Why do the various white communities that coalesce in the novels, from the Klan to white Americans to "the English-speaking people . . . of the world," as they are called in *The Leopard's Spots*, do so only in precipitous fashion (413)? And why do such key scenes as the ones that conclude *The Clansman* begin and end with barely a half-page's worth of narration, instantly resolving conflicts that had sometimes required several chapters to set up?

These aspects of Dixon's narrative style might seem peculiar but are not necessarily enigmatic. Dixon wrote so hastily and revised so halfheartedly that these moments of abrupt, sometimes unprecedented action and transformation can be seen simply as instances of bad writing; foreshadowing, we might say, was one of the many literary devices that eluded him. Yet suddenness is suggestive of something more important going on in Dixon's novels. It is symptomatic, in fact, of the anxieties that underlie his fiction. One of these is his fear that "the white race" might neither be as unified nor as perpetual as he imagines it to be at the end of each novel. Another, which is related, is his concern that the United States' imperial moment may have passed. To tackle the first issue first, though: Dixon tries to imagine "the white race" as eternal at several points, referring to it in *The Traitor* in terms of its "culture and . . . inheritance of centuries of knowledge" and again in *The Clansman* in terms of its "heritage of centuries of heroic blood from the martyrs of old" (221, 101). In *The Leopard's Spots*, he even tries to quantify this heritage, referring early in the novel to "the proudest and strongest race of men evolved in two thousand years of history" and then later to "the manhood of the Aryan race, with its four thousand years of authentic history" (98, 440). Dixon could be inconsistent with his dates and still "authentic" in his historiography because his point was simply to imagine the white race as possessing a deep, coherent past.

What his novels enact, however, is the perpetual dissolution of the white race. Scenes of dissension, inertia, and even effeminacy within the race occupy far more space in the novels than scenes of white triumph over racial others. Indicative of the magnitude of these problems for Dixon is the fact that he seems only to know how to resolve them "suddenly," only through scenes of transcendent, almost magical assertions of whiteness. Early in *The Leopard's Spots*, for example, a Confederate veteran who had lost a leg during the war (and thus exemplifies a kind of incapacitated white manhood) is unable to protect his daughter from a black mob that intrudes "[s]uddenly" into their cabin and kidnaps her. Later, he loses a second daughter to a lone black rapist. Both daughters die, but neither death deters Dixon from celebrating the fact that white rescue parties had assembled rapidly in their defense. "Within a half hour," he writes after the second kidnapping, emphasizing the suddenness of the event, "a thousand white people were in the crowd":

In a moment, the white race had fused into a homogeneous mass of love, sympathy, hate, and revenge. The rich and the poor, the learned and the ignorant, the banker and the blacksmith, the great and the small, they were all one now. The sorrow of that old one-legged soldier was the sorrow of all;

every heart beat with his, and his life was their life, and his child their child. (372)

Dixon imagines the white community that consolidates itself in response to black violence as a family, the daughter they are seeking to rescue becoming "their child." They come together across class boundaries, and they do so "[i]n a moment," the professional and educational lines that separate them disappearing temporarily in the face of racial imperatives. That they also become like an "old one-legged soldier" and fail for a second time to rescue the girl seem not to faze Dixon. The point is instead that they demonstrate the momentary capacity to "sympath[ize]" with each other, which Dixon treats as evidence of larger racial and historical bonds.

Parallel incidents receive similar treatment in *The Clansman*, with white communities continually having to reassemble rapidly because their disunion had permitted black characters to insult or injure them. In *The Traitor*, dissension within the white race becomes so great that the Klan itself splits into rival factions. Its older, more genteel members decide their mission has been accomplished and agree to disband while its younger, generally poorer members refuse to relinquish their robes. The rogue Klan members scuffle at several points with the veterans who had agreed to the disbanding. They also abet the cold-blooded murder of a scalawag judge, and, in perhaps the novel's most interesting scene, they raid the cottage of a well-to-do Jewish shopkeeper named Nickaroshinski. In terms of the racial epistemologies that govern Dixon's texts, the "problem" with each of these incidents is that they involve white-on-white rather than white-on-black violence. In the case of the Jewish shopkeeper, Dixon wants to subscribe to so Manichean a view of race that, at least in the South, a nonblack is white regardless of religion or ethnic origin. There are no other ethnic minorities in Dixon's Carolina foothills to trouble this racial scheme. Nickaroshinski thus emerges as the trilogy's lone character with the potential to destabilize the strict white-black divide that makes possible Dixon's defense of Klan violence, his faith in the one-drop rule, and so forth. Yet Dixon stages his absorption into the white community by having the disbanded Klan members ride to his defense—suddenly, of course—and thrash the upstarts. The scene concludes with the disbanded "knights" tying their foes to trees and hanging signs from their necks upbraiding them for "disgracing the uniform." The spectacle is reminiscent of the lynching scenes in the first two novels, both of which involved black men being displayed as warning signs with notes affixed to their bodies. The two obvious differences, though, are that the victims in Dixon's final "lynching" scene are allowed to live and, more to the point, that they are white.

As an attempt to restore racial order within the South, the scene only serves to magnify the idea that the white race was prone to deep divisions, however. Dixon was no doubt immanently aware of this fact, especially after the publication of *The Leopard's Spots*, for he himself had recently become a divisive figure among white writers and intellectuals. If he could imagine a perfect white union at the end of each of his Klan novels, he must have had trouble doing so after reading his reviews and seeing some refer to him as gallant and others as hateful. Only once in his career had he experienced something resembling the kind of white unity he wants to enact in his novels, which brings me to the second anxiety that I believe motivates his fiction: his concern that the spirit of white reunion and sectional reconciliation that had exploded at the outset of the Spanish-American War might already be passing away. Historians have debated the causes of the war, with some emphasizing the problem of economic overproduction and the need among American capitalists for new markets overseas, others stressing the importance of yellow journalism and the manipulation of public sentiment against Spain, and still others pointing toward various crises surrounding race, class, and gender at home. However, many agree that, whatever the causes, something remarkable had happened between late 1897 and early 1898, transforming a widespread American ambivalence over imperial expansion into a widespread enthusiasm.

Here, then, it is worth turning to the scenes in *The Leopard's Spots* in which Dixon actually describes the war. In them, we see yet another rapid response of whites to a threat of barbarism, and we hear the unmistakable echoes of the imperialist rhetoric that had fueled *Dixon's Sermons*. We also witness Dixon once again collapsing race, region, nation, and empire into one another by arguing that the war had created a country consisting of "no North, no South—but from the James to the Rio Grande the children of the Confederacy rushed with eager, flushed faces to defend the flag their fathers had once fought."

> America, united at last and invincible, waked to the consciousness of her resistless power.
>
> And, most marvellous [*sic*] of all, this hundred days of war had reunited the Anglo-Saxon race. This sudden union of the English-speaking people in friendly alliance disturbed the equilibrium of the world, and confirmed the Anglo-Saxon in his title to the primacy of racial sway. (410–12)

Dixon's decision to frame the events of the war in terms of national reunion was thoroughly conventional.[30] His emphasis upon the racial nature of re-union, if unusually forthright, nevertheless possessed precedent as well. What makes Dixon's use of the trope noteworthy is the stress he places on the sud-denness of this reunion: its miraculous, alacritous quality, which suggests more conspicuously than any other aspect of the novels that Dixon understood the "Invisible Imperialism" of the Klan and the more manifest imperialism of the United States to be related, mutually constitutive phenomena.

He goes on to write that there was but "a moment's pause" between the destruction of the battleship Maine in Havana harbor and the United States' response. "The war lasted but a hundred days," he records, "but in those hun-dred days was packed a harvest of centuries," a statement that parallels Dixon's observation in *The Clansman* that "the white race" could experience a century's worth of its heritage "[w]ithin the span of a week." Evanescent as it is, Dixon's "white race" needs imperial circumstances—at home or abroad, metaphoric or real—in order to sense its own history, to feel itself confirmed in its mission to continue spreading "civilization" to the less advanced populaces throughout the world. Absent these circumstances, it cannot prove that it exists. Empire thus represents to Dixon a system of fantasized social relationships predicated above all upon racial hierarchies. This is why Dixon ignores almost completely such issues as expanding markets and even territorial acquisitions. In terms of how he represents it, empire is less about such material circumstances as these and more about the spread of "civilization" and the pursuit of "racial instinct." Within a system of legitimate imperial dominion, white subjects can maintain safe, regulated contact with racialized others. They need this contact because, according to the simplest of dialectical relationships, they cease to be a coher-ent community (and probably commence the sort of infighting characteris-tic of *The Traitor*) because they lack an alien rival. Without the regulations characteristic of empire, meanwhile, contact between the races can become contaminating and the social order can be "turn[ed] . . . upside down," as he warns in *The Leopard's Spots*, making the "negro, but yesterday taken from the jungle, the ruler of" what Dixon supposes to be his evolutionary betters.

Walter Hines Page, the publisher who would give Dixon the opportunity to become a novelist in 1902 (but did so, if Dixon is to be believed, only after having bled on his manuscript) shared his soon-to-be author's sense of what was happening to the country in early 1898. In an editorial published in the *Atlantic* in June and prepared simultaneously with Dixon's earliest war sermons, Page writes approvingly of "[t]he inspiring unanimity of the people" and "old outdoor spirit of the Anglo-Saxon" that seemed to be manifesting itself throughout the nation as it pursued its new imperial course. He even wonders whether "[i]n literature . . . we have well nigh lost the art of constructive writing, for we work too much on indoor problems, and content ourselves with adventures in criticism." Some old-fashioned outdoor imperialist gallivanting, Page speculated, might do the nation's literature some good. Yet even as he endorsed the changes in U.S. society and culture that seemed to be underway as a result of the war, he wondered whether Americans fully grasped what they meant, whether indeed they were sufficiently grappling with the question. "Has [the change] come without our knowing the meaning of it?" he asks. "The very swiftness of these events and the ease with which they have come to pass are matters for more serious thought than the unjust rule of Spain in Cuba, or than any tasks that have engaged us since we rose to commanding physical power."[31]

Dixon experienced no such inklings, no sense that the nation needed at least to pause and consider whether, just because it felt exhilarating to win a war fought in a far-off land, it meant that empire was compatible with the United States' most fundamental ideals and institutions. Rather, he sensed in the rapidity of the changes taking place proof that "America" had at long last charted its proper course, that in fact it had laid claim to a destiny he regarded as almost genetic and, in so doing, had lived up to the achievements of its founders, earned the respect of its European peers, and even proved worthy of the blessings of Jesus (who, for Dixon's purposes, comes to seem the embodiment of burdened white manhood; Jesus's "race" poses no questions with which he opts to deal). Indeed, as Walter Hines Page maintained his pro-imperialist views mindful of the problems empire created for the United States—and as such other public figures as Mark Twain, who had initially supported a war to liberate Cuba, came to be disillusioned by the bloody occupation of the Philippines—Dixon kept churning out romances of the white man's burden, celebrating bloodshed and fetishizing bloodlines in a self-consciously revolutionary literary effort to make white southerners and, when they came to see the light, the rest of white "America" seem like culminating figures in white world history.[32]

What comes finally to characterize the Klan novels, then, is something one encounters in abundance in the plantation fiction of the late nineteenth century, namely a sense of nostalgia couched in a vision of progress, an idea that, *in order to move forward, we must return to how they did things back then.* In Dixon's case, though, the nostalgia was directed less toward the Old South than toward a relatively brief moment in early 1898 when the bitter "[p]arty divisions" that had once characterized U.S. debates over "Cuba's struggle" had seemed to disappear—a magical transformation he records in his earliest published sermon on the subject. "To-day," he writes in "The Battle Cry of Freedom," "sword in hand, face to face with the barbarism and tyranny of Spain, we are one people. . . . With this glorious battle cry our nation shall go forth to war . . . without a single selfish purpose, with everything to lose and nothing to gain save the consciousness of duty noble done" (1). No proponent of turn-of-the-century U.S. imperialism could have articulated the idea of the "white man's burden" any better. Borrowing language that he might have remembered from the fiction of Thomas Nelson Page and would in any event soon incorporate into his own brand of plantation novel, Dixon represents empire as a selfless, perhaps thankless "duty" rather than a self-serving enterprise. If empire were something he pretended to begrudge in 1898, however, it was a "burden" he continued to try to "take up" throughout the first decade of the twentieth century. As the next chapter will suggest, the examples of white southern manhood introduced by Page and Grady and embellished by Dixon had come to seem dominant in U.S. culture by 1907, the year Dixon published the final novel in the Klan trilogy. They would thus provide a succeeding generation of southern writers a paradigm to work within as well as against, among them a writer from Mississippi who wrote with fewer illusions about what the plantation represented but also with his own romantic sense of the white southern man as burdened.

CHAPTER 4

"White Babies . . . Struggling"

William Faulkner and the

White Man's Burden

The fiction of William Faulkner is replete with images of burdened white manhood. In *The Unvanquished* (1938), for example, a young Bayard Sartoris is informed by his aunt of the scandal caused by his cousin Drusilla's having dressed as a man and fought under the command of Bayard's father during the Civil War. The only solution, his aunt informs him, is for his father and Drusilla to marry: "Bayard, I do not ask your forgiveness for this because it is your burden too; you are an innocent victim as well as . . . I."[1] In "Old Man," the novella that composes one half of *The Wild Palms* (1939), the "tall convict" who is freed temporarily from prison when the Mississippi River floods and then is commissioned to rescue a pregnant woman stranded in a tree struggles at one point to convince the woman to leave the security of their small boat in order to try to reach a stretch of dry land. "Let me down!" she tells him as he resorts to carrying her. "But he held her, panting, sobbing . . . his now violently unmanageable burden . . . the burden with which, un-witting and without choice, he had been doomed."[2] In *The Reivers* (1962) a man recollects how, when he turned ten, he was informed by his father that it had come time for him to go to work, "to carry the burden of the requisite economic motions" and "assum[e] responsibility for . . . the space he occu-pied, the room he took up, in the world's (Jefferson, Mississippi's, anyway) economy."[3] Yet in *As I Lay Dying* (1930), a man who barely works at all—Anse Bundren, who makes it his life's mission to move so little that, in the words of his daughter, he "dassent sweat"—nevertheless convinces his neighbor, Ver-non Tull, that he himself constitutes an encumbrance: "the only burden Anse Bundren's ever had is himself."[4]

In keeping with the figures studied thus far in this book, these images are all of white southern men and boys. They constitute only a partial list, moreover, of the representations of burdened white manhood to be found in

Faulkner's Yoknapatawpha County novels. Some of these will seem familiar. Bayard Sartoris, for example, is the son of a planter and Confederate officer, and at fifteen years old at the end of the Civil War, he is almost identical in age to Henry W. Grady. A man of the "New South," therefore, he goes on to become a banker and politician rather than simply following in his father's footsteps. Like Grady also, however, he turns out to be an Old South revivalist when it comes to matters of race: as mayor of Jefferson during the 1890s, he "father[s] the edict that no Negro woman should appear on the streets without an apron," a fact revealed in the short story "A Rose for Emily" (1930).[5] Other images of burdened white manhood in Faulkner's fiction are new. One might cite again from "A Rose for Emily" and the fact that Miss Emily herself is represented as "a tradition, a duty, and a care; a sort of hereditary obligation upon the town" as a result of Bayard Sartoris's having remitted her taxes "into perpetuity" in 1894.[6] Or one might recognize in Anse Bundren a white man's burden of a different sort—a poor white man's burden, which his "humped" back and shoulders seem to embody and about which he complains in his mutterings to himself ("Nowhere in this sinful world can a honest, hardworking man profit") even as he schemes successfully to avoid physical labor.[7] Or one might cite Quentin Compson, son of an even newer "New South" than Bayard Sartoris, born as he is in 1891, which is to say, shortly before Bayard's attempts as mayor to preserve what remains of the Old South's public image by legislating all black women into mammies. Similarly devoted to an image of the old order—and by all means a figure who seems weighed down by his heritage—Quentin nevertheless does not think of himself as saddled with the burden of uplifting African Americans or performing any of the other self-sacrificial civic acts supposed by such figures as Grady and Thomas Nelson Page to be the natal obligations of southern men of his social class. Instead he feels a responsibility to discern the motivations of his white forebears, to wonder why they have bequeathed to him the world they did. This sense of burden is expressed in multiple ways in the two novels in which Quentin figures centrally: in "the chill pure weight of the snow-breathed New England air" he feels on his skin while a student at Harvard in *Absalom, Absalom!* (1936), for example, or, much more somberly, in the heavy flat-irons he purchases in *The Sound and the Fury* (1929) to ensure that, once he drowns himself in Boston's Charles River, his body will not rise to the surface.[8]

So prevalent are these images in Faulkner's fiction that, when C. Vann Woodward chose to include a chapter on him in the third edition of *The Burden of Southern History* (1993), he titled it simply "The Burden for William Faulkner." In it he wonders whether the weightiness of Faulkner's fiction was fundamentally the result of his having written so much "about the South, about people living in its unique culture"; whether it reflected instead his impressions of the nation, making his fiction thus "an indictment not only of the South but of America"; or whether in fact Faulkner's deepest, darkest concerns were with the universal—"the same stink no matter where in time," as Faulkner once referred to it—which might explain "why the Mississippian's accomplishment was appreciated widely abroad before it was at home."[9] Based on the cultural history I have sought to reconstruct in this book, I am less eager to separate out these three imaginaries and wonder whether local, national, or global problems and concerns weighed heaviest upon Faulkner. His fiction addresses all three, with some of what are arguably his most "localized" novels (1929's *Sartoris* and 1962's *The Reivers*, for example) appearing within a few years of some of his most "global" ones (1926's *Soldier's Pay* and 1954's *A Fable*).[10] More to the point, the region about which he wrote in most of his fiction, the plantation and postplantation South, had become by 1900 a space in which writers and readers routinely beheld the local, national, and global simultaneously. In the Uncle Remus books readers had encountered what Joel Chandler Harris believed to be the uniquely hybridized regional culture produced by the plantation system and the global economic mechanism that had made it possible, the transatlantic slave trade. In Grady's and Page's writings about the New South they had been made aware, moreover, of a "negro problem" said to present a unique regional predicament—"a burden no other people bears to-day," according to Grady—yet one whose resolution would represent a national contribution to world civilization: "The American Republic . . . will have nothing better to render into the keeping of universal history than the progress made by the two races in the South . . . [toward] the solution of the problem that is theirs."[11] And in Thomas Dixon's Ku Klux Klan novels they had glimpsed a reductionist view of history in which the world and the South were made to seem mirror images of one another, the plantation districts near Dixon's Appalachian hometown becoming battlegrounds in an epic story of white conquest. Each writer had perceived the region at least somewhat distinctly, with Harris's penchant for irony contrasting sharply with Dixon's unambiguous white supremacy, for example. Yet each had also authored what could be called a "romance of the white man's burden," a phrase invented by Dixon yet applicable to the writings of all four since each saw in the South's plantation past a purpose and indeed future for white southern men.

Faulkner reproduces none of these visions exactly in his own fiction. What he does do, however, is to write about *this* South, a South that had been reimagined after Reconstruction as a space of national centrality and said by Grady in 1890 to have attracted the attention of the world ("The promise of her great destiny . . . is no longer blurred or indistinct, and the world draws near to read") for reasons that actually included its "race problem . . . the only shadow that rests on the South."[12] Faulkner writes about a famously "freakish" South, too, and perhaps an even worse one: "a society that is too often vicious, depraved, decadent, corrupt," as the *New York Times* complained in 1950.[13] Yet among the Souths that register in Faulkner's writings—indeed among the Souths in which Faulkner grew up—is a South that during the late nineteenth and early twentieth centuries was defined more in terms of its proximity to U.S. nationality than its alterity or deficiency, a South celebrated by Page in 1897, the year of Faulkner's birth, as having both "largely contributed to produce this nation" and "maintained the supremacy of the Caucasian race, upon which all civilization seems now to depend."[14]

This chapter thus reads Faulkner's fascination with the white man's burden as a form of engagement with a mythology that had made the plantation South seem "universal" by the turn of the century. Whereas his fiction has long been read as signaling a decisive break between what had come before in southern literature and what would come after, this chapter argues that, at least in this one respect, Faulkner was much more deeply involved with southern literary tradition than has often been appreciated. In terms of his experimentations with form, his explorations of his characters' psyches, his critique of traditional modes of historiography, and above all his interrogation of the idea of the plantation as a model society, there can be no doubt: Faulkner was not like his predecessors. Yet in terms of his depictions of white southern men (and, as it turns out, women, too) as unusually freighted by racial responsibility, Faulkner was, as Eric Sundquist has said of his "white mind" and the novels that resulted from his trying to express it, divided.[15] He shows signs in his fiction of repudiating the idea of a white man's burden yet also signs of embracing it, signs even that he was seduced by its potential for "romance." To read him in this light, as a writer wrestling with one of the founding myths of post–Civil War southern literature—that white men had been made by slavery and postslavery to serve a purpose whose consequences were unusually far-reaching—is thus to recognize one way in which a postbellum plantation tradition outlives itself. The actual plantations that had once dominated Yoknapatawpha County had by the twentieth century mostly "reverted to the cane-and-cypress jungle from which their first master had hewed them" or, less romantically, had simply been subdivided into plots of real estate. Plantation fiction, however, may be said to have survived by continuing to structure the stories about the South that white men felt compelled to tell.

That Faulkner was aware of the white man's burden as an idea that expressed the United States' historic mission vis-à-vis the world is suggested in one of his later novels, *Requiem for a Nun* (1951). Its lengthy section titled "The Jail" contains this vision of an "America" expanded to such vast proportions that it seems scarcely supportable or even recognizable by its citizens:

> One nation: no longer anywhere, not even in Yoknapatawpha County, one last irreconcilable fastness of stronghold from which to enter the United States, because at last even the old sapless indomitable unvanquished widow or maiden had died and the old deathless Lost Cause had become a faded (though still select) social club or caste, or form of behavior when you remembered to observe it . . . one world: the tank gun: captured from a regiment of Germans in an African desert by a regiment of Japanese in American uniforms, whose mothers and fathers at the time were in a California detention camp for enemy aliens . . . one universe, one cosmos: one towering frantic edifice poised like a card-house over the abyss of the mortgaged generations; one boom, one peace: one swirling rocket-roar filling the glittering zenith as with golden feathers, until the vast hollow sphere of his air, the vast and terrible burden beneath which he tries to stand erect and lift his battered and indomitable head.[16]

Such a sequence of images compares interestingly to those encountered in Grady, Page, and Dixon, all of whom were fond of recounting expansive histories in matters of only a few hundred words. In their visions, however, the South radiates outward from the plantation toward a horizon of empire. In the penultimate paragraph of Page's *Social Life in Old Virginia before the War* (1897), published the year Faulkner was born, Page travels from "the Old South" through "the great West" to "all civilization" in fewer than two hundred words. In this passage from "The Jail," however, the South is being subsumed by the "one nation" as it expands to become "one universe, one cosmos" with a mass media and consumer culture ("the babbling pressure to buy and buy and still buy arriving" via the "ululance of radio," Faulkner calls it) that are limitless in their capacity to absorb and transmit.[17] The "vast and terrible burden" borne by Americans in 1951 is that their nation has developed the capacity to remake the world in its image or, if it resists, to blow it up: "one boom, one peace."[18]

That Faulkner was interested in the white man's burden as an idea that pertained to southern race relations is revealed much earlier in his career. Indeed, it is revealed in the novel that, according to Sundquist, represents "the extraordinary deepening of style and theme" that separates such later novels as *Absalom, Absalom!* and *Go Down, Moses* (1942) from such earlier ones as *The Sound and the Fury* and *As I Lay Dying*—triumphal novels, to be sure, yet not the intense explorations of race that, in the views of Sundquist and several other critics, made for Faulkner's best work.[19] The novel that marked this "deepening" was *Light in August* (1932). The longest of Faulkner's early published works, it focuses initially on Lena Grove, a young white woman who has traveled from Alabama to Mississippi in search of the man who has left her an unmarried mother-to-be. A major theme is signaled early in the novel when Lena is described as bearing a "swelling and unmistakable burden" by the time she reaches Yoknapatawpha County—a literal white woman's burden that contrasts with a more figurative one presented later in the novel and discussed at length below.[20] The novel also includes among its major characters Gail Hightower, a white man and former preacher deposed from his ministry, in part because of something akin to what Woodward terms "the burden of southern history." Hightower's grandfather was a Confederate cavalryman killed in Jefferson during the war, but like a Henry Grady or a Thomas Dixon trapped within the opening sentences of one of his writings and unable to move beyond them, Hightower can speak of nothing from the pulpit except the war and the day of his grandfather's death in battle. For him the Old South founds nothing; it instead becomes the setting for a story he tells only so that he may tell it again, apparently without variation. And like Anse Bundren, his body seems to show how weighed down he has become by his life: "He was thin once. But he is not thin now. His skin is the color of flour sacking and his upper body in shape is like a loosely filled sack falling from his gaunt shoulders of its own weight, upon his lap" (78–79).

Yet at the center of *Light in August* is Joe Christmas, a man rumored to be of mixed racial descent who has more or less accepted the rumor as fact: "I think I got some nigger blood in me. . . . I dont know. I believe I have" (196–97). At the center of his story, meanwhile, is his relationship with a white woman named Joanna Burden. As the novel presents it, their relationship is literally over before it has started: the first suggestion that Joe and Joanna might have known each other intimately comes only after Joanna's house has burned to the ground and her nearly decapitated body has been found inside. It is then that stories begin to circulate that Christmas and another man, a transient going by the name of Joe Brown, have been living in a former slave cabin on the Burden property and running a bootlegging operation. After Christmas goes missing and Brown is captured, Brown saves his own skin and implicates his fellow bootlegger by alleging that Christmas is not white:

> Because they said it was like he had been saving what he told them next for just such a time as this. Like he had knowed that if it come to a pinch, this would save him. . . . "Go on. Accuse me. Accuse the white man that's trying to help you with what he knows. Accuse the white man and let the nigger go free. . . ."
>   "Nigger?" the sheriff said. "Nigger?"
>   It's like he knew he had them then. (97–98)

It is at this point in the novel that Christmas's racial identity ceases to be a secret (and a secret uncertainty at that) and becomes a form of public knowledge about which no doubt can be expressed. A lynch mob forms, tracks him down, chases him into Hightower's house, and kills him. By the end of the novel Christmas's story, which had begun in rumor, becomes almost a form of trivia, a bit of sordid local history about which out-of-towners are reminded when they hear the name "Jefferson" and are moved to respond, as a furniture dealer from eastern Mississippi does in the novel's final pages, "Oh. Where they lynched that nigger" (496–97).

    That the lynch mob should form so instantaneously and the story of Joe Christmas become trivial so quickly is not surprising. One way in which Dixon's Klan novels manage something like accuracy is in showing how little evidence was required to provoke a white supremacist response, hence how relatively commonplace the lynching of African American men became between the 1890s and 1920s, the years during which both Faulkner and the major characters of *Light in August* lived.[21] To the extent that it is comprehended by the community, the Joe-Joanna story could perhaps have been transplanted into one of Dixon's novels, and Faulkner, who had been given a copy of *The Clansman* (1905) by his first-grade teacher, may well have had Dixon in mind when he developed it.[22] Yet the true stories of Joe and Joanna, about which the community knows little and cares even less, could not have worked at all in Dixon's novels. For one thing, Christmas is not "black." He is described as the color of "parchment" when he is first introduced, a color that likely differs only slightly from Hightower's "flour sacking" (34). Indeed, Brown mocks the sheriff for thinking Christmas merely a "foreigner" when he accuses him of Joanna's murder, and the sheriff is not immediately convinced that his own eyes have deceived him: "You better be careful what you are saying, if it is a white man you are talking about" (98). Christmas's having passed for white would have upset Dixon's fantasy of black biology, which rested on the assumption that "one drop of Negro blood makes a Negro. It kinks the hair, flattens the nose, thickens the lip," and so on.[23] His not even knowing his racial identity, meanwhile, would have suggested that, in some cases, race is not fundamentally knowable, that at the color line it is more a social and legal category than a biological one. Thus, while Dixon's novels contain the occasional mulatta temptress, they contain no one at all who would have proved as upsetting to a white supremacist social imaginary as Christmas.

For another thing, the Joe-Joanna story would have been too complicated for a Klan novel because Joanna is not a white southern woman, at least not according to the standards of Jefferson. Though she was born in the same house in which she is killed, and though she experiences "homesickness for [its] sheer boards and nails, the earth and trees and shrubs" during the few brief intervals in which she must be away from it, she is nevertheless descended from a family with New England roots and—much worse for her, as far as Yoknapatawphans are concerned—a history of militant abolitionism and advocacy for freedmen (240). Her grandfather Calvin Burden, father Nathaniel, Nathaniel's first wife (and her namesake) Juana, and their son (and her half-brother) Calvin II had relocated to Jefferson from Missouri in 1866, at the outset of Reconstruction. They had arrived, moreover, because of Reconstruction: they had first traveled to Washington, D.C. and received "a commission to come down here, to help with the freed negroes" (251). Within a few years the grandfather and father had tried to organize the African American vote in support of a black candidate, and John Sartoris, the father of Bayard, had killed both the grandfather and grandson (the two men named Calvin, in other words) as a result of their interference. The details of this episode are revealed in *The Unvanquished*, a novel published six years after *Light in August*. Joanna's recall of the events in *Light in August* is much hazier, for she says only that her relatives had been "killed in the town two miles away by an ex-slaveholder and Confederate soldier named Sartoris, over a question of negro voting" (248).

"Over a question of negro voting": Joanna's vagueness is startling yet explicable, first, because the deaths of her grandfather and half-brother had taken place more than a half-century earlier. She had never known either man and possessed a different mother than the younger Calvin: Joanna was born to her father's second wife in the late 1880s, fourteen years after the bloody event that represented Jefferson's refusal to reconstruct itself. Juana, the first wife, had died soon after her son and father-in-law. Joanna's connections to both a familial and communal past are thus vexed. She is a native Mississippian—one indeed whose love for its "earth and trees and shrubs" compares to Scarlett O'Hara's for Georgia and "the green bushes starred with fleecy white . . . the raw color of the red earth and the dismal dark beauty of the pines" of the plantation Tara in *Gone with the Wind* (1936).[24] Yet she is not a "southerner" by any definition of the word valid during her lifetime, which means she can share neither her forefathers' hatred of the South nor Jefferson's leading white citizen's hatred of her forefathers. As a woman, moreover, she has little access to the mechanisms for revenge that might give meaning to a young southern man's life, her proper role instead being lamentation. Yet since she cannot exactly mourn the losses of men she never knew, she grows up regarding them as abstractions—symbols surely, yet of what she could not exactly say.

Her complexity is thus similar to Christmas's. Their meeting may not be fated (though *Light in August* is suffused with a language of fate, most notably in Christmas's belief that "*Something is going to happen. Something is going to happen to me*") (118). After they do meet, however, the relationship assumes a momentum of its own, progressing through a series of "phases" in ways that Christmas can foresee until he finally murders her. It is at the beginning of "the second phase," the two having already begun and suspended a sexual relationship, that Joe informs Joanna that he believes himself "part nigger" while Joanna reveals her family's long and violent history of entanglement with causes related to "negro" uplift (254–56). After this their sexual relationship, which had already involved a fair amount of scripting and playacting, becomes almost a parody of a scene out of Dixon, with Joanna staging her own rape night after night and "breathing 'Negro! Negro! Negro!'" as Joe performs his part: "It was as if she had invented the whole thing deliberately, for the purpose of playing it out like a play" (259–60). During the third phase of their relationship Joanna seeks to redeem Joe (and perhaps herself) by encouraging him to attend one of the "negro" colleges she supports. He refuses and some time later declines even to kneel and pray with her. By asking him to pray, Joanna transforms herself into a white missionary of sorts—this after having failed to become his sponsor and ceased to imagine herself his rape victim. When he refuses and she brandishes a gun, she becomes like a white colonizer of the earliest period of European contact with the New World, one who demands religious conversion with a cross in one hand and sword in the other. Their relationship thus regresses from something too radical for the 1920s to something that seemingly dates back to the sixteenth or seventeenth century. As Joanna struggles to identify a role to play ("She's trying to be a woman and she don't know how," Joe thinks to himself at one point), she in effect reverts backward from one role to another, from spinster-lover (this before she knows Joe's reputed race) to defiled white woman to would-be white benefactor to missionary to virtual conquistador (240). The fact that Joe murdered Joanna is revealed in the subsequent scene, though the murder scene itself is omitted. What matters to Faulkner more are the *mechanics* of their relationship, the ways in which it follows a script from the time that Joe first reveals his race and Joanna her life's mission, that night setting in motion a patterned series of events as Joanna tries to determine which romance of the white man's burden she wishes to pursue.

It is worth paying closer attention to the sense of mission that consumes Joanna, which, in the criticism on *Light in August*, has attracted far less attention than the sense of fatalism that surrounds Joe Christmas.[25] Faulkner elaborates upon Joanna's mission in what amounts to her most revelatory scene in the novel—and, as it turns out, the scene that occupies the novel's actual center.[26] Since she knew neither her grandfather nor her half-brother, her concept of them is mediated by her father, who shares his own father's abolitionism but is at least somewhat less inclined toward radicalism during Reconstruction. Nevertheless, he takes Joanna when she is four years old (which is to say, during the early 1890s) to visit the graves of her deceased relatives. He has had to hide the graves out of fear that they would be desecrated by the white citizens of Jefferson. When he shows them to her, he explains to her what they mean. Joanna's recall of his words is notably more vivid than her remembrance of why the men had been killed in the first place ("over a question of negro voting"):

> "'Remember this. Your grandfather and brother are lying there, murdered not only by one white man but by the curse which God put on the whole race before your grandfather or your brother or me or you were even thought of. A race doomed and cursed to be forever and ever a part of the white race's doom and curse for its sins. Remember that. His doom and his curse. Forever and ever. Mine. Your mother's. Yours, even though you were a child. The curse of every white child that ever was born and that ever will be born. None can escape it.' And I said, 'Not even me?' and he said, 'Not even you. Least of all you.'" (252–53)

By assigning the white man's burden to a white woman of New England ancestry Faulkner may have been attempting any of several things. He may have
wanted to show how diffuse the myth had become by the turn of the century.
Alternatively, he may have wished to show how it implicated women in particular, how they were expected to uphold the burden yet remain within a domestic sphere: Joanna spends much of her time at a roll-top desk carrying on
correspondences with representatives of "a dozen negro schools and colleges
through the south," having become a virtual one-woman charitable foundation (233). He may also have sought to make Joanna's gender identity seem
all the more complex, for during their sexual encounters Joe initially feels "as
if he struggled physically with another man" (235). Or he may have wished to
suggest that, all along, the myth of the white man's burden had been deeply
erotic, with Joanna's desires toward her colonial subject (Christmas is called
"heathenish" at one point) representing an absurd version of the fantasy at
the heart of the civilizing mission: that the colonizer *desires* to be colonized
whether he acknowledges it or not. Joanna may provoke Joe's anger repeatedly
as part of the routine of their coupling, yet he keeps coming back, night after
night, apparently resenting her all the while.

    Yet perhaps the most interesting possibility is that Faulkner encumbers
Joanna with the white man's burden to articulate what it feels like—what it
feels like to *him*, even—without having to inject into his novel an obvious
stand-in for himself. Faulkner's earlier masterpieces are appreciated for including such characters as Quentin Compson and Darl Bundren whose levels of
self-reflexivity and poetic self-expression invite consideration of the extent to
which they speak for Faulkner. *Light in August* includes no such character,
unless it is Joanna. Her reminiscence continues, and in a manner one can
imagine Faulkner himself might have spoken had he been allowed to give full
voice to what it felt like to be a white man who did not support Jim Crow yet
recently had become so focused on the question of race as to write an entire
novel about the problem of the color line:

> "I had seen and known negroes since I could remember. I just looked at them
> as I did at rain, or furniture, or food or sleep. But after that I seemed to see
> them for the first time not as people, but as a thing, a shadow in which I
> lived, we lived, all white people, all other people. I thought of other children
> coming forever and ever into the world, white, with the black shadow already
> falling upon them before they drew breath. And I seemed to see the black
> shadow in the shape of a cross. And it seemed like the white babies were

struggling, even before they drew breath, to escape from the shadow that was not only upon them but beneath them too, flung out like their arms were flung out, as if they were nailed to the cross."(253)

In *The Sound and the Fury* Quentin comes to recognize "a nigger [as] not a person so much as a form of behavior; a sort of obverse reflection of the white people he lives among."[27] One could argue that Faulkner never arrives at a more incisive or at least more succinct statement of what it means to be "black" in all of his novels—not in *Absalom, Absalom! Go Down, Moses, Intruder in the Dust* (1948), or any other novel in which race figures as a central theme. Yet Quentin's remark says very little about what it means to be "white"—to be one of the white people among whom "niggers" live, whom they reflect, and to whom they provide a sense of identity and purpose. Joanna's comments go much further. To imagine "white babies . . . struggling" long before they were born—and even longer before they might ever develop a concept of themselves as "white"—is to recognize how absurd *and* how inevitable the concept of whiteness was for someone such as Faulkner.

Light in August may therefore be read as Faulkner's first and perhaps even his most sustained exploration of what it meant to be white—indeed, what it meant to identify as white, as Faulkner did—yet not to embrace white supremacy. If read in this light, then the conclusion to Joanna's reminiscence becomes all the more meaningful:

"I saw all the little babies that would ever be in the world, the ones not even yet born—a long line of them with their arms spread, on the black crosses. I couldn't tell then whether I saw it or dreamed it. But it was terrible to me. I cried at night. At last I told father, tried to tell him. What I wanted to tell him was that I must escape, get away from under the shadow, or I would die. 'You cannot,' he said. 'You must struggle, rise. But in order to rise, you must raise the shadow with you. But you can never lift it to your level. I see that now, which I could not see until I came down here. But escape it you cannot. The curse of the black race is God's curse. But the curse of the white race is the black man who will be forever God's chosen own because He once cursed him.'" (252–53)

One gains an idea of what is happening in this passage simply by citing the first significant words of each sentence: "I . . . I . . . But . . . I . . . At last I . . . What I . . . 'You' . . . 'You' . . . But . . . But . . . I . . . But . . . The curse . . .

But." The passage contains as many affirmations of what Joanna's "I" feels and desires as it does qualifications or negations: "But . . . But . . . But . . . But . . . But." That Joanna feels both so ennobled and so imprisoned by her white skin makes her the truest embodiment of the white man's burden yet cited in this study. That she is a woman who seems also at times "another man" and a native Mississippian who manages still to seem a Yankee makes her oddly universal—a parody of the figures we have encountered throughout the study—and, in the end, an outsider: a person who belongs even less to any society than the famously outcast man who comes to know and then kill her.

In death Joanna becomes something much simpler, namely a white woman who has been victimized by a black beast in Mississippi. She is in the end incorporated into Jefferson's white community because, when word of her death is followed by rumors of Christmas's "blackness," the community knows—even more assuredly than the woman whose honor they are supposed to defend and the man whose life they consider themselves bound to take the script they are supposed to follow:

> Within five minutes after the countryman found the fire, the people began to gather. . . . Within thirty minutes [there were] produced, as though out of thin air, parties and groups ranging from single individuals to entire families. . . . Among them the casual Yankees and the poor whites and even the southerners who had lived for a while in the north, who believed aloud that it was an anonymous negro crime committed not by a negro but by Negro and who knew, believed, and hoped that she had been ravished too: at least once before her throat was cut and at least once afterward. . . .
>
> They were gathering now about the sheriff . . . with faces identical one with another. It was as if their all their individual five senses had become one organ of looking, like an apotheosis. (287–88, 291)

At no point in Faulkner's novels does he come closer than this to suggesting that he knew Dixon. The alacrity with which the mob forms recalls the many scenes of sudden union that occur in the Klan novels, as does the fact that it fuses into a single organism. In *The Leopard's Spots* (1902) Dixon describes the formation of a lynch mob in similar terms, calling it a "crowd [that] seemed to melt into a great crawling swaying creature, half reptile half beast, half dragon half man, with a thousand legs, and a thousand eyes, and ten thousand gleaming teeth, and with no ear to hear and no heart to pity!"[28] Yet of course he also depicts the Klan as an embodiment of a divine energy and purpose, apotheosizing them in a manner Faulkner may have had in mind when his novel shifts so suddenly from its final scenes involving Joe and Joanna to scenes in which the white people of Jefferson seek to play the role that, by the late 1920s, they knew not because of biological instinct but rather because they had encountered it in novels, films, newspaper stories, and other forms of mass communication.

One person in particular who has gotten the message is Percy Grimm, a national guardsman in his middle twenties who might be among the least Faulkner-like of all men in Yoknapatawpha expect for one fact: like Faulkner, he had been unable to fight in World War I. This was not because he was too small, which had been Faulkner's curse, but rather because he had simply been "too young . . . he would never forgive his parents for that fact" (450). What redeems him is the opportunity created when the U.S. National Guard is formed after the war. Grimm finds in Guard service the same sense of purpose that Dixon's white male characters discover when they join the Klan or, as happens at the end of *The Leopard's Spots*, become swept up in a political movement to assert white supremacy. When Christmas is captured and escapes, Grimm is thus presented a chance to live out the sort of fantasy envisioned by Dixon, one in which, by killing a "black" man, he is saving his town, his state, the South, "America," and the idea of civilization itself while avenging white womanhood in the process: "Now you'll leave white women alone, even in hell," he tells Christmas after having shot then emasculated him (464).

It is the language in which Faulkner describes Grimm's discovery of his life's mission that proves most relevant to the present chapter, however. Well before he gains the opportunity to prove himself by killing Christmas, he assumes what Faulkner describes as a very peculiar version of the white man's burden:

> It was the new civilian-military act which saved him. He was like a man who had been for a long time in a swamp, in the dark. . . . Then suddenly his life opened definite and clear. . . . He could see his life opening before him, uncomplex and inescapable as a barren corridor, completely freed now of ever again having to think or decide, *the burden which he now assumed and carried as bright and weightless as his insignatory brass*: a sublime and implicit faith in physical courage and blind obedience, and a belief that the white race is superior to any and all other races and that the American is superior to all other

white races . . . and that all that would ever be required of him in payment for this belief, this privilege, would be his own life. (451; emphasis added)

A "burden . . . bright and *weightless*": Faulkner's most explicit reference to the white man's burden in all of his fiction makes clear what the idea had become by the early twentieth century and the moment such figures as Dixon began using it to describe the South's relationship to the nation and world. It was hardly a burden at all, not in the sense that Kipling had described the supposedly thankless work of maintaining an empire. It was instead a way of making white supremacy seem momentous and white privilege seem like hard work. It gave weight to whiteness and made being white seem like work itself. In short, it allowed such white men as Grimm to *feel* their own skin, which, since it had never been tasked to the same extent as black skin, might otherwise have seemed insignificant, "weightless."

Percy Grimm and Joanna Burden—two characters that, in the end, are presented in only a handful of the novel's 500-plus pages—are nevertheless central to *Light in August*, Faulkner's first novel to make race its central theme and his most thorough and explicit interrogation of the idea of the white man's burden.[29] Grimm embodies the concept as Dixon had imagined it: the white man's burden as a form of race consciousness that discovers in the bi-racial South a place where men may pursue what they fantasize as a global mission. Joanna, by contrast, reflects a different sense of the phrase: the white man's burden as a set of responsibilities that *by design* one can never fulfill, hence "a shadow in which . . . we lived, all white people, all other people." Faulkner obviously did not choose to take up the white man's burden as it was understood by Grimm. Though both felt they had missed out on something by not being able to serve in World War I, and though both took to wearing uniforms because they were denied the opportunity, Grimm assumes the identity he does because it seems "uncomplex," one that "free[s]" him "of ever again having to think or decide." Faulkner tended in a different direction. Yet while he may have come much closer to resembling Joanna, he uses her and her father's memorable speech to her to highlight the absurdity of the other sense of the white man's burden, which permits white men and women to "rise" only insofar as they *fail* to elevate "negroes" ("You must raise the shadow with you. But you can never lift it to your level") and thus dooms "white babies" before they are ever born. The fact that Lena Grove and her white child seem so unencumbered at the end of the novel perhaps shows that Faulkner was working to envision an alternative to the idea of whiteness-as-burden. The fact that Lena's sense of freedom is made possible by her being *white*—one cannot imagine a black woman traveling the same paths with the same feelings of delight and irresponsibility—may however show Faulkner's awareness that the encumbrances of race cannot be escaped so easily.

If Lena does represent an alternative to the idea of whiteness-as-burden, hers is a path ("a peaceful corridor paved with unflagging and tranquil faith and peopled with kind and nameless faces and voices," Faulkner calls it) that few other white characters travel in the novels published after *Light in August* (7). This is especially true of the next novel in the Yoknapatawpha sequence, *Absalom, Absalom!* published four years later. The dilemma with which Faulkner begins wrestling in the earlier novel—whether one can one identify as "white" without being particularly proud or particularly regretful of the fact—also confronts Quentin Compson, the central character of *Absalom, Absalom!* as he tries to understand the story of Thomas Sutpen, a Yoknapatawpha planter and Confederate officer who had been dead more than twenty years by the time of Quentin's birth in 1891. Unrelated to Sutpen by blood, Quentin's connection to Sutpen is entirely imaginary. It is in a sense a literary fascination, for Quentin's first exposure to Sutpen as someone who might be worthy of his contemplation comes when Rosa Coldfield, an old townswoman and one-time sister-in-law to Sutpen, summons Quentin to her home and presents to him her version of the Sutpen story as a kind of literary present, a narrative Quentin himself might wish to reproduce should he "enter the literary profession as so many Southern gentlemen and gentlewomen too are doing now."[30] More than this, the most compelling chapters of *Absalom, Absalom!* involve Quentin and his Harvard roommate, the Canadian Shreve McCannon, in effect writing the Sutpen story themselves, filling in its gaps and fleshing out its characters using their own powers of deduction and imagination. Perhaps as much as half of what Quentin finally "knows" about the Sutpen saga, he invents. The task of having to compose so much of the narrative himself, which is to say, to become so involved with it, weighs upon Quentin, who observes after concluding his retelling of the Sutpen story that he now feels "older at twenty than a lot of people who have died." He says this after having mused earlier in the novel that "he was not a being, an entity" but rather "a commonwealth," a sum total of a community's stories, none of them uplifting (301, 7).

Provoking an even greater feeling of encumbrance, however, is that Quentin is able to complete Sutpen's story (and to complete it in two senses of the word: both to finish his retelling of the story and to supply the information missing in the stories handed down to him by his elders) only because he knows the South so well. The questions at the heart of Sutpen's story that, for a time, transform Quentin and Shreve into literary detectives—why does Sutpen leave his first wife after the birth of their son, and why does his second son kill the first (which is to say, his own half-brother) after the first becomes engaged to his half-sister—turn out to be almost too easy to answer, too predictable to someone who knows the South as intimately as Quentin does. The answer to both questions is the same as the answer to why the Jefferson community comes together and lynches Joe Christmas after the murder of Joanna Burden: because Christmas and Sutpen's first wife and son are believed to be nonwhite, their appearances notwithstanding. The fact that versions of the same story keep repeating themselves—both in the sense that *Absalom, Absalom!* repeats elements of *Light in August* and that the Sutpen story was still being played out in various ways in the Mississippi Quentin had known since his 1890s childhood—leads Quentin by the end of the novel to feel almost doomed by his racial and regional heritage. Whereas Shreve can solve the mysteries of the Sutpen saga and experience a sense of elation as a result ("The South. Jesus," he exclaims after he has put all of the story's pieces together), Quentin can only feel as if white southern men of his social rank have been condemned to uphold a society structured in such a way that it was destined to keep collapsing in on itself (301). It is an absurd task, and one not unlike the Sisyphean challenge presented to Joanna by her father ("You must struggle, rise. But in order to rise, you must raise the shadow with you. But you can never lift it to your level") during the early 1890s, about the time Quentin was becoming old enough to think of himself as white, southern, and male.

His sense of fatigue is communicated most clearly when he and Shreve begin to ponder in earnest why Henry Sutpen, Thomas's second son, murders Charles Bon, his first. This junction in the Sutpen story marks the moment that Sutpen, like the South, must start over after the Civil War. Perceiving one too many new beginnings in a tale that seems always to be heading toward the same conclusion, Quentin recoils:

"And so [Sutpen] came home and found—"

"Wait," Quentin said.

"—what he must have wanted to find or anyway what he was going to find—"

"Wait, I tell you!" Quentin said, though he still did not move nor even raise his voice—that voice with its tense suffused restrained quality: "I am telling." *Am I going to have to hear it all again* he thought *I am going to have*

to hear it all over again I am already hearing it all over again I am listening to
it all over again I shall have to never listen to anything else but this again forever
so apparently not only a man never outlives his father but not even his friends
and acquaintances do. (222)

Quentin's dismay does not stem merely from the fact that, by this point in the
novel, he has already told and retold Sutpen's story multiple times (including
even to his own father, who begins the novel as one of Quentin's sources but
ends up learning as much from his son as his son from him). It stems also
from his realization that the Sutpen's saga, for all of its ironies and moments of
high drama, is at its heart a story that had been repeated countless times in the
plantation South, one he may even regard as definitive of his home region. It
is a story in which a planter, possessing unusual access to black women's bodies
because of the forms of power inherent in slavery, produces two lines of descent, one white and legitimate, the other "black" and illegitimate. The one he
claims and even makes a point of teaching its members to regard themselves
as the upholders of a long and distinguished tradition (one thinks of Henry
W. Grady's and Thomas Nelson Page's many writings about proud planter
lineages, their own ancestries especially). The other he disavows and—often
enough to make this a part of the story, too—bequeaths them to his legitimate
heirs, creating possibilities for even more incestuous and more miscegenated
lineages (which is to say, for darker stories) than had existed before.

The story had been repeated often enough—white man affirms white supremacy and expects his wife and daughters to reproduce white purity while
at the same time he begets a "black" progeny—that Quentin and Shreve both
perceive it as tending toward white racial doom. In one of the novel's final
and most provocative passages, Shreve extrapolates it and envisions a future in
which "black" blood will be so pervasive that "white" blood will no longer be
able to compete: "and so in a few thousand years I who regard you will have
sprung from the loins of African kings" (302). The story might thus even be
considered cliché—a set of events that have been repeated so often that they
should no longer even seem surprising—except that it has always been unspeakable, a part of a plantation everydayness that nevertheless refuses to be
acknowledged. Once it has been spoken—indeed once Quentin and Shreve
have embroidered and embellished it into something resembling literature—
it immediately becomes to Quentin demoralizingly *common*. He knows, for
example, that black women continue to serve as prostitutes to white men (a
fact that may even have dawned upon him during his childhood, as is suggested in the 1931 short story "That Evening Sun," which a young Quentin

narrates). He knows also—indeed he has grown up in a community in which the visual evidence still exists—that slaveowners had produced children by both their white wives and black slaves (and slaveowners' sons had done so by both *their* white wives and the daughters of their *fathers'* slaves: facts explored more deliberately in two later Faulkner novels, *Go Down, Moses* and *Intruder in the Dust*). Were he given any of the hundreds of examples of plantation fiction that had proved so popular during his adolescence and young adulthood (and surely he, like Faulkner, had been exposed to them if not actively consumed them), he would have seen it as a form of denial, a way of celebrating the old plantation by *not* discussing what went on before and after its scenes involving belles and ballrooms, its vignettes centered around bird hunts, hound dogs, horses, "darkies," and the other more decorous elements of plantation life.

If *Light in August* thus presents characters groping among a set of narratives in search of the story that will teach them how to conduct their lives, *Absalom, Absalom!* presents something else: the story of a young southern man who sets out to solve the mysteries surrounding a deceased nonrelative only to discover himself implicated in a recurring story about a region and its plantation past. It is a story that represents the antithesis of, say, *Gone with the Wind*, which was published the same year as *Absalom, Absalom!* but in many ways extends the plantation tradition that had been so popular during the previous half century.[31] In answer to the text's final pressing question—Shreve's query to Quentin, "Why do you hate the South?" in the novel's penultimate paragraph—one might surmise that, his disavowals notwithstanding, Quentin hates the South in large part because Sutpen's story, which had in some respects ended with the planter's death in 1869, still seems so relevant. It seems so, moreover, in 1910, the year in which Quentin and Shreve complete their reconstruction of its events. Its relevance seemed undiminished to Faulkner a quarter century later as he wrote the novel. As recent criticism has shown, furthermore, *Absalom, Absalom!* has lost none of its resonance, with Sutpen's narrative and all that surrounds it providing, in the words of Barbara Ladd, "a study in implication": a novel in which efforts to avow difference or affirm distance only reveal how closely connected supposedly separate entities really are.[32] Perhaps Faulkner himself knew he had discovered in the story of Sutpen what *Absalom, Absalom!* has come to seem in American literature, namely, its modern parable of the plantation South.

Quentin's concluding observation that he feels "older at twenty than a lot of people who have died" echoes something said of Rosa Coldfield at the outset of the novel: that she exemplifies "children born too late into their parents' lives and doomed to contemplate all human behavior through the complex and needless follies of adults" (15). Since Quentin's parentage is so extensive, however, including as it does both Rosa and Sutpen among the virtual ancestors to whom he feels attached, he imagines himself even more "doomed" than she. Rosa, after all, sees the Sutpen saga and the white southern epic it embodies from inside of it and, more importantly, from a single vantage point. Quentin on the other hand sees the story both from within and without, possessing forms of distance—temporal, geographical, and genealogical—that she does not. Yet he feels no greater capacity to escape what amounts to its gravitational pull, making *Absalom, Absalom!* a romance of the white man's burden of a different sort. Quentin's initial quest is to discover why Rosa has even bothered to tell him Sutpen's story at all, "What is it to me that the land or the earth or whatever it was got tired of him at last and turned and destroyed him?" (7). His next is to resolve as best he can the mysteries that surround Sutpen's life: why he left his native Virginia to become an overseer on a plantation in Haiti, why he left Haiti and his first wife and son for Mississippi, how and why he becomes "the biggest single landowner and cotton-planter in the county," and why his "design" ultimately fails (56). Having for the most part resolved these questions, he finds himself in the end still questioning whether a new and different South might emerge from the one Sutpen and his fellow planters had built, one that might afford young men of his generation more opportunities to chart their own courses (or simply more room to breathe: Quentin is perpetually short of breath in the novel, at one point "lying . . . in the Massachusetts bed . . . breathing fast now" and in the novel's final paragraph "panting in the cold air, the iron New England dark") (295, 303). In the end he concludes that there is no such possibility, that in a sense Henry W. Grady had been right when he had argued in 1889, only two years before Quentin's birth, that "the new South is simply the old South under new conditions."[33] What this phrase might have meant to Quentin, however, is almost the opposite of what Grady intended. To Quentin, the Old South had at least been a land of opportunity and relative "innocence," the word upon which he finally settles in order to explain Sutpen's actions. The New South, by contrast, is a space in which white men may know better—in which some of them may even grow to conceptualize "a nigger" as merely "a form of behavior; a sort of obverse reflection of the white people he lives among"—yet still feel powerless to be "white" any differently than had their fathers.

That Quentin feels trapped within a southern story that seems to be looping endlessly back on itself is all the more noteworthy given the narrative he finally writes for Sutpen. It is, it can be said, a new story, one whose images of a planter and the society he creates around him are significantly unlike those that had been propagated in the fiction of the late nineteenth and early twentieth centuries. Sutpen is depicted as a world-builder, and to this extent Faulkner was perhaps engaging directly with the mythology we have encountered repeatedly in earlier texts, one in which planters are represented as miniature emperors and founding fathers of regions and nations. (To know that this mythology remained resonant in 1936, one need look no further than Margaret Mitchell's descriptions of Gerald O'Hara, Scarlett's father, in *Gone with the Wind*. Though an Irish immigrant and a character of much greater vitality than the staid patriarchs typical of earlier plantation fiction, he is nevertheless depicted as founding something much larger than a mere plantation, a fact that prompts Rhett Butler to tell Scarlett that "your family and my family . . . made their money out of changing a wilderness into a civilization. That's empire building."[34]) Yet singularly missing from Sutpen's profile is that quality I have sought throughout this book to identify as central to a post–Civil War plantation mythology. At no point in any of the versions of his story rehearsed in *Absalom, Absalom!* is Sutpen presented as an embodiment of a white man's burden. He is called many things, from Rosa's opening descriptions of him as a devil incarnate to Shreve's insistence on seeing him as "the demon" to Quentin's final recharacterization of him as an innocent. He is, moreover, without question a white supremacist, though an "innocent" sort, if Quentin is to be believed: Sutpen seeks the powers and privileges associated with his race and gender not because he necessarily envisions white manhood as superior—he likely does, yet in none of the lines of dialogue Quentin writes for him does he make this a point—but rather because the powers and privileges are simply there to be had.

Spurned as an inferior after his family descends from the mountains of western Virginia and he makes his first visit to a Tidewater plantation, he formulates his design: to found his own plantation, marry and produce at least one (necessarily white) son, become wealthy, and be done with it. For all of Rosa Coldfield's attempts to persuade Quentin to conceive the creation of Sutpen's Hundred in biblical terms—to imagine it like the creation story of Genesis (Quentin envisions Sutpen saying *Be Sutpen's Hundred* like the oldtime *Be Light*") or better yet like the establishment of a veritable Hell by a "*demon . . . who came out of nowhere*" and "*tore violently a plantation*" from a virgin Earth—the motivations that Quentin finally ascribes to Sutpen are remarkably insignificant (4–5). They could even be called insular, for as far as Sutpen seems concerned, his story has only to do with himself and, to the extent that they matter to his design, his wife and children. It has little to do with empire-building as a thankless task that beckons white men, less to do the with the Manifest Destiny of the United States, and only to do with the South to the extent that the South was where slavery had remained legal and plantations continued to grow throughout the first half of the nineteenth century. Had things gone according to plan in Haiti, one imagines, Sutpen would have been content to pursue his design there.[35] His commitments were never nationalistic, certainly not when he was founding Sutpen's Hundred and likely not even when he became a colonel in the Confederate army. He seems instead to have joined the war effort in order to preserve the possibility for attaining his goals as he had originally envisioned them, not because of any particular patriotic feeling toward "Dixie."

Above all, Sutpen seems to have no feelings about his slaves. He regards them instead as units of labor expected to do as they were ordered (including, for his female slaves, submitting to sexual exploitation and producing additional slaves; Quentin's father speculates that Sutpen "probably chose them with the same care and shrewdness with which he chose other livestock") (48). He by no means endeavors to uplift them, however. The early citizens of Yoknapatawpha County watch as his "legend[arily] . . . wild negroes" advance from seeming "wild men" to becoming only "somewhat tamed" (27, 33). They are not depicted as having benefited from the civilization afforded them by plantation life, however, and they by no means resemble the "happy darkies" of plantation fiction, nor is Sutpen ever shown expecting them to conform to these roles. Rather, they seem to share his understanding that his whiteness opens up possibilities in Mississippi that their blackness precludes, and they labor accordingly (though whether they do so contentedly the novel never bothers to say—an indication that, rather than posing critiques of the plantation myth, *Absalom, Absalom!* more often simply refuses even to engage it, dismissing it as a fabrication by declining even to offer up its central images as worth debunking).

Because he travels from Virginia to Haiti to Mississippi, crossing national boundaries before settling on a plantation site that *could* have been depicted as an outpost in a westward-moving United States, Sutpen would have been an almost perfect expression of the white southern planter as bearer of the burden of empire, had Faulkner chosen to represent him in this way. Indeed, he could have seemed like the figures Page idealizes at the end of *Social Life in Old Virginia* (or even like the almost comically burdened white man George Cary Eggleston writes about in *Love Is the Sum of It All*, the one who masters "negro problems" everywhere from Virginia to South America to Africa). He potentially represents the western pioneer, hence nation-builder; the Civil War hero, hence defender of home and tradition; and the master obeyed by his slaves, hence bringer of civilization to "Africans." Yet rather than raise his slaves to his level, Sutpen routinely "descends" to "theirs." Or, as the novel represents it, he and they simply occupy the same plane, a space reminiscent of one of the novel's descriptions of Haiti: "a little island . . . which was the halfway point between what we call the jungle and what we call civilization" (202). Sutpen is described early in the novel as having labored alongside his slaves to build his plantation, the lot of them "plastered over with mud against the mosquitoes and . . . distinguishable from one another by his beard and eyes alone" (28). In an even more memorable scene, he fights with one of his slaves for sport, apparently neither giving nor expecting any quarter from his opponent. In Quentin's imagination they appear as parallel figures, "a white one and a black one, both naked to the waist and gouging at one another's eyes as if their skins should not only have been the same color but should have been covered with fur too" (20–21).

Nor is the era of Reconstruction presented as a racial melodrama, as it had been in such novels as Page's *Red Rock* and Dixon's *The Leopard's Spots* and *The Clansman*. In *Absalom, Absalom!* it seems instead a continuation of the same personal and increasingly futile history of Sutpen's pursuit of his original design. Sutpen loses his slaves and lives an additional four years after his return from the Civil War. His attempts to rebuild his plantation, however, just like his efforts to build it in the first place, seem to Quentin remarkably devoid of symbolism, certainly of the conventional sort. Sutpen is not portrayed as having inherited a "negro problem" of global significance, which is how Page and Dixon among others had been imagining Reconstruction. Instead, his new trials seem simply additional impediments to the realization of his plan. Sutpen himself, meanwhile, rather than becoming a sympathetic figure charged with solving a race problem, is represented as an increasingly desperate and pathetic character who, after the setbacks he experiences when his second wife dies and son Henry disowns him, will do anything to produce a legitimate white male heir.

In short, his story possesses much in terms of its settings and structure that mimics the stories about planters in circulation in U.S. culture, yet almost nothing in terms of its plot or characterization resembles the fiction that had made the plantation so popular a site for fictional exploration. Neither Sutpen nor his "Hundred" lend themselves to evocations of the white man's burden as an idea that explains the plantation South. Yet Quentin, though he never tries to force Sutpen to "fit" this image, still feels oppressed by what he discovers. It is as if, by having told Sutpen's story, he has become aware of an overwhelming responsibility, yet to whom and of what kind he cannot say. He comes in the end to envy Sutpen's "innocence," imagining himself, not unlike the "white babies . . . struggling" in the vision of white obligation imparted to Joanna Burden by her father, born into a world in which the injustices associated with race have become transparent yet seem no less inevitable. Unlike Joanna, however, Quentin does not indulge in one or another fantasy that he is burdened by "negroes." The weight he feels has been produced instead by the actions of white men. And unlike Sutpen, he can neither possess nor pursue white male privilege innocently. As he says already by the novel's midpoint, long before he has completed his retelling of Sutpen's tale, "*I have heard too much, I have been told too much; I have had to listen too much, too long*" (168).

It is beyond the scope of this chapter to explore the additional ways Faulkner takes up the white man's burden, so to speak, in the novels published later in his career. One might note briefly that, just as *Absalom, Absalom!* did not lay to rest his questions about the color line, the connections between race and violence, or the legacies of the plantation, it did not mark the end of his exploration of white southern manhood as a kind of weighty inheritance, a form of responsibility that obligated one to face the past yet did not clarify what one was supposed to do with the knowledge gained as a result. Questions of how white southern men should comprehend the actions of their ancestors emerge in *The Unvanquished*, for example, the next novel in the Yoknapatawpha sequence and the one in which the murders of Joanna Burden's grandfather and half-brother by John Sartoris are dramatized. The novel makes clear the community's response to Sartoris's violent defense of southern white supremacy ("Yaaaaaay, John Sartoris! Yaaaaaaay!" they exclaim at the end of the chapter in which the murders are committed).[36] It makes much less clear, however, how the event should be interpreted in retrospect, leaving readers to play a role similar to Quentin's in *Absalom, Absalom!* and ponder the extent to which such an event, which essentially inaugurates the Jim Crow era of politics in Yoknapatawpha County, might have shaped the history in which they now live.

Questions of whether white southern men are called upon to make amends for the actions of the ancestors are latent in *The Unvanquished* and made much more explicit in *Go Down, Moses*, a novel in which white male characters seem involved in an almost perpetual interrogation of the South's racial past. Among its oldest generation of characters are Buck and Buddy McCaslin, who keep a ledger noting the dates of the births and deaths of the family's slaves yet discover by way of the information contained in it—and via an act of imaginative reconstruction similar to what Quentin and Shreve perform in *Absalom, Absalom!*—the ways in which rape, miscegenation, and incest have figured into their family's history. Among the novel's next generation of characters is Isaac McCaslin, Buck's son, who uncovers the same history from the same ledger and repudiates his plantation inheritance as a result, proclaiming as he does, "Don't you see? This whole land, the whole South, is cursed, and all of us who derive from it, whom it ever suckled, white and black both, lie under its curse?"[37] An echo in some ways of Nathaniel Burden's admonition to his daughter, Ike's speech and subsequent actions raise questions of whether a plantation past can be repudiated and whether one of its beneficiaries can ever become "innocent" again. Among Ike's final acts in the novel is to distribute an inheritance to the descendants of two of the McCaslin plantation's slaves, an attempt to pay off a debt that only illustrates to him more clearly the depths of his obligations. As one of the descendants reminds him when he hands her an envelope, "That's just money."[38]

Questions of indebtedness and whether the South's past can ever be "paid for" also arise in *Intruder in the Dust* and *The Reivers*. In the former a young Chick Mallison, nephew to the lawyer Gavin Stevens, resents the fact that he is rescued from drowning by Lucas Beauchamp, one of the nonwhite McCaslin descendants of *Go Down, Moses*. He resents even more the fact that his efforts at compensating his rescuer with money are rejected, forcing him thereafter to live fully conscious of how much he owes to a "nigger." When Beauchamp fails to make eye contact with him on the street one morning, he feels like a weight has been lifted, expressing the sensation in a language relevant to this chapter: "He was free. Lucas was no longer his responsibility, he was no longer Lucas' keeper; Lucas himself had discharged him."[39] In the latter a young Lucius Priest comes to recognize in Ned McCaslin, yet another of the "negroes" related by blood to the white McCaslins, one of the sharpest men in all of Yoknapatawpha County. Upon the successful completion of an elaborate scheme involving a borrowed automobile, a stolen racehorse, and several duped white men, Lucius recognizes that Ned had been responsible for their every success, "had carried the load alone, held back the flood, shored up the crumbling levee with whatever tools he could reach."[40]

Exploring the ways in which white men become indebted to black men— to exceptionally capable black men, in the cases of Lucas Beauchamp and Ned McCaslin—Faulkner inverts the image seen in much plantation fiction, in which "negroes," some moderately capable, most not, are depicted as owing what levels of advancement they possess to their white male caretakers. By the end of the book that marked the end of his career (*The Reivers* was published in June 1962, one month before his death), Faulkner was perhaps seeking to repay a debt he felt to black southerners by writing a novel in which Ned is clearly the most admirable and arguably the central character—the figure whose influence on the young Lucius Priest seems even greater than that of his own grandfather, "Boss" Priest, who is otherwise the person Lucius professes most to revere. (In so doing Faulkner creates with his last novel a text that bears comparison to the one I identify as the first in a postbellum plantation tradition, *Uncle Remus, His Songs and His Sayings* [1880]. In both, young white boys come to regard older black men as wise teachers, especially in terms of how they negotiate racial expectations. *The Reivers* even makes reference to Harris's creation, with a racist constable's referring to Ned as "Uncle Remus" at one point and, soon after, Lucius's asserting that "when it was just me and members of his own race around," "he was not Uncle Remus now.")[41]

Yet even *The Reivers*, which seems Faulkner's most deliberate attempt to represent a young white man who is the heir to a planter's fortune as *unen-cumbered* by the past, concludes with an image that will appear familiar. After Lucius has been discovered by his grandfather to have lied in order to go on a joyride to Memphis, he is admonished and told that his punishment is to "live with" a full acknowledgment of his wrongdoing:

> "Live with it," Grandfather said.
> "Live with it? You mean forever? . . . Don't you see I can't?"
> "Yes you can. . . . You will. A gentleman always does. . . . A gentleman accepts the responsibility of his actions and bears the burden of their conse-quences, even when he did not himself instigate them but only acquiesced to them, didn't say No thought he knew he should. Come here." Then I was crying hard, bawling, standing (no kneeling; I was that tall now) between his knees. (302)

The subject of this exchange is not explicitly racial, for "Boss" Priest is more concerned with his grandson's having lied than his having become caught up in a scheme that involved, among other pursuits too old for him, horse racing and gambling, all under the direction of a "negro." Indeed, Lucius's grand-father, like most of the other respectable white characters in *The Reivers*, seems to regard Ned as an intellectual if not necessarily social equal. Yet the subtext of the passage may have something to do with race, for "Boss" Priest is speak-ing to Lucius (and Lucius to his own grandson: *The Reivers*, subtitled *A Remi-niscence*, is narrated by an elderly Lucius Priest to his own grandchild) about what it means to be a "gentleman," a word that does not necessarily denote race and class yet may in this context suggest them. For what is being passed down from one to the next among five generations of Priest men, in effect, is a code of conduct that identifies "acquiesce[nce]" as a form of guilt. Upon receiving this insight at the end of his novel, the young Lucius Priest does not collapse into his bed in a fit of panting and violent shivering, as Quentin does in the final pages of *Absalom, Absalom!* He does end up on his knees, however, "bawling" because he "bears the burden of . . . consequences" of actions he "did not himself instigate" but to which he "only acquiesced." That, in a phrase, is Quentin's burden, too, just as it is Joanna's: all three are born into worlds in which a system of race relations has afforded them privileges and demanded little in return other than their tacit consent, their acquiescence to tradition if not their full-fledged commitment to racism. What propels their stories—what creates for each a kind of quest narrative in pursuit of answers to the question, *so what do I do differently?*—is that by the early twentieth century the old ways of being "white" and "southern" seemed inadequate yet no new ways had presented themselves as viable alternatives. Faulkner's best fiction records the frustrations characters feel when they try to break free of the ways of the old plantation only to find themselves, like Quentin when he dismays at having "*to hear it all over again,*" trapped within a story that refuses not to be repeated.

The romance of the white man's burden thus proves difficult to elude. By the time it finds its way into *The Reivers* and a young Lucius Priest's discovery that Ned McCaslin "was not Uncle Remus now," Faulkner had been writing about it since 1932's *Light in August* and perhaps even since 1929's *The Sound and the Fury* and Quentin Compson's realization that "a nigger" was "a form of behavior." Both Lucius's and Quentin's moments of recognition lead them to wonder whether whiteness is also an artifice, and if so, what kind. Faulkner's later novels attempt various answers to this question, but the metaphor to which he keeps returning is one of burden, of whiteness itself as a kind of weight.

Speaking as himself, Faulkner voiced an insight similar to Quentin's and Lucius's in an address delivered at the University of Virginia in 1958: "the white race can never really know the Negro, because the white man has forced the Negro to be always a Negro rather than another human being in their dealings."[42] This insight, however—the one that governs so much of his best fiction writing about race—produces something else in his University of Virginia address. It would be too much to suggest that the ghosts of Henry W.

Grady and Thomas Nelson Page, Virginia alumni both, possessed him at times as he spoke. But it would make a point. Faulkner's address concerned the race problem, which he notes was "still unsolved" and had lately become a crisis that northerners accused white southerners of perpetuating. "Let us say to the North: All right, it is our problem, and we will solve it," Faulkner responds— and in so doing unwittingly reproduces the same formulation we have seen earlier, most conspicuously in the title to Thomas Nelson Page's 1904 treatise *The Negro: The Southerner's Problem.*

In highly qualified and speculative language, almost as if he were refusing to commit to his own thoughts, Faulkner then outlines a solution to the problem:

> For the sake of argument, let us agree that as yet the Negro is incapable of equality for the reason that he could not hold and keep it even if it were forced on him with bayonets; that once the bayonets were removed, the first smart and ruthless man black or white who came along would take it away from him, because he, the Negro, is not yet capable of, or refuses to accept, the responsibilities of equality.
>
> So we, the white man, must take him in and teach him that responsibility. . . . Let us teach him that, in order to be free and equal, he must first be worthy of it, and then forever afterward work to hold and keep and defend it. He must learn to cease forever more thinking like a Negro and acting like a Negro. This will not be easy for him. *His burden will be that,* because of his race and his color, it will not suffice for him to think and act just like any white man: he must think and act like the best among white men. . . .
>
> So we alone can teach the negro the responsibility of personal morality and rectitude. (157–58; emphasis added)

Faulkner was speaking on the same campus where, seventy years earlier, Grady had beheld "the vision of this Republic—its mighty forces in balance, and its unspeakable glory falling on all its children . . . working out its mission under God's approving eye, until the dark continents are opened . . . and under one language, one liberty, and one God, all the nations of the world hearkening to the American drum beat."[43] It was the same sort of vision of "one nation: no longer anywhere" that Faulkner would later parody in *Requiem for a Nun.* Yet while there was nothing of Grady's imperialism or naked white supremacy in Faulkner's 1958 address, there was most assuredly an articulation of the white man's burden, indeed of the white man's burden as, for the time at least, a peculiarly southern responsibility, a task that "we alone" can assume. He foists the burden also upon African Americans—"*His burden will be that*"—and requires of them a peculiar performance. For if "the Negro" were essentially a performative category to begin with—"a sort of obverse reflection of the white people he lives among," as Quentin calls it—then what would it have meant for him then to "act like the best among white men"? Had not his own examples of Joe Christmas, Charles Bon, and Lucas Beauchamp made clear the deep risks involved when "the Negro" acts white?

By ending this chapter with these questions and this speech, I do not mean to suggest that Faulkner regressed in his old age or that, in his response to the growing civil rights movement, he sought solace in the southern fantasies of Grady, Page, and others. *The Reivers*, his last novel, may have been his most cheerful, but it was no plantation romance. Yet the concept of the white man's burden seemed seductive to Faulkner to the end. It seemed worthy of romance, even: the sort of idea that could sustain novel after novel and could even prove useful as a means of structuring a speech on the "negro problem." Perhaps in all of his literary explorations he had discovered no alternatives for imagining a whiteness he could inhabit, one that described how he had felt from the moment that, like Joanna Burden, he himself had become conscious of "negroes" as a race, "not as people, but as a thing." His novels are replete with examples of African Americans emerging from "thingness" to become people again, from that of Dilsey in *The Sound and the Fury* to that of Ned McCaslin in *The Reivers*. Yet they are also replete with images of white people, white men in particular, imagining themselves as less human and more mechanical, more thinglike, because of the responsibilities placed upon them by their whiteness. Perhaps the only alternative to imagining whiteness as a burden would have been to imagine whiteness as not inherently significant, whiteness as an undeniable social and historical fact yet not a sign or symbol of one's destiny or relationship to history. Perhaps this would have been desirable, since it would have made it impossible to see "the negro" as in any way "ours." Yet it may have been that this was simply not Faulkner's inclination—to see less significance in something when his tendency was always to see more—or it may have been that, during the years and places in which he lived, seeing whiteness as insignificant was simply not a possibility.

Conclusion

Plantation Nationhood and the
Myth of Southern Otherness

One narrative of how southern literature achieved national and global recognition during the 1930s and afterward goes like this. In 1917 H. L. Mencken, the Baltimore-born editor and essayist who by that time had become a fixture of a New York based literary establishment, published "The Sahara of the Bozart," an essay disparaging the South for its failure to have contributed to American "civilization" since the end of the Civil War. Broad in its indictment, the essay makes fun of white southern backwardness from what Mencken regards as the society's bottom—its "mob of peasants" whose aspirations toward "culture" rise no higher than "the gospel hymn" and "the phonograph"—to its top—its "ghost[s] of the old aristocracy" whom Mencken concludes the essay by pitying as "in the main . . . pleasant. . . . But a bit absurd. . . . A bit pathetic." What differentiates the South's best white citizens from its worst, according to Mencken, is simply the form of retardation each has chosen to embrace. Its "old aristocracy" is backward-looking. Its new commercial leaders are philistines. And its poor white underclass, whose political ascendancy he can already sense and very much dreads, disdains all forms of intellectual exertion as "scoundrelly damnyankee" and potentially "Bolshevik Jew"—as unsouthern and potentially un-American, in other words. Put the pieces together, Mencken concludes, and one beholds a society destined never to produce anything of lasting cultural value. The South of 1917 represents not the foundational space one encounters in the popular literature of the previous four decades but rather a "vast . . . vacuity," a "stupendous region of worn-out farms, shoddy cities, and paralyzed cerebrums . . . almost as sterile, artistically, intellectually, and culturally, as the Sahara Desert."[1]

A generation of young southern writers read Mencken's essay, so the story goes, and were moved to respond in one of two ways. Either they sought to defend the old regimes against the charge of cultural sterility by citing such figures as Joel Chandler Harris, George Washington Cable, and Sidney Lanier as proofs that the postbellum South had contributed at least something to national culture.[2] Or they sought to prove him wrong going forward, perhaps even agreeing with and feeling liberated by his denunciation of the stultifying nature of southern literary and cultural traditionalism.[3] What he had annihilated they could now rebuild, and in a new image. Thus, within a decade the Vanderbilt Fugitives were publishing poetry intended to impress readers as erudite and cosmopolitan as Mencken, and by 1930 they and others had taken their stands as the Nashville Agrarians against a dehumanizing modernity while William Faulkner had invented a modern South of his own in his first three Yoknapatawpha County novels: *Sartoris* (1929), *The Sound and the Fury* (1929), and *As I Lay Dying* (1930). The Southern Renaissance would be fully underway by the end of the following decade, prompting Mencken, in a note appended to a 1949 reprinting of "The Sahara of the Bozart," to claim some credit for what had happened since the essay's initial appearance: "On the heels of the violent denunciations of the elder Southerners there soon came a favorable response from the more civilized youngsters, and there is reason to believe that my attack had something to do with the revival of Southern letters which followed in the middle 1920s" (184).

Mencken's claims have been challenged and the narrative of southern literary emergence based on them superseded by the work of literary historians and critics over recent decades. In addition to constructing literary genealogies that include among the South's writers such figures as Edgar Allan Poe and Mark Twain, critics have called attention to the works of such women writers as Kate Chopin and Ellen Glasgow, both of whom Mencken could have read and by whom he might have been forced to reevaluate his sense of southern culture as "paralyzed." Of equal importance, critics have insisted upon recognizing the contributions made to a revised and expanded notion of southern literature by such African American writers as William Wells Brown, Charles Chesnutt, Frances E. W. Harper, Alice Dunbar Nelson, W. E. B. Du Bois, and James Weldon Johnson, some of whom were born in the South, all of whom had lived there at least briefly, and all of whom had written about it in the revisionary and aspirational ways that, had he cast his attention toward them, might have moved Mencken to recognize that southern "cerebral" activity had not ceased but lately and in several respects had become more impressive than it had ever been.

If recent criticism has understood that southern literature before the "Renaissance" was much more varied and interesting than Mencken allows in "The Sahara of the Bozart," however, it has been less mindful of another fact represented by the essay, namely that the idea of a "backward" South had to be invented, too—that indeed it represented a counterimage to the dominant view of the region that had developed during the prior forty years. It was exactly four decades earlier, or during the final year of Reconstruction, that Thomas Nelson Page's "Uncle Gabe's White Folks" (1877) had presented in a national magazine a vision of the Old South's return via a poem about a "young marste[r] done come back!" It was during this same year that Joel Chandler Harris had begun contributing Uncle Remus sketches to Henry W. Grady's *Atlanta Constitution* and only three years after this that *Uncle Remus, His Songs and His Sayings* (1880) had attracted audiences worldwide with its portraits of plantation life as, whatever else one might say about it, culturally productive. It was during the following decade that Grady himself had become a national figure with his New South speeches and Page with his *In Ole Virginia* (1887) and other writings. And it was during the 1890s and early 1900s that such texts as Page's *Red Rock* (1898) and Thomas Dixon's *The Leopard's Spots* (1902) and *The Clansman* (1905) had promulgated narratives of national history by imagining plantations as nations in miniature.

Taking advantage of the popularity of local color, these and other writers had concentrated on what might have been the most individuated spaces in U.S. culture—spaces that seemed differentiated from national norms in almost every way possible, from their agrarian economies to their histories of defeat to their hybridized cultures to simply the ways their denizens spoke—and beheld in them "empires" evocative of a truer "America." In the case of Page's novel the plantation came complete with a history of fighting Indians. In the case of Dixon's it was made to seem symbolic of the proper management of "Africa." In both writers' visions—and in the visions of others, some of whom were not southerners and a few of whom were not even Americans—the plantation came to seem worth preserving because of what it *meant*.[4] Whether it were viable economically mattered less than what its loss would mean culturally to the South, the nation, and the world—the lesson made explicit in George Cary Eggleston's *Love Is the Sum of It All* (1907) when its central figure capitalizes on his planter heritage to take charge of construction crews in South America and Africa. The preservationist's impulse that motivated much local color writing during the period was thus paired in much plantation fiction with drives toward nationalism and empire. By the time Mencken felt moved to excoriate it, "the South" connoted to many nonsoutherners not a space of cultural "vacuity" or radical alterity but rather a locality representative of them.

The region had been on quite a run, in other words. Its range of meanings and associations had expanded in ways analogous to how Margaret Mitchell would later describe the growth of the plantation Tara in *Gone with the Wind*. Pursuing his dream of a homeland in which "the white walls of Tara should rise" above a landscape "white as eiderdown in the sun," Gerald O'Hara, Scarlett's father and the novel's patriarch, devotes himself in the early chapters to realizing a vision that Mitchell expresses via a language of manifest destiny:

> Gerald closed his eyes and, in the stillness of the unworked acres, he felt that he had come home. Here under his feet would rise a house of whitewashed brick. Across the road would be new rail fences, inclosing fat cattle and blooded horses, and the red earth that rolled down the hillside to the rich river bottom would gleam white as eiderdown in the sun—cotton, acres and acres of cotton! . . .
>
> He cleared the fields and planted cotton and borrowed more money from [his brothers] to buy more slaves. . . . They lent Gerald the money and, in the years that followed, the money came back to them with interest. Gradually the plantation widened out, as Gerald bought more acres lying near him, and in time the white house became a reality instead of a dream.[5]

As *Gone with the Wind* itself shows, moreover, the plantation South's run in U.S. culture had not come to an end in 1917. In fact, as Mencken was writing, D. W. Griffith's *The Birth of a Nation* (1915) was still showing in theaters. The film and the novel on which it was based, Dixon's *The Clansman*, would later provide inspiration to Mitchell.[6] The plantation nation, in short, both predated and postdated "The Sahara of the Bozart" as a way of conceptualizing the South and explaining its meanings to "America." In his essay Mencken compares the South to fully fifteen foreign spaces in order to express southern backwardness—spaces ranging from Serbia to Nicaragua to the Gobi Desert to the Yangtze River regions of China. He goes so far at one point as to urge "a survey of the population by competent ethnologists and anthropologists" (187). He did so, however, to the exclusion of the other images of the South still very much in circulation during the 1910s. While Mencken was imagining white southerners as in need of civilizing, others were still representing them as the original bearers of the white man's burden, hence the examples to be followed in bringing civilization to the world.

That Mencken does not discuss recent literary expressions of the South as national is not surprising. Regardless of what he might have wanted to say about them, he could not have addressed them and still claimed that the South had had no impact on U.S. culture. For good or for ill—and very likely he would have argued the latter, had he taken it up—the impact of white southern writers' visions of "America" upon broader conceptualizations of U.S. nationhood had been considerable. They had been strong enough to produce waves of responses from African American writers seeking to disentangle southern white supremacy from U.S. nationality. One thinks of Frances E. W. Harper's *Iola Leroy* (1892) and the remarks made by a fugitive slave who regards the United States as a giant plantation: "It seemed to me that the big white men not only ruled over the poor whites and made laws for them, but over the whole nation."[7] The character's words echo an observation made by an actual escaped slave, William Wells Brown, who in *My Southern Home* (1880) writes of "the success of the slave-holders in controlling the affairs of the National Government for a long series of years" prior to the Civil War: "the admitted fact that none could secure an office in the national Government who were known to be opposed to the *peculiar* institution, made the Southerners feel themselves superior to the people of the free States."[8] These words, in turn, repeat one of the central themes of Martin R. Delany's *Blake; or the Huts of America* (1861–1862), namely that slaveholders controlled the country (called at one point in the novel "the Newnited States uv the South"), which required African Americans to contemplate a separate nationhood.[9] This impulse toward black sovereignty would receive its most radical expression in fiction almost forty years later, when Sutton R. Griggs's *Imperium in Imperio* (1899) would advocate that "the Negro have an empire of his own." Arguing that "the Negro finds himself an unprotected foreigner in his own home," Griggs imagines the black colonization of Texas and establishment of an independent "Negro" nation-state—a republic in which the U.S. Constitution's principles of equality, liberty, and justice might be attempted once again.[10] Like many others, Griggs had lost hope that such ideals could be resurrected in the near future in a Jim Crow "America."

The existence of an African American tradition recognizing in the United States a veritable "greater South"—a tradition that might be thought of as culminating in Malcolm X's 1964 observation that "Mississippi is anywhere south of the Canadian border"—shows that, to some, the idea of an imperial South was nothing new during the 1890s, the decade in which imperial images of the old plantation began to proliferate.[11] It was certainly no idea to celebrate. Thus, Harper's *Iola Leroy* muses at some length about the connections between slaveholders' political power and antebellum U.S. expansionism:

> When [the South] wanted the continuance of the African slave trade the North conceded that we should have twenty years of slave-trading for the benefit of our plantations. When we wanted more territory she conceded to our desires and gave us land enough to carve out four States, and there yet remains enough for four more. When we wanted power to recapture our slaves when they fled North for refuge, Daniel Webster told Northerners to conquer their prejudices, and they gave us the whole Northern States as a hunting ground for our slaves (88).[12]

Such remarks offer a very different interpretation of the history glorified by Thomas Nelson Page in "Social Life in Old Virginia before the War," the essay first published in 1892, the same year as *Iola Leroy*. Whereas Page imagines an Old South expanding and "largely contribut[ing] to produce this nation," Harper depicts it as self-consuming: a monster feeding on liberty rather than promoting it, and one incapable ever of being satisfied. Her vision thus anticipates one Charles Chesnutt would incorporate into *The Marrow of Tradition* (1901) a decade later. A novel based on the actual overthrow of the elected government of Wilmington, North Carolina, by white supremacists in 1899, *The Marrow of Tradition* worries that a white South is overtaking the nation once again. One of the architects of the coup argues early in the novel that Wilmington must be made the first battle in a much broader war: "We must be armed at all points . . . and prepared for defense as well as attack,—we must make our campaign a national one." Standing in Wilmington but imagining an entire nation his field for battle, the same character later beholds the South from the opposite perspective—from the outside in, the imperial to the local: "The nation was rushing forward with giant strides toward colossal wealth and world-dominion. . . . The same argument that justified the conquest of an inferior nation could not be denied to those who sought the suppression of an inferior race."[13]

If it had become paradigmatic in much plantation fiction by 1900 that the plantation South represented a truer and even an original "America," then such texts as *The Marrow of Tradition* may be thought of as contesting the narrative of origins that made white southern men seem directly descended from the nation's Founding Fathers. The black radicals who colonize Texas in Griggs's *Imperium in Imperio* even claim them as their own. Celebrating "the teachings of Thomas Jefferson" and chiding white Americans for having forgotten them, the novel goes so far as to fantasize that a secret government run by African Americans and adhering more closely to Jeffersonian principles "has been organized and maintained within the United States for many years." It simply "needed a George Washington" in order to realize its manifest destiny and go from an underground movement to an aboveground one.[14] The call to return to the principles (and not the plantations) of the Founders is repeated later in James Weldon Johnson's *The Autobiography of an Ex-Colored Man* (1912). Discussing "the man of the South" and his fixation on "the ever present Negro question" (the "one narrow channel" through which "most of his mental efforts run"), Johnson's narrator pities those about whom he writes: "Here, a truly great people, a people that produced a majority of the great historic Americans from Washington to Lincoln, now forced to use up its energies in a conflict as lamentable as it is violent."[15]

An even more complex appropriation of an image of the Old South as preferable to the New comes in the poetry of Paul Laurence Dunbar, specifically in "To the South on Its New Slavery" (1903). Published in what seems like the incongruously titled *Lyrics of Love and Laughter* (and preceding in that volume the somewhat more famous and even darker poem, "The Haunted Oak"), "To the South on Its New Slavery" blasts white southerners for having failed to live up to the examples of their forefathers. Whereas their ancestors had once earned wide renown, the present generation had become the object of international scorn:

> What art thou, that the world should point at thee,
> And vaunt and chide the weakness that they see?
> There was a time they were not wont to chide;
> Where is thy old, uncompromising pride?
> . . . .
> Oh, Mother South, hast thou forgot thy ways,
> Forgot the glory of thine ancient days,
> Forgot the honor that once made thee great,
> And stooped to this unhallowed estate? (ll. 9–12, 69–72)[16]

Whether Dunbar was fully committed to a vision of the antebellum plantation as idyllic has been a matter of critical debate.[17] What seems clearer in light of the cultural history I have been tracing in this book, however, is that Dunbar was disagreeing absolutely with the image of a modernizing, even "globalizing" South promoted by Henry W. Grady. Grady depicts a region developing rapidly and pursuing "unhindered comradeship with the world" in *The New*

South (1890). By contrast, "To the South on Its New Slavery" suggests that, in some ways, southern culture had changed little since the Civil War, and in other ways it had only declined, "stooped to this unhallowed estate." Images of the New South as linked in "comradeship with the world"—indeed, images of the region as an extension of "the Old South under new conditions"—deserved what Dunbar hoped would be the world's criticism.[18]

That many academic as well as popular discussions of the South still stress the region's alterity and overlook the kinds of images to which Dunbar and others were responding thus requires redress. The claim to be made here is *not* that the South is the same as everywhere else, that it somehow fails to live up to the legend of its own difference. It is also not that America has been "Dixified" or that plantation fiction reveals that "the southernization of America" has been happening since an early date.[19] And it is certainly not the argument of this book that the writers of plantation fiction were correct when they had imagined the region the true center of "America." Yet it is worth arguing in light of the images presented here that the idea of the South as the nation's outlier, the nation's problem, or (most broadly and perhaps most commonly) the nation's "other" can assume shape only when one forgets how common and indeed influential were a set of representations that circulated a century ago and depicted the southern plantation as the United States' true source, its touchstone. The idea of southern otherness has become its own myth, too, in other words—not a "myth" in the sense that it bears no relation to the truth but rather a "myth" in that it constitutes a story whose coherence requires that one not examine more fully an alternate set of possibilities.[20] In the case of many late nineteenth- and early twentieth-century writings about the South, these counternarratives emphasize not southern otherness but rather southern similitude, southern synecdoche—in short, the idea that the plantation South *meant* "America."

These chapters have offered glimpses into the different ways the South was being conceptualized as national during the decades that followed the legendary failure of Reconstruction to transform the region into something more like the North. These efforts to nationalize the South varied. They include Harris's image of the plantation as having produced, rather by accident, a cross-racial culture that could have emerged only in the United States. They include Dixon's, Page's, Grady's, and Eggleston's images of the plantation as a space that made men fit for empire. And they include Faulkner's images of the plantation as always doomed yet not yet dead, an institution whose ghosts promise to haunt all of America for years to come. These are different representations, sharing as they do the idea that the plantation South proves a key to understanding "America" but diverging from each other radically in terms of how finally they construe the relationship between region and nation. Yet even this set of images is far from comprehensive. It may thus be fitting to offer as a final image—and as one that provides a different kind of guidance into how the plantation South was being "nationalized" during the very early twentieth century—one from Du Bois's *The Souls of Black Folk* (1903). One of many African American responses to the idea of plantation nationhood, its critique is made even more salient when one situates it against the various other claims being made about plantations at the time.

The chapter titled "Of the Black Belt" describes Du Bois's tour of a stretch of southwestern Georgia during the very early 1900s. Two hundred miles south of Atlanta by train, the space he was visiting was located at some distance from what was still being called the capital of Henry W. Grady's New South. Yet it was very much within the realm—the South's surviving plantation districts— that Grady had sought to imagine as contiguous culturally with the region's new economic and social order, within the spaces that allowed him to assert that "the New South is simply the Old South under new conditions."[21] What Du Bois discovers, however, is a space in the midst of radical reconfiguration, one composed of

> the scattered box-like cabins of the brick-yard hands . . . the long tenement-row facetiously called "The Ark," and . . . the confines of the great plantations of other days. There is the "Joe Fields place"; a rough old fellow was he, and had killed many a "nigger" in his day. Twelve miles his plantation used to run,—a regular barony. It is nearly all gone now; only straggling bits belong to the family, and the rest has passed to Jews and Negroes. Even the bits which are left are heavily mortgaged, and, like the rest of the land, tilled by tenants.[22]

Du Bois's description compares interestingly to Mencken's, first of all, for in addition to the material decline Mencken would later observe, Du Bois also perceives forms of adaptation and endurance—not a space of sunny new beginnings, by any means, yet at least "a land of rapid contrasts and of curiously mingled hope and pain." In addition to its black tenant farmers who labor under the "pall of debt [that] hangs over the beautiful land," he discovers "here and there . . . black freeholders," one of whom, a man named Jackson who

owns one hundred acres, impresses the Harvard-trained Du Bois as a philoso-
pher in his own right: "'I says, "Look up! If you don't look up you can't get
up,"' remarks Jackson, philosophically. And he's gotten up" (154).

Du Bois's mention of the "Joe Fields place," meanwhile, compares in-
triguingly to *Absalom, Absalom!* and the additional Faulkner novels in which
Sutpen's Hundred no longer exists as a physical entity yet still is invoked in
language and narrative, a sign of both how distant and proximate the antebellum South could seem. That the place had once seemed "a regular barony"
anticipates how Faulkner would describe the Sutpen manor as it was being
built and its owner lived in it: "He lived out there . . . in masculine solitude in
what might be called the halfacre gunroom of a baronial splendor. He lived in
the Spartan shell of the largest edifice in the county, not excepting the court-
house itself."[23] Several of the ruined plantation homes Du Bois passes on his
tour seem similarly vast yet similarly incomplete—signs of a cultural impulse
that Du Bois attributes to antebellum Georgia yet that one might just as easily
imagine as describing the Mississippi of *Absalom, Absalom!*: a "life of careless
extravagance reigned among the masters. . . . And yet with all this there was
something sordid, something forced,—a certain feverish unrest and reckless-
ness; for was not all this show and tinsel built upon a groan?" (152).

What proves most interesting, however, are not the ways in which Du
Bois anticipates Mencken or Faulkner but rather the ways in which he engages
writers of his own time and their images of the plantation as having produced
"America." Dixon's *The Leopard's Spots* (1902) had appeared just one year prior
to the publication of *The Souls of Black Folk*. By the time copies of *Souls* were
finding their way to their first readers, Dixon and his publisher were watching
as the sales of *The Leopard's Spots* grew into the hundreds of thousands. Du
Bois does not address Dixon or his novel in his own book, *The Leopard's Spots*
having perhaps been issued too late in the preparation of *Souls* to allow Du
Bois to comment. (He does say at one point that it is "the imperative duty of
thinking black men" to "argu[e] with Mr. Thomas Nelson Page," whose white
supremacy was rather less venomous than Dixon's; one assumes that, had he
had the chance, Du Bois would have advocated an even stronger response to
the author of the Klan novels.)[24] What Du Bois does do, however, is envision
a plantation landscape in which the once-grand designs of white southern
men are legible only in forms of hollowed-out buildings, overgrown fields,
and spaces where fences used to be. The voids left behind—Du Bois describes
at one point how "the houses lie in half ruin, or have wholly disappeared; the
fences have flown, and the families are wandering the world"—are being filled

by new landowners and laborers whose relationships with the land are different (146). He by no means depicts the new order as representing unqualified progress; indeed, he attends to several ways in which old plantation problems are proving persistent. Yet he is resolute in explaining southwestern Georgia's present state of things—its scenes of desolation as well as its occasional signs of black advancement—as consequences, unintentional though they might be, of what white southern planters had *failed* to accomplish during the nineteenth century. Against the argument that planters had built "America," Du Bois arrays evidence that they had indeed brought about a new world, yet one not at all like they had projected.

It is a view of southern cultural creativity and cross-racial reactivity not unlike what Harris had once hinted at in the Uncle Remus books. While plantations had failed to become the civilizational anchors of the vast empires for slavery once imagined by antebellum planters, they had served as the birthplaces of a folk culture unlike anything else in the world, hence something worth recognizing in both Harris's and Du Bois's views as uniquely "American." In Harris's books this unique culture could be recognized in the folktales. In *The Souls of Black Folk* it finds expression in the form of the "sorrow songs," the negro spirituals that were born during slavery but had survived to become what Du Bois calls "the sole American music . . . the most beautiful expression of human experience born this side the seas" (265). He writes this at the beginning of the final chapter of his book, titled simply "The Sorrow Songs." Toward the chapter's end he asks whether "America [would] have been America without her Negro people?" (270). To amplify this point, he challenges his white readers to imagine their nation the much less miscegenated space that, in some of their more popular recent works of fiction, an idealized "America" had been imagined to be. He does so, moreover, using precisely the same terminology they were using to conceptualize the plantation as the model for a new American imperium. And as if he were responding quietly yet nonetheless firmly to Thomas Nelson Page, he even includes a subtle reference to Jamestown in his reconstruction of American history and culture as having always been to a significant extent "black":

Your country? How came it yours? Before the Pilgrims landed we were here. Here we have brought our three gifts and mingled them with yours: a gift of story and song—soft, stirring melody in an ill-harmonized and unmelodious land; the gift of sweat and brawn to beat back the wilderness, conquer the soil, and lay the foundations of this vast economic empire two hundred years earlier than your weak hands could have done it; and third, a gift of the Spirit. Around us the history of the land has centered for thrice a hundred years. (275)

It would be wrong to argue that what Du Bois is proposing here is a reclamation of the plantation as African American, too. His earlier record of his travels within Georgia's Black Belt make clear his contentedness to see so much of an old plantation order turned upside down and so many plantations simply gone to waste. Yet it would also be wrong to ignore that Du Bois's concluding argument in *The Souls of Black Folk* is centered around the plantation—indeed that it seeks to recenter the plantation around black labor and creativity and therefore relocate the institution within U.S. history. To the extent that the plantation *has* been fundamental to the development of the United States, Du Bois contends, African American contributions must be seen as vital to the process. His rewriting of U.S. history in this manner might indeed be called a romance of the black man's burden were it not for his insistence on developing images connoting generosity, images of gifts given rather than burdens borne. It is in any event a representation to keep in mind as students of southern literature, U.S. culture, and the conceptual territories wherein concepts of race, region, and empire intersect seek further to uncover the meanings of plantations—spaces that were rarely what writers claimed them to be during the late nineteenth and early twentieth centuries yet still may be seen as generative of cultural forms that have not gone away.

Notes

INTRODUCTION

1. Eggleston, *Love Is the Sum of It All*, 12–14. Subsequent references are cited parenthetically.
2. Tourgée, "The South as a Field for Fiction," 406–7.
3. Daniel, "A Visit to a Colonial Estate"; Coleman, "The Homes of Some Southern Authors."
4. Foster, *The Old Plantation Melodies*, back cover.
5. Page, "Social Life in Old Virginia before the War," 184–85. Page expanded and republished the essay complete with illustrations as *Social Life in Old Virginia before the War* in 1897.
6. Avirett, *The Old Plantation*, 201–2.
7. Grady, *The New South*, 232, 252. Subsequent references are cited parenthetically.
8. Harris, "Observations from New England," in *Joel Chandler Harris: Editor and Essayist*, 165.
9. Grady, "The South and Her Problems," 96.
10. Adams, *Democracy*, 197, 100.
11. Faulkner, *Light in August*, 451.
12. For an excellent discussion of the links between plantation imagery and the Spanish-American and Philippine-American Wars, see Santiago-Valles, "'Still Longing for the Old Plantation.'"
13. Dixon, *The Leopard's Spots*, 312.
14. Austin, "The Kipling Hysteria," 327–28.
15. "Kipling Had This Celebrity in Mind,'" 2; "Rudyard Kipling," 490–91.
16. Qtd. in Weston, *Racism in U.S. Imperialism*, 35.
17. "'The White Man's Burden,'" *New York Evangelist*, 24.
18. Tillman, "Are We to Spread the Christian Religion with the Bayonet Point," 122–23.
19. "The Negro in the South," *New York Times*, 8.
20. Brown, *The Lower South in American History*, 247–71.
21. Page, *The Negro: The Southerner's Problem*, 296.
22. Riley, *The White Man's Burden*, 17, 179.

23. Ibid., 13.

24. The notion of postcolonial "writing back" is drawn from Ashcroft, Griffiths, and Tiffin, eds., *The Empire Writes Back*. Scholarship on the idea of the United States and its literature as "postcolonial" is abundant. The debates that have propelled this scholarship may best be glimpsed in Singh and Schmidt, eds., *Postcolonial Theory and the United States*. A debate over whether the literature of the U.S. South may be productively construed as "postcolonial" has emerged more recently. At its center are several of the essays collected in Smith and Cohn, eds., *Look Away! The U.S. South in New World Studies*. See also the fall 2003 and winter 2003/2004 issues of the *Mississippi Quarterly* (56, no. 4, and 57, no. 1), which contain several articles that test the possibilities of postcolonial theory for southern study.

25. X-Ray, "Charity Begins at Home," 4.

26. Qtd. in Gatewood, *Black Americans and the White Man's Burden*, 184. The phrase "Pile on the Black Man's Burden" may have been adapted from an even earlier parody of Kipling, the English writer Henry Labouchère's "The Brown Man's Burden," published in *Truth* in February 1899 (which is to say, during the same month that Kipling's poem first appeared in *McClure's*). Labouchère's poem begins "Pile on the brown man's burden / To gratify your greed / Go, clear away the 'niggers' / Who progress would impede." Another example of the African American response to "The White Man's Burden" undertakes what Patrick Brantlinger calls "less a mocking of Kipling's poem than an expression of the theme of 'black uplift' or self-improvement." Written by the North Carolina–born, Kansas City–based black journalist and educator James Dallas Bowser, the poem appeared, like "Charity Begins at Home," in the *Colored American* (and, like Johnson's "The Black Man's Burden," in April 1899): "When yours—his chances equal / Give him the fairest test. / Then, 'Hands off!' be your motto / And he will do the rest" (ll. 13–16). The best discussions of these and other parodies may be found in Brantlinger, "Kipling's 'The White Man's Burden' and Its Afterlives," and Mitchell, *Righteous Propagation*, 51–74. See also Gatewood, *Black Americans and the White Man's Burden*, 183–84; Painter, *Standing at Armageddon*, 153–66; and Blum, *Reforging the White Republic*, 242–43. For a fuller discussion of Bowser and his poem, see Coulter, *"Take Up the Black Man's Burden,"* 21–24.

27. Fields, "The White Man's Burden," 19. In the original, line 14 reads, "Kaze trou de longtrwl daw." "Daw" must be a misprint, however, since "say" (l. 16) is the word with which "daw" ("day") is supposed to rhyme. "Longtrwl" may translate as "long, cruel." My thanks to Stan Wells for the translation.

28. Baker, *Modernism and the Harlem Renaissance*, 25–27.

29. Kelley uses the phrase both in his introduction to *Race Consciousness: African-American Studies for the New Century* (1997) and in *Yo' Mama's Disfunktional! Fighting the Culture Wars in Urban America* (1997).

30. Harrison, "The Black Man's Burden (A Reply to Rudyard Kipling)," 3. Harri-

son went so far as to adopt the pseudonym "Gunga Din" when the poem was first published in the *Colored American Review*, making the parody of Kipling even more involved. "Gunga Din" is the eponymous figure in an 1892 poem by Kipling: a "regimental *bhisti*" (Indian water carrier) whom the English soldiers look down upon until he proves heroic in sacrifice. "You're a better man than I am, Gunga Din!" thus parallels the portraits of self-sacrificing slaves and ex-slaves one encounters in U.S. plantation fiction—a connection that resembles those I discuss toward the end of Chapter 1.

31. The essay also bore the title "The Black Man's Burden," originally appearing in the *International Socialist Review* in 1912. Among the additional sources it cites is a 1910 study revealing that in the former Confederate states, black schools received so comparatively little funding that black taxpayers, relatively poor though they were, were in effect subsidizing white education. See Harrison, "The Black Man's Burden [II]," 68, 71. For additional discussion of the essay, see Perry, *Hubert Harrison*, 177–79.

32. Du Bois, *The Quest of the Silver Fleece*, 190.

33. A novel that tests the possibilities of naturalism for black literary representation, *The Quest of the Silver Fleece* wonders whether black southerners are determined by the historical forces that surround them, namely the South's cotton economy, its links to northern capital and federal political power, and its absolute dependence on cheap black labor. As Maurice Lee has argued, the novel strongly resembles the fiction of Frank Norris, especially *The Octopus* (1901) and *The Pit* (1903), the first two of Norris's uncompleted "Epic of the Wheat" trilogy. In the chapter containing the passage just cited, in fact, the cotton market is cornered, much like wheat is cornered in Norris's *The Pit*. In Du Bois's novel this causes a white landowner to fear that he will lose his fortune, hence his class status. To his mind, this descent would mean the virtual loss of his race as well: "Slowly the blood crept out of his white face leaving it whiter, and went surging and pounding in his heart. Poverty—that was what those figures spelled. Poverty—unclothed, wineless poverty, to dig and toil like a 'nigger' from morning until night, and to give up horses and carriages and women; that was what they spelled" (197). See Lee, "Du Bois the Novelist," 390.

34. It is worth citing here another prose work titled *The Black Man's Burden*, this one an autobiography written by William Henry Holtzclaw, a graduate of Booker T. Washington's Tuskegee Institute, who went on to found the Utica Normal and Industrial Institute in south-central Mississippi. Holtzclaw had originally hoped to found a Tuskegee-modeled institute in the Mississippi Delta, but the planters there discouraged him. One explained forthrightly that he thought black education in general "good work," though not in the Delta: "What I want here is Negroes who can make cotton, and they don't need education to help them make cotton. . . . Such a school as you speak of is needed, but not here. . . . I advise you to go out of the Delta into the hill country farther east and establish

your school" (75–76). This passage is suggestive of why Holtzclaw's work deserves greater attention.

35. Du Bois, *The Souls of Black Folk*, 240. The moment occurs when Crummell is told by an Episcopal bishop in Philadelphia that "no Negro priest" would be allowed to serve equally alongside his bishopric's white clergymen. Subsequent references to *Souls* are cited parenthetically.

36. Rousseau, *The Black Woman's Burden*, 4–5.

37. Jacobs, *Incidents in the Life of a Slave Girl*, 100.

38. Du Bois, "The Burden of Black Women," 31. The poem was published again in the *Crisis* in 1914 before being incorporated into *Darkwater* as "The Riddle of the Sphinx" in 1920. Some changes were made in the final version, including one of particular relevance here. The line that originally began "But out of the past of the Past's grey past" was changed to "But out of the South,—the sad black South." For a discussion of this change and other aspects of this rich poem, see Sundquist, *To Wake the Nations*, 582–612; Smith, *American Body Politics*, 284–93; and Gillman, *Blood Talk*, 190–94.

39. "Burden" derives more directly from the Old English *byrðen*, "birth" from the early Middle English *byrþ* (which itself derived more directly from the Old Norse *byrðr* rather than the Old English *gebyrd*, though the linkage to *beran* exists here, too). My thanks to Dan Wiley for help with this etymology.

40. On this transition in meaning, see Williams, *Keywords*, 248–50.

41. The allusion here would be to the allegorical figure of the pelican, a bird that in medieval bestiaries was represented as capable of resurrecting its own young: "the mother pierces her breast, opens her side, and lays herself across her young, pouring out her blood over the dead bodies. This brings them to life again." This invited parallels to Christ's blood and its salvific powers. The fact that this belief predated Christianity and was then reconciled with Christian orthodoxy makes the allusion seem more likely, since Du Bois's poem emphasizes that African belief systems are older than many others. The fact that the pelican was, according to the twelfth-century *Book of Beasts*, "a bird which lives in the solitude of the River Nile" makes the allusion seem even richer, since Du Bois specifically mentions Egypt and Ethiopia in the poem, celebrating them as birthplaces of civilization. See White, *The Book of Beasts*, 132–33.

42. The studies to which I allude are Griffin and Doyle, eds., *The South as an American Problem*; Smith and Appleton, eds., *A Mythic Land Apart*; Binding, *Separate Country*; and Gray, *Southern Aberrations*.

43. Among the South's defenders, however, there were disagreements over whether the South should remain different within the nation or whether it should secede and seek even to reproduce itself by expanding into the Caribbean, Mexico, and Central and South America—a "region" that seemed to some to form a more natural nation-state given the plantation and its centrality to local economies. A

growing body of scholarship is focused on antebellum southern nationalism and the Old South's cultures of empire. Michael O'Brien's *Conjectures of Order* (2004) makes the important point early on that "Southerners were also imperial. . . . Virginians and others had not rebelled against George III to repudiate the venture of European imperialism, but to take the matter into their own hands" (5). Adam Rothman's *Slave Country* (2005) attends similarly to the complexities that arose as U.S. expansionism resulted not in the gradual elimination of slavery, as some founders had hoped, but rather in its considerable growth. Matthew Pratt Guterl's *American Mediterranean* (2008) explores the hemispheric visions planters developed during the late antebellum and early postbellum periods. Eric Sundquist's *Empire and Slavery in American Literature, 1820–1865* (2006) considers how these intersecting problems register in antebellum U.S. literature, especially in texts produced by now-neglected white southern writers. Brady Harrison's *Agent of Empire* (2004) focuses much more narrowly on the Tennessee filibusterer William Walker and his image in U.S. literature, yet it arrives at the same set of issues, namely how slavery both propelled and complicated the drive toward expansion in the antebellum United States. Last, Robert E. Bonner's *Mastering America* (2009) attends perhaps most closely to the same subject matter that I discuss in this book, for though it is a study of antebellum U.S. history, its concern is with "Proslavery Americanism" and how, as Bonner discusses at the very end of his study, "in having sought to master not only their plantations but the American nation as a whole, these men and women set in motion a process that would lead toward a new world" (xix, 328). The present volume may be considered one study of this "new world."

44. Pollard, *The Lost Cause*, 751. For a brief discussion of Edward A. Pollard as a proponent of antebellum southern expansionism, see Sundquist, *Empire and Slavery in American Literature*, 147. For a fuller discussion of him as an exemplar of the South's "rage to explain" and adjustment to the collapse of the antebellum expansionist dream, see Hobson, *Tell about the South*, 85–91.

45. The scholarship on local color has been abundant since the early 1990s, years in which Judith Fetterley and Marjorie Pryse's anthology of *American Women Regionalists* (1992) proposed the recovery of late nineteenth-century regionalist fiction on feminist grounds, Richard Brodhead's *Cultures of Letters* (1993) reexamined it in the context of an emerging bourgeois tourism industry, and Amy Kaplan's "Nation, Region, and Empire" (1991) encouraged its reconsideration in light of an emerging scholarship on race and nationality. The conversation that followed has been among the richest in recent U.S. literary studies. For an overview of how considerations of region have reconstituted the field of American literary studies, see Crow, *A Companion to the Regional Literatures of America*. Among the additional works that have most shaped my thinking about regionalism and local color are Foote, *Regional Fictions*; McCullough, *Regions of Identity*;

Jones, *Strange Talk*; Evans, *Before Cultures*; Zagarell, "Troubling Regionalism"; Dainotto, "'All the Regions Do Smilingly Revolt'"; and Howard, "Unraveling Regions, Unsettling Periods."

46. Gatewood, *Black Americans and the White Man's Burden*, x. It is worth noting that Kipling's poem provided the title for another historical study published within a year of Gatewood's: Winthrop Jordan's *The White Man's Burden: Historical Origins of Racism in the United States* (1974), the condensed version of his *White over Black: American Attitudes toward the Negro, 1550–1812* (1968).

47. Also worth noting is Eric T. L. Love's *Race over Empire: Racism and U.S. Imperialism, 1865–1900* (2004). Love's thesis—that white supremacy complicated rather than abetted U.S. expansionism during the late nineteenth century—provides an important corrective to what he describes as "the conventional narrative": "that white supremacy—elaborated in history, culture, tradition, custom, law, and language—armed the imperialists of 1898 with a nearly impenetrable rationale" for expansion (xi). Yet Love does discover that "after 1893 . . . imperialists began to develop a strategy that finally enabled them to exploit race to their advantage" (106). The turning point revolved around Hawaii and debates over whether it should be annexed. Love argues that U.S. policy makers who favored annexation began to promote "sympathy" for the island's white minority and conjure dark visions of a Japanese takeover of the islands. The present study may illuminate further why the early 1890s saw a change in prevailing U.S. attitudes toward expansion. As I hinted at earlier in this introduction and argue more directly in Chapter 2, it was during the late 1880s that plantation fiction became a certifiable national phenomenon. With it came the argument that, though interracial contact may not always be desirable, it is inevitable; and, given this, the plantation provides the best model for white Americans to take responsibility for their racial inferiors—the idea of "the white man's burden." Love reads Kipling's poem differently than I. I concede its "irony and cynicism" but think that Kipling was saying that, in spite of the difficulties empire will entail, it still must be pursued (6). Love conceptualizes "the white man's burden" as a post-1898 rationalization of what had just happened vis-à-vis the Philippines. I argue in this book that it was an ideology developed a decade earlier, one legible in plantation fiction (even though it had not yet been assigned the name given to it by Kipling in 1899).

48. Kaplan, "'Left Alone with America,'" 11, 14. Kaplan actually identifies three "absences" in her essay: the one just named as well as "the absence of culture from the study of U.S. imperialism . . . and the absence of the United States from the postcolonial study of imperialism." As I suggest below—and thanks in large part to Kaplan's essay and the volume it introduces—such lacunae no longer characterize the study of U.S. culture. See, for example, Briggs, *Reproducing Empire*; Renda, *Taking Haiti*; and the essays collected in Stoler, *Haunted by Empire*.

49. Rowe, *Literary Culture and U.S. Imperialism*, 11.

50. Kaplan, *The Anarchy of Empire in the Making of U.S. Culture*, 22.

51. Streeby's study is focused on the decades surrounding the Mexican-American War (1846–1848) and includes a chapter ("The Hacienda, the Factory, and the Plantation") particularly relevant to the present study because it shows how dime novels of the middle nineteenth century reflected debates about the extension of slavery, hence of southeastern planter power, into the territories gained as a result of the Treaty of Guadalupe Hidalgo. See also Rivera, "Embodying Greater Mexico," and Pérez, "Remembering the Hacienda," both collected in Smith and Cohn, *Look Away!*

52. Baker and Nelson, "Preface: Violence, the Body and 'The South,'" 233.

53. Hall, "When Was 'The Post-Colonial'?" 247.

54. Adams, "Introduction: Circum-Caribbean Performance, Language, History," 2.

55. Both quotations represent translations. See Glissant, *The Poetics of Relation*, 72, and Benítez-Rojo, *The Repeating Island*, 5. Of the two, Glissant writes more often about linkages between the Caribbean and the U.S. South, most notably in *Faulkner, Mississippi* (1996). In *The Repeating Island* Benítez-Rojo attends more to what differentiates the Caribbean plantation and makes it "this extraordinary machine . . . [that] repeats itself endlessly": "Apart from the fact that the plantation economy existed in other zones of the American continent, it is only in the Caribbean region that its dynamics produce a kind of socioeconomic instability whose morphology is repeated, becoming more or less ascendant from colonial times until the present" (11, 38). An interesting counterargument to Benítez-Rojo's thesis that the Caribbean plantation has proved unusually durable might be supplied by Clyde Woods's *Development Arrested* (1998), which examines the Mississippi Delta and how the plantation remains "painfully alive among those still dominated by the economic and political dynasties of the South which preserved and reproduced themselves through diversification and through numerous new mobilizations" (4). Woods explores how successive political and economic programs for reconstructing the Delta, each of which aimed to modernize the region, have instead perpetuated a power structure that resembles closely the one founded prior to the abolition of slavery. Interestingly, Woods's study resonates with Benítez-Rojo's in another way as well, for Woods's analysis of how the plantation repeats itself in the Delta serves to explain the birth there of the blues (and, more generally, of what Woods terms a "blues epistemology") (16–21). Benítez-Rojo's analysis of the how the plantation repeats itself in the Caribbean serves similarly to explain the births there of multiple musical forms, each defined by polyrhythm and improvisation: "the mambo, the cha-cha-cha, the bossa nova, the bolero, salsa, and reggae happen[ed]; that is to say, Caribbean music did not become Anglo-Saxon but rather the latter became Caribbean within a play of differences" (21).

56. Loichot, *Orphan Narratives*, 3. Handley and Russ also address the irony that the plantation produced, in addition to so much violence and suffering, so many forms of creative response and resistive culture, "a trans-American poetic imagi-

nary that has emerged from this brutal, dehumanizing past," as Russ elegantly describes it (*The Plantation in Postslavery Imagination*, 3).

57. Handley, *Postslavery Literatures in the Americas*, 14. On illicit plantation relations of a different sort, see Hodes, *White Women, Black Men*.

58. Jennifer Rae Greeson's "Colonial Planter to American Farmer" tests the limits of a postcolonial rereading of the region by examining Crèvecoeur and the image of the South in early national writings. Her "Expropriating *The Great South* and Exporting 'Local Color'" does this by examining postbellum southern travel narrative. Jon Smith's "Postcolonial, Black, and Nobody's Margin" does this by way of a review essay on several titles published during the early 2000s. Also worth mentioning here are several recent studies that, though they are not as engaged with questions of U.S. nationalism, nevertheless reexamine plantation culture from new perspectives and inform my thinking. See Costello, *Plantation Airs*; Cowan, *The Slave in the Swamp*; Bibler, *Cotton's Queer Relations*; McPherson, *Reconstructing Dixie*; Vlach, *The Planter's Prospect*; and Mack and Hoffius, *Landscape of Slavery*.

59. Adams, *Wounds of Returning*, 3–4, 7–11; Stecopoulos, *Reconstructing the World*, 17.

60. Schmidt's is a noteworthy exception. Focused on a period similar to the one that defines my own study, Schmidt examines how debates about education, primarily the education of ex-slaves and colonial subjects, shaped and were shaped by theories of race and ideologies of empire. In what is most compelling about the study, it locates in literary texts scenes in which teaching of one sort or another takes place, thus revealing how ideas about pedagogy circulated not only in books specifically on the subject but also in mass culture.

61. Stecopoulos, *Reconstructing the World*, 4.

62. Metcalf, "George Cary Eggleston," 1529.

63. "Geo. C. Eggleston's Southland Story," 548.

64. "Ambassador to Italy," 8.

65. Du Bois, *The Souls of Black Folk*, 93.

66. The increased, much deserved attention given to Charles Chesnutt over the past decade accounts for much of this. See, for example, Cowan, "Charles Waddell Chesnutt and Joel Chandler Harris"; Baker, "Jamming with Julius"; Stecopoulos, "The Geography of Reunion" (in *Reconstructing the World*); and Gilligan, "Reading, Race, and Charles Chesnutt's 'Uncle Julius' Tales."

67. Sundquist, *Faulkner: The House Divided*, 158.

CHAPTER 1

1. My information derives from Powell, *The Dictionary of North Carolina Biography*.

2. Gaines, *The Southern Plantation*, 2. Subsequent references are cited parenthetically.

3. Brown, *The Negro in American Fiction*, 18.

4. Vlach, *The Planter's Prospect*, 1.

5. Harris, "The Negro as the South Sees Him," in *Joel Chandler Harris: Editor and Essayist*, 114.

6. Lowe, "Reconstruction Revisited," 14.

7. Hale, *Making Whiteness*, 52.

8. Theodore Roosevelt, letter to Julia Collier Harris (June 28, 1917), in Julia C. Harris, *The Life and Letters of Joel Chandler Harris*, 514.

9. Harris, *Uncle Remus, His Songs and His Sayings*, 3, 12. When the source is clear, subsequent references are cited parenthetically.

10. The present discussion builds upon a great deal of scholarly work on Harris, on whom there has existed a sort of scholarship since even before he first rose to national fame. As Kathleen Light notes, John Wesley Powell, an ethnologist who worked at the Smithsonian Institution, contacted Harris in 1879 to inquire further about some of the folktales Harris had published in the *Constitution*. Harris would later be honored in the first issue of the Journal of American Folklore. Since then, studies of the relationships between the Remus collections and various folk and oral traditions have been one of the main branches of the scholarship on Harris. See especially Baer, *Sources and Analogues of the Uncle Remus Tales*. See also Light, "Uncle Remus among the Folklorists"; Bone, "The Oral Tradition"; and (on Harris briefly and the figure of Brer Rabbit more extensively) Roberts, *From Trickster to Badman*. I address the other branches of the scholarship on Harris later in this chapter and in the notes below.

11. Brown, *The Negro in American Fiction*, 53.

12. Baskervill, *Southern Writers*, 67. Such remarks echo something said by the narrator of James Weldon Johnson's *The Autobiography of an Ex-Colored Man* (1912) when he identifies the songs sung by the Fisk Jubilee Singers, ragtime, the cake walk, and "the Uncle Remus stories" as the "four things which refute the oft-advanced theory that [the colored people of this country] are an absolutely inferior race. . . . They have originality and artistic conception, and, what is more, the power of creating that which can influence and appeal universally" (63). That the stories were recorded and published by a white man is an irony Johnson's narrator does not acknowledge, perhaps because of his own vexed racial identity.

13. Lanier, "'Million' Books and 'Best' Books," 382.

14. In a 1932 essay Allen Tate kept alive the idea of Harris as among American literature's representative figures: "The agitation in the last fifteen years for a 'native' American literature has been based almost exclusively on Whitman, but a far sounder text could have been found in a few passages from the writings of Joel Chandler Harris." See Tate, "The Cornfield Journalist," 59.

15. Bryan Wagner's *Disturbing the Peace* (2009) came to my attention late in the preparation of the manuscript for this book. This chapter does not sufficiently account for his brilliant rereading of Harris as an exponent of the state's appropriation of a police power that had once been exercised privately by planters on their

plantations. Wagner does read Remus's return to the Putnam County plantation as a sign of how much worse things were becoming for African Americans in the city as a result of police surveillance and violence. Like me, Wagner sees Uncle Remus as having played a "leading role in redefining what counted as culture and what counted as politics" in the post-Reconstruction South and later United States. Like me also, Wagner emphasizes Harris's assumption of "the moral authority of insider knowledge." Unlike me, Wagner tends to perceive Remus (or at least the Remus of the early newspaper columns) as an unironic spokesman for Harris. In the analysis that follows, I insist that Remus may be seen as either sincere or ironic, hence that he may be voicing opinions to which Harris subscribed but which Remus may be speaking only because he is in the presence of white male auditors. The character may thus be said to lack an "essence." See Wagner, *Disturbing the Peace*, 126, 154.

16. The references are from, in order, Connolly, "Crossing Borders from Africa to America," 151; Kodat, "Disney's Song of the South and the Birth of the White Negro," 115; Miller, *Backgrounds to Blackamerican Literature*, 280; and Guererro, *Framing Blackness*, 11.

17. Brown, *The Negro in American Fiction*, 54. Brown's dilemma is illuminated by a remark made by Bryan Wagner, namely that "there is something grotesque about inheriting your tradition from somebody like Uncle Remus." See Wagner, *Disturbing the Peace*, 177.

18. Hemenway, "Author, Teller, and Hero," 23.

19. Painter, *Standing at Armageddon*, x, 141–42.

20. Meer, *Uncle Tom Mania*, 253.

21. On "Tom shows" see Williams, *Playing the Race Card*, 85. On *Uncle Tom's Cabin*'s publication history, see Parfait, *The Publishing History of Uncle Tom's Cabin, 1852–2002*. On *Uncle Tom's Cabin*'s international reputation, see, in addition to Meer, the essays collected in Kohn, Meer, and Todd, eds., *Transatlantic Stowe*.

22. Harris's praise for Stowe's having defended slavery seems less perverse when one considers that numerous twentieth-century critics would arrive at a similar interpretation of the novel. Two have been cited already in this chapter. Francis Pendleton Gaines would argue in 1924 that *Uncle Tom's Cabin* "was a plantation novel . . . in certain important respects . . . congruous with that already presented in literature," while Sterling Brown would note in 1937 that its two central planter figures, Arthur Shelby and Augustine St. Claire, "are kindly owners, in the plantation tradition, whose humanity was overpowered by the system." Brown argues further that "Joel Chandler Harris goes too far in calling [the novel] a defense of American slavery as Mrs. Stowe found it in Kentucky, but his comment has point." Gaines, *The Southern Plantation*, 38; Brown, *The Negro in American Fiction*, 37–38.

23. Stowe, *Uncle Tom's Cabin*, 18. Louis Rubin pursues a similar comparison in "Uncle Remus and the Ubiquitous Rabbit," 159.

24. Ibid., 213, 224; Harris, *Uncle Remus, His Songs and His Sayings*, 120, 108.

25. Stowe, *Uncle Tom's Cabin*, 224.

26. Ibid.

27. Cartwright, *Reading Africa into American Literature*, 114, 18.

28. The more accurate count might be five and one-half. In 1889 Harris published *Daddy Jake the Runaway and Short Stories Told after Dark by "Uncle Remus," Joel Chandler Harris*. The title story, a novella about a runaway slave, was not an Uncle Remus story. Remus folktales do make up half of the volume, however. The other collections were *Nights with Uncle Remus* (1883), *Uncle Remus and His Friends* (1892), *The Tar-Baby and Other Rhymes of Uncle Remus* (1904), *Told by Uncle Remus: New Stories of the Old Plantation* (1905), and *Uncle Remus and Brer Rabbit* (1907).

29. Wells, "The Southern American Renaissance," 124; Rev. of *Uncle Remus*, *Eclectic Magazine*, 279; Cone, "Women in Literature," 117; Banks, "The Brotherhood of All Creatures," 407. Another note of nationalism was sounded later in folklorist Richard Chase's foreword to his 1955 compilation, *The Complete Uncle Remus Tales*: "It might be a good thing nowadays to consider lasting elements in the cultural heritage of our nation. We have grown too self-conscious and our sense of values has gone astray." See Chase, Foreword, xi.

30. Allen, "The Gentleman in American Fiction," 120. For the best discussion of Allen's own plantation fiction and its curious gender play, see Gebhard, "Reconstructing Southern Manhood."

31. Allen, "The Gentleman in American Fiction," 118.

32. This last argument is made by Mixon in "The Ultimate Irrelevance of Race: Joel Chandler Harris and Uncle Remus in Their Time." The debate over whether Harris subverts a plantation tradition forms a second major branch of the criticism on Harris. Ellen Douglass Leyburn was among the first scholars to emphasize Brer Rabbit's connections to a tradition of fable in which animals satirize humans. Jefferson Humphries has performed a similar reading more recently. See Leyburn, "Satiric Allegory in the Uncle Remus Tales"; and Humphries, "Remus Redux." Other readings that highlight how Harris subverts the literary traditions within which he wrote include Bier, "Duplicity and Cynicism in Harris's Humor"; Cochran, "Black Father: The Subversive Achievement of Joel Chandler Harris"; Cartwright, "Creole Self-Fashioning" (in *Reading Africa into American Literature*); and Pamplin, "Plantation Makeover." For an early study that positions Harris primarily as a reactionary, see Turner, "Daddy Joel Harris and His Old-Time Darkies," which argues that Harris's fiction "molded actual Negroes into the old-time slaves essential to the romantic myth of a utopian plantation, governed by a kingly and paternal master" (128). For more recent discussions that build upon this view, see Ellis, "Enacting Culture"; Cowan, "Charles Waddell Chesnutt and Joel Chandler Harris"; and Hale, *Making Whiteness*, 54–60. For an early reading that positions Harris on both sides of this argument, see

Wolfe, "Uncle Remus and the Malevolent Rabbit," which argues that Harris both "loved" and "virulently hated the Negro" (83). Louis Rubin's "Uncle Remus and the Ubiquitous Rabbit" does not imagine the poles of Harris's ambivalence as quite so far apart, yet it does insist that the Uncle Remus collections be read in terms of their both subversive and reactionary potentials. For more recent readings that argue that Harris is fundamentally ambivalent, see MacKethan, "Joel Chandler Harris: Speculating on the Past" (in *The Dream of Arcady*); Sundquist, *To Wake the Nations*, 323–47; and especially Ritterhouse, "Reading, Intimacy, and the Role of Uncle Remus in White Southern Social Memory." Like the present chapter, Ritterhouse's article insists that Harris's meanings and messages reside not primarily within his books themselves but rather within their receptions among multiple reading publics. Her argument that Harris's reputation as a romancer of the plantation was an effect fundamentally of what a majority of early readers wanted to see in his texts resonates powerfully with the argument I develop here.

33. On Harris's reception among parents and children, see Connolly, "Crossing Borders from Africa to America."

34. Brown, *The Negro in American Fiction*, 53. At times Harris was even presumed to have been black. As Mark Twain reports in *Life on the Mississippi*, a group of schoolchildren gathered to hear Harris read in 1881 was disappointed when the author materialized: "They said:—'Why, he's white!' They were grieved about it." See Twain, *Life on the Mississippi*, 330.

35. Stowe, *Uncle Tom's Cabin*, 155.

36. Birnbaum, "Dark Dialects," 36. Michael North reads Harris's and others' uses of dialect as a "challenge to the dominance of received linguistic forms"—a challenge that would be taken up once again by such modernist writers as T. S. Eliot and Ezra Pound, both of whom borrowed from Harris when they themselves produced lines of poetry in "negro" dialect. See North, *The Dialect of Modernism*, 78.

37. Excepting the remarkable short story "Where's Duncan?" (from the 1891 collection *Balaam and His Master, and Other Sketches and Stories*), Harris almost never writes about master-slave sexual relations, interracial progeny, and the problem of the color line. "Where's Duncan?" does confront these issues in the person of a mixed-race man who passes as white and, not unlike Charles Bon does in Faulkner's *Absalom, Absalom!*, returns to his father's plantation to demand recognition. The story registers Harris's comprehension of the sexual dimensions of the plantation, though it stands out because these are issues Harris rarely addresses in his other works.

38. As Robert Bone noted succinctly a number of years ago, "Joel Chandler Harris was a complicated man, full of neurotic conflicts and self-deceiving ways." Louis Rubin concurs, imagining even that "there were two Joel Chandler Harrises—the journalist, citizen of Georgia, and man of letters who wrote pleasant, optimistic,

and moral tales . . . and the fiercely creative artist, his uncompromising realism masked to the world." See Bone, "The Oral Tradition," 131, and Rubin, "Uncle Remus and the Ubiquitous Rabbit," 171. A tradition of reading Harris's stories as windows into his own complex psychology and personal history forms the third major branch of Harris criticism. For additional sources that commit to this approach, see Wolfe, "Uncle Remus and the Malevolent Rabbit"; Martin, "Joel Chandler Harris and the Cornfield Journalist"; Flusche, "Underlying Despair in the Fiction of Joel Chandler Harris"; Griska, "In Stead of a 'Gift of Gab': Some New Perspectives on Joel Chandler Harris's Biography"; and Wyatt-Brown, "The Trickster Motif and Disillusion" (from *Hearts of Darkness*). See also the many sections of Harris's biographies (Cousins, *Joel Chandler Harris*; Bickley, *Joel Chandler Harris*; and Brasch, *Brer Rabbit, Uncle Remus, and the "Cornfield Journalist"*) that speculate about the links between Harris's psychology and his writings.

39. Scott Romine develops a similar reading of Thomas Nelson Page's *In Ole Virginia* tales in *The Narrative Forms of Southern Community*, 90–111.

40. Harris, *Uncle Remus and His Friends*, 35–36.

41. See Julia Collier Harris, *The Life and Letters of Joel Chandler Harris*, 164.

42. Harris, *Uncle Remus and His Friends*, 81.

43. Harris, *Nights with Uncle Remus*, xiii–xiv. Claire Pamplin reads this scene as evidence of Harris's remarkable ability to don masks and "reinven[t] himself." See Pamplin, "Plantation Makeover," 47.

44. Cassidy, *Dictionary of American Regional English*, 771.

45. Walter M. Brasch, Harris's most recent biographer, believes that 1846 is the most likely birthdate. Earlier biographers, including Robert Lemuel Wiggins and Bruce Bickley, have cited 1848 as the year. See Brasch, *Brer Rabbit, Uncle Remus, and the "Cornfield Journalist,"* 18.

46. Julia Collier Harris, *The Life and Letters of Joel Chandler Harris*, 7.

47. Harris, *On the Plantation*, 21.

48. Douglass, *Narrative of the Life of Frederick Douglass*, 13.

49. Washington, *Up from Slavery*, 1.

50. Harris, "Observations from New England," in *Joel Chandler Harris: Editor and Essayist*, 165.

51. Harris, "The Old Plantation," in *Joel Chandler Harris: Editor and Essayist*, 90.

52. Ibid., 90, 92.

53. The Spectator review is mentioned in an advertisement D. Appleton and Company included in the back pages of a number of titles it published during the 1890s, for example, Frank Lebby Stanton's *Song of the Soil* (1894), a book of poetry for which Harris wrote the introduction.

54. Rev. of *Uncle Remus* in *Publisher's Weekly*, 432–33.

55. Stead, introduction to *The Wonderful Adventures of Old Brer Rabbit*, by Harris, i.

56. Avary, *Joel Chandler Harris and His Home: A Sketch*, 25.

57. Wiggins, *The Life of Joel Chandler Harris*, 4.

58. Bickley has counted more than twenty foreign-language translations. My thanks to the staff at Emory University's Robert W. Woodruff Library, especially Kathy Shoemaker, as well as Lain Shakespeare of the Wren's Nest museum in Atlanta and Lanelle Frost of the Uncle Remus Museum in Eatonton for aiding me with research into the international editions of Harris's books.

59. Kipling, letter to Joel Chandler Harris (Dec. 6, 1895), in *The Letters of Rudyard Kipling*, 217. Kipling wrote at least one additional letter to Harris, describing in it, among other things, his pleasure that Harris had written a book as appealing to his daughter as to him.

60. Kipling, *The Complete Stalky & Co.*, 144–47.

CHAPTER 2

1. M. B. Hillyard claimed some ownership of the term in his 1887 study *The New South*, observing that the term had already become "quite hackneyed" of late. But the term had begun to be used even before the end of Reconstruction. Grady's first use of it was probably in an editorial dated March 14, 1874. Other newspapers would use it as well. As C. Vann Woodward notes, the term was competing with other appellations (the "Solid South," the "Redemption" South, etc.) to describe what had become of the region since the Civil War and Reconstruction. See Hillyard, *The New South*, 1–3; and Woodward, *Origins of the New South*, ix–x. For additional general information on the term and the era, see Ayers, *The Promise of the New South*, and Gaston, *The New South Creed*.

2. "Henry W. Grady," 4.

3. Harris, "Biographical Sketch of Henry W. Grady," 12.

4. Rev. of *In Ole Virginia*, 165–66.

5. Brooke, *English Literature*, 217–19.

6. "Provinciality" was the word Harris himself used to describe his art, though he believed that this connoted something authentic rather than something narrow or limited. See Harris, "Provinciality in Art: A Defense of Boston." Lucinda Mac-Kethan expresses the differences between Page and Harris nicely, noting that Page's plantations tend to represent "the gracious homeplace" whereas Harris "puts the plantation version of Arcady down in the middle of the briar patch." See MacKethan, *The Dream of Arcady*, 36, 38.

7. Unless otherwise noted, all biographical information for Grady derives from Nixon, *Henry W. Grady: Spokesman of the New South*, and for Page, from Gross, *Thomas Nelson Page*. Grady's writings have drawn relatively little attention from students of U.S. culture recently. Page's have attracted more. For discussions that resonate with the one I pose here, see Romine, "The Plantation Community" (in *The Narrative Forms of Southern Community*); MacKethan, "Thomas Nelson Page: The Plantation as Arcady" (in *The Dream of Arcady*); Lowe, "Re-creating a Public for the Plantation"; Hagood, "'Prodjickin', or Mekin' a Present to Yo' Fam'ly";

Myers, "Desirable Immigrants"; and especially Romine, "Things Falling Apart," and Michaels, "Anti-Imperial Americanism."

8. Qtd. in Nixon, *Henry W. Grady*, 56.

9. Page, *Two Little Confederates*, 1.

10. Page, *The Old Dominion*, 198–99.

11. Page, "Two Old Colonial Places," 211. Rosewell, the Page family plantation at which Jefferson may have drafted the Declaration, may also have been built on the same lands where Pocahontas once performed her legendary "rescue" of John Smith. See Mayer, "The Spot Where Pocahontas Rescued Captain Smith," 472.

12. Grady, "Against Centralization," 143.

13. Ibid., 153.

14. Page, "The Old South," 6.

15. Page, "Uncle Gabe's White Folks," 882. The short story for which Page would later become best known, "Marse Chan: A Tale of Old Virginia," begins similarly. In it a former slave recounts the story of how he had accompanied his master to the battlefront and then returned to the plantation to tell his family and sweetheart of the man's death. He tells the story to a visitor who arrives on horseback. His first words to the man are identical to Uncle Gabe's first words to his auditor: "'Sarvent, marster,' he said, taking his hat off." The story was first published in the *Century* in April 1884 and was later featured in *In Ole Virginia; or, Marse Chan and Other Stories*. Interestingly, the story was accepted for publication by the editors of the *Century* in 1881 but not published until later—evidence, perhaps, that it was not entirely clear until later in the decade that plantation fiction might be so phenomenally popular.

16. This shift from conversation to reverie might also be described as a shift from a more self-conscious to a less self-conscious mode of narration, which would be to invite a comparison to Scott Romine's smart analysis of how black performativity either registers or fails to register in Page's dialect fiction: "The narrative work of *In Ole Virginia* . . . is to recuperate the former slave's authentic, rather than performative, commitment to the social order." Like Harris, Page recognizes a black capacity to signify, especially when talking to whites who project power. Yet whereas Harris's writings tend to leave open questions of whether Uncle Remus is being sincere when he speaks to white men, Page's writings work to arrive at moments when his black storytellers seem unquestionably earnest. See Romine, *The Narrative Forms of Southern Community*, 97.

17. Grady, "The New South," 87. Subsequent references are cited parenthetically.

18. On the existence of "simple police regulations" on the antebellum plantation and the conflicts that arose when, in a modernizing "New South," the state sought to assume the powers once exercised privately by planters, see Wagner, *Disturbing the Peace*, especially 127–35, in which Wagner discusses the important roles Grady and the *Constitution* played in advocating for this controversial new form of police power in the South.

19. For a discussion of the Freedmen's Bureau in Athens and elsewhere in Georgia, see Cimbala, *Under the Guardianship of the Nation*.

20. Grady, "The South and Her Problems," 96.

21. Tourgée, "The South as a Field for Fiction," 406–7.

22. Page, "Marse Phil," 897; Harris, "Ananias," 699.

23. Harris, *Gabriel Tolliver*, 111.

24. Page, *Red Rock*, 1. Subsequent references are cited parenthetically.

25. Page wrote to a friend that "after having written a third or more of the novel I discovered that I had drifted into the production of a political tract. I bodily discarded what I had written, and going back beyond the War, in order to secure a background and a point of departure which would enable me to take a more serene path, I rewrote it entirely." See Gross, *Thomas Nelson Page*, 78–79.

26. As MacKethan argues, "the plantation, for Page, was the breeding ground for heroes." Where I differ from her interpretation is in her description of planter heroism as a relic of a bygone age. "All of Page's major characters exhibit the traits of feudal lords, and all of them are involved in a crusade to preserve an ideal way of life against the forces of inevitable change," MacKethan contends (*The Dream of Arcady*, 48). The argument in the present chapter is that both Page and Grady saw planter power as much more adaptive, much more in sync with modernity, and therefore much more a national resource that needed to be spread, not simply conserved.

27. Jacquelin's achievement of a symbolic full manhood may possess additional significance. As Carolyn Gebhard has argued, numerous works of postbellum plantation fiction invite readers to pity and indeed cry over white aristocratic men: "The spectacle of a white man's body in a scene designed to evoke tears and admiration placed readers in a sentimental relation to a site that had formerly been reserved for women and slaves." Such scenes involve elements of "camp," Gebhard argues, and *Red Rock* occasionally drifts toward camp—and certainly toward a sentimental—aesthetics, especially in scenes involving the younger Jacquelin. By becoming a man capable of violence—one who inspires fears rather than invites tears—Jacquelin becomes a different sort of plantation protagonist than the one discussed by Gebhard. He may also become more manly than his own name, more "Jack" than "Jacquelin"—a facet of the novel helpfully pointed out to me by John Mayfield. See Gebhard, "Reconstructing Southern Manhood."

28. *Red Rock* thus presents an interesting variation upon a theme that Jessica Adams has identified as central to a U.S. plantation imaginary: "The ownership of people has generated a culture in which people may become possessed by what we call history, and the plantation itself remains haunted by property." In Page's novel, however, "becom[ing] possessed by . . . history" is an affirmative condition, not a disabling one, while "haunting" becomes a means quite literally of repossessing "property." See Adams, *Wounds of Returning*, 11. For a related discussion of the

ways in which "the haunted plantation" proves central to the fiction of William Faulkner, see Duck, *The Nation's Region*, 146–55.

29. To read the novel in this manner is thus to arrive at a different conclusion than those reached by Walter Benn Michaels, who regards *Red Rock* as an example of "the major anti-imperialist literature of the turn of the century," and Scott Romine, who reads the novel as analogous to other works of postcolonial fiction in which narratives of community are developed and sustained as reactions against imperial takeovers (and thus may be threatened with dissolution unless the "emperor," figuratively speaking, is kept always in view). My objection is not that "anti-imperialism" fails to describe white southern attitudes toward the North nor that postbellum southern fiction may be read as "postcolonial." Rather, I want to attend to those ways in which such writers as Page are anti-imperialist, postcolonial, and *imperialist* simultaneously. That is, they object to white northern control over white southerners but propound white control over black southerners and develop narratives of national history in which the white South seems always to generate expansionist energies. The problem with the nation during Reconstruction, Page believes, is that it had embraced the wrong form of imperialism—one contrary to the form first established by John Smith and perpetuated by Thomas Jefferson and other southerners, especially Virginians, throughout U.S. history, or at least up until the mistake of Reconstruction. See Michaels, "Anti-imperial Americanism," 365–72; and Romine, "Things Falling Apart," 178–86. I engage Michaels's argument at greater length in Chapter 3.

30. Though he does not address Page or Grady, Blum's discussions of religious missions and U.S. imperialism resonate with the analyses I am presenting of the religious imagery that pervades both men's writings. See Blum, *Reforging the White Republic*, 51–86 and 209–43.

31. Williams, *Keywords*, 248–49.

32. Page, *The Negro*, 80, 310. The final word in this passage from Page, "character," is central to Cathy Boeckmann's study of how during the late nineteenth century, racialist thinkers came to emphasize character traits over bodily differences as the elements that differentiated one race from the next. This argument helps to clarify further how such writers as Grady and Page could make white planter paternity—a concept that seems specific to one race, class, gender, and region—more universally available as an imagined point of cultural origins. "White" Americans of many backgrounds may lay claim to the character of the South's planter patriarchs and then imagine *this* as a sign of racial connectedness. See Boeckmann, *A Question of Character*, 1–62.

33. Grady, "The South and Her Problems," 96, 100–101.

34. Grady, "At the Boston Banquet," 180–81, 185.

35. Ibid, 180.

36. Grady, *The New South*, 146. Subsequent references are cited parenthetically.

37. "Henry W. Grady," 4.

38. Interestingly, Page also was drawn to the Franco-Prussian War (1870–1871) and the ways in which France resembled the U.S. South because it represented a proud regime losing in battle to a more efficient military machine. In "A Soldier of the Empire," a short story published in the *Century* in 1886, he goes so far as to build a story around an aged yet proud soldier who had fought for and received a medal for military valor from Napoleon trying to rally young Frenchmen to fight in this later war. Significantly, given the focus of this chapter, the story also centers around the old soldier's relationship with his son, who wishes not to fight and is thus unworthy of his paternity. In the story's climactic scene the old soldier aims his own musket at his son, who is fleeing from battle. He is relieved of the responsibility of having to kill him when a Prussian shell explodes nearby and kills the son. He himself dies afterward, and in the story's final scene a group of Prussian officers praise his valor, recognizing him as "a brave soldier . . . a *soldier of the empire*" (954).

39. Grady, "At the Boston Banquet," 197–98; and "Against Centralization," 157.

40. Page, "The Dragon of the Sea," 731–32.

41. Page, "Social Life in Old Virginia before the War," 184–85.

CHAPTER 3

1. Dixon, *Southern Horizons*, 265.

2. Cooper, *Walter Hines Page*, 168–69. Cooper notes that Walter Hines Page (perhaps a distant cousin to Thomas Nelson Page and, like Dixon, a native of North Carolina) was embarrassed by Dixon's racial politics but nonetheless saw in *The Leopard's Spots* and its proposed successors potential moneymakers for his publishing company. Only a few months earlier the firm had published Booker T. Washington's *Up from Slavery*.

3. Dixon, *Southern Horizons*, 265.

4. Dixon, *The Leopard's Spots*, 455. Subsequent references are cited parenthetically.

5. Dixon, *The Clansman*, 374. Subsequent references are cited parenthetically.

6. Dixon, *Southern Horizons*, 263.

7. Romine, "Thomas Dixon and the Literary Production of Whiteness," 125–26. For additional readings of how Dixon's novels are propelled by anxieties surrounding whiteness, see Rogin, "'The Sword Became a Flashing Vision'" (in *Ronald Reagan, the Movie*); Gunning, "Re-Membering Blackness after Reconstruction" (in *Race, Rape, and Lynching*); Stokes, "White Sex" (in *The Color of Sex*); Clymer, "The United States of Terrorism" (in *America's Culture of Terrorism*); Gillman, "Procrustean Bedfellows" (in *Blood Talk*); Stecopoulos, "The Geography of Reunion" (in *Reconstructing the World*); Magowan, "Coming between 'The Black Beast' and 'The White Virgin'"; Fossett, "(K)Night Riders in (K)Night Gowns";

Richardson, " 'The Birth of a Nation'hood' "; and the essays collected in Gillespie and Hall, eds., *Thomas Dixon Jr. and the Birth of Modern America*.

8.   Readers may even have been reminded of several local color short stories, most famously Thomas Nelson Page's "Marse Chan" (1884), in which an ex-slave performs the same duty as Dixon's "Nelse," returning to "de ole home" after the war to report that his master was killed in battle yet to deliver "a braver message," too, as one of Dixon's white characters conceives it, "in [his] honest black face of faith and duty and life and love." "Thankee," Nelse replies, in perfect keeping with the codes of plantation fiction: "I wuz erbleeged ter come home." See Page, *In Ole Virginia*, 7.

9.   That the words are in Latin, the Grand Dragon who speaks them a man of Scotch-Irish descent, the setting of his novel South Carolina, and the secret association he heads one that had arrived at its name by adapting a Greek word, kuklos, and combining it with a Scottish one, clan, in order to create a phrase that meant, roughly translated, "family circle"—these sorts of conflations contribute to the Klan novel's representation of whiteness as a universal force. In *The Clansman*, for example, Dixon celebrates the men who don the robes as descendants of those who "had defied the Crown of Great Britain a hundred years from the caves and wilds of Scotland and Ireland, taught the British people how to slay a king and build a commonwealth, and, driven into exile into the wilderness of America, led our Revolution, peopled the hills of the South, and conquered the West" (342).

10.   Page, "Social Life in Old Virginia after the War," 184, and *Red Rock*, 1.

11.   Stricklin, " 'Ours Is a Century of Light,' " 105.

12.   Dixon, *Southern Horizons*, 265.

13.   Ibid., 265–66.

14.   All biographical information derives from Dixon's *Southern Horizons* and Cook's *Thomas Dixon and Fire from the Flint*.

15.   Dixon, *Dixon's Sermons*, 114. Subsequent references are cited parenthetically.

16.   Dixon's sermons have been neglected. The most thorough discussion of them comes in Stricklin, " 'Ours Is a Century of Light,' " though his concern is more with their embodiment of the idea of a Social Gospel than their endorsement of U.S. imperialism. See also Lyerly, "Gender and Race in Dixon's Religious Ideology."

17.   "A Week of Victories," 1.

18.   Dixon would make a similar argument in a 1905 article in the *Saturday Evening Post*, explaining that the so-called Liberian solution would prove much less expensive to the U.S. government than attempts to educate and uplift black Americans at home. Dixon, "Booker T. Washington and the Negro," 1–2.

19.   Michaels, "Anti-Imperial Americanism," 366. Michaels makes versions of this argument in *Our America*, 16–23, and "The Souls of White Folk," 185–88, as well.

20.   During the past ten or so years Dixon has been the subject of numerous works

of scholarship, including a biography (Anthony Slide's *American Racist*, 2004), a collection of essays bearing the telltale title *Thomas Dixon Jr. and the Birth of Modern America* (Gillespie and Hall, eds., 2006), and a slew of scholarly articles and book and dissertation chapters. The *MLA International Bibliography* currently indexes twenty-five entries under the subject heading "Dixon, Thomas" from the year 2000 onward. The total from 1950 to 1999 is only twenty-six, and ten of these were published during the middle-to-late 1990s. Most of the more recent discussions are focused on Dixon's own writings, moreover, not on his relationship with Griffith. Of those published prior to the middle 1990s, roughly half concentrate as much or more on *The Birth of a Nation* as they do on Dixon himself.

21. On how white supremacy complicated the drive toward U.S. imperialism, see Love, *Race over Empire*.

22. Tillman, "Are We to Spread the Christian Religion with the Bayonet," 123.

23. Indeed Dixon despised Tillman, who believed that the threat of black rapists had produced too few lynchings during the 1890s, the sizable recent increases in the number of black men lynched notwithstanding. In "A Friendly Warning to the Negro" he distances himself from Tillman's extremism, calling him "a freak. He is an abnormality, even in South Carolina. He has no parallel in the history of the state or the nation, and he will never have an imitator. . . . Mr. Tillman no more represents the Southern white race than the wildcat represents the animal life in the South." See *Dixon's Sermons*, 117. On Tillman's extreme racism, see Kantrowitz, *Ben Tillman and the Reconstruction of White Supremacy*.

24. For a discussion of how Dixon's rendition of the events in Wilmington compares to Charles Chesnutt's in *The Marrow of Tradition*, see Wilson, *Whiteness in the Novels of Charles Chesnutt*, 121–27, and Stecopoulos, "The Geography of Reunion" (in *Reconstructing the World*).

25. Grady, *The New South*, 161.

26. Dixon, *The Traitor*, 18.

27. Ibid., 87. Subsequent references are cited parenthetically.

28. Fossett, "(K)Night Riders in (K)Night Gowns," 37–39, 42.

29. Miller, *The Empire of the Eye*, 3–13.

30. See Silber, *The Romance of Reunion*, 159–96.

31. Page, "The War with Spain and After," 725–27.

32. Dixon perhaps had reason to feel that he was carrying a torch. Massachusetts Senator Henry Cabot Lodge would observe in 1903, for example, that the "American people ha[d] lost all interest in" the subject of imperialism. See May, "American Expansionism," 150. On Walter Hines Page's attitudes toward U.S. foreign policy, see Cooper, *Walter Hines Page*, 135–39. On the development of Twain's anti-imperialism, see Zwick, *Confronting Imperialism*.

CHAPTER 4

1. Faulkner, *The Unvanquished*, 203.

2. Faulkner, *The Wild Palms*, 149.

3. Faulkner, *The Reivers*, 4. The man speaking is Lucius Priest, a grandfather recollecting the story of his boyhood to his grandson, which is the form *The Reivers* assumes.

4. Faulkner, *As I Lay Dying*, 26, 73.

5. Faulkner, "A Rose for Emily," 392.

6. Ibid.

7. Faulkner, *As I Lay Dying*, 110.

8. Faulkner, *Absalom, Absalom!* 290; and *The Sound and the Fury*, 85.

9. Woodward, *The Burden of Southern History*, 269, 278, 267. The "same stink" quotation derives from a letter Faulkner wrote to Malcolm Cowley. See Cowley, *The Faulkner-Cowley File*, 15.

10. Studies of Faulkner in international and imperial contexts are now numerous. Taylor Hagood's *Faulkner's Imperialism* (2008) resonates particularly powerfully with the present study, for while its interest is more in space and its adumbrations in myth, it attends to how Faulkner's fictions may be read as both "a rhapsody on the inexpugnable voice of the imperialist and the equally inexhaustible cries of the narratives of subversion" (31). This insight resembles one Leigh Anne Duck voices in "From Colony to Empire," namely that Faulkner's "transnational analysis" of the relations among race, labor, and capital produce "skepticism" as well as "a totalizing view of inequality in which local struggles seem almost inevitably ineffectual" (38). It also echoes George B. Handley's observation in *Postslavery Literatures in the Americas* that Faulkner recognizes how "modern forms of imperialism . . . imitate the former plantation in a postslavery context" (114). I liken these arguments to mine because, in this chapter, I identify how Faulkner both moves beyond the imperial discourse of the white man's burden and continuously embraces it. Following John T. Matthews, one might conclude that ambivalence is what happens when one "recognizes the South as a historical phenomenon of global imperialism" when one has grown up reading stories in which the South is depicted as having been colonized by the North. See Matthews, "Many Mansions," 5. For additional approaches to Faulkner as a postcolonial, imperial, and/ or anti-imperial (and in any event transnational) writer, see Glissant, *Faulkner, Mississippi*; Baker, *William Faulkner's Postcolonial South*; Cohn, "The Vase of Fabricated Facts" (in *History and Memory in the Two Souths*); Aboul-Ela, *Other South*; Trefzer, "Postcolonial Displacements in Faulkner's Indian Stories of the 1930s"; See, "Southern Postcoloniality and the Improbability of Filipino-American Postcoloniality"; the essays in the section devoted to Faulkner in Smith and Cohn, *Look Away!*; and the additional essays included in Trefzer and Abadie, eds., *Global Faulkner*.

11. Grady, "The South and Her Problems," 96; and *The New South*, 252.

12. Grady, *The New South*, 141, 231.

13. "Nobel Bedfellows," 12. The complaint was issued in an otherwise laudatory opinion piece praising the Nobel committee for having awarded the 1950 prize for literature to Faulkner. Interestingly, the piece worries that Faulkner's "enormous vogue . . . in Latin America and on the European Continent, especially in France, does not mean that foreigners admire him because he gives them the picture of American life they believe to be typical and true."

14. Page, *Social Life in Old Virginia before the War*, 106. The book represented an expanded version of the essay published in *The Old South* (1892) and cited in Chapter 2.

15. See Sundquist, *Faulkner*, especially chapter 6.

16. Faulkner, *Requiem for a Nun*, 212–13.

17. Ibid., 210.

18. On Faulkner's (uneasy) complicities with cold war–era U.S. expansionism, see Matthews, "Many Mansions"; Cohn, "Combating Anti-Americanism during the Cold War"; and Stecopoulos, "Mississippi on the Pacific" (in *Reconstructing the World*).

19. Sundquist, *Faulkner*, 67. Among the additional studies of Faulkner and race that most illuminate my own thinking in this chapter are Williamson, *William Faulkner and Southern History*; Irwin, *Doubling and Incest / Repetition and Revenge*; Davis, *Games of Property*; Michaels, "*Absalom, Absalom!* The Difference between White Men and White Men"; and the chapters on Faulkner in Ladd, *Nationalism and the Color Line*; Duck, *The Nation's Region*; McKee, *Producing American Races*; and Duvall, *Race and White Identity in Southern Fiction*. In addition to Duvall, articles useful on the subject of Faulkner and whiteness include Jackson, "American Emergencies," Entzminger, "Passing as Miscegenation," and especially Hagood, "Negotiating the Marble Bonds of Whiteness," which considers Faulkner's treatments of whiteness in the context of U.S. and European imperialisms. Particularly helpful on the question of Faulkner's responses to the civil rights movement, which I discuss briefly at the end of this chapter, is Peavy, *Go Slow Now*.

20. Faulkner, *Light in August*, 9. Subsequent references are cited parenthetically.

21. On the subject of how lynching figured in U.S. cultural production of the period, see Gunning, *Race, Rape, and Lynching*; Goldsby, *A Spectacular Secret*; and Wood, *Lynching and Spectacle*.

22. See Blotner, *Faulkner*, 20. Blotner also speculates that Faulkner may have seen a stage production of the novel that came to Oxford, Mississippi, in 1908. See Blotner, *Faulkner*, 33.

23. Dixon, *The Leopard's Spots*, 244.

24. Mitchell, *Gone with the Wind*, 1037.

25. Exceptions include Owada, "Who Is Joanna Burden?" and Fowler, "Joe Christ-

mas and 'Womanshenegro,' " both of which recognize the importance of Joanna's unusually marginalized character within the Yoknapatawpha scheme.

26. Of the 505 pages that compose the Vintage International edition of the novel, for example, the passages described below span pages 252–53. In terms of the novel's twenty-one chapters, the passages come at the end of chapter 11. Ten chapters precede and ten follow.

27. Faulkner, *The Sound and the Fury*, 86.

28. Dixon, *The Leopard's Spots*, 380.

29. Interestingly, Valérie Loichot reads *Light in August* as the novel of Faulkner's that "gets as close as he can to a romancing of the African-American past." See Loichot, *Orphan Narratives*, 118.

30. Faulkner, *Absalom, Absalom!* 5. Subsequent references are cited parenthetically.

31. Faulkner claimed not to have read *Gone with the Wind* because of its length. On the relationships between Faulkner's and Mitchell's views of the plantation, see Sundquist, *Faulkner*, 110–12; and Railton, " 'What Else Could a Southern Gentleman Do?' "

32. Ladd, *Nationalism and the Color Line*, 155.

33. Grady, *The New South*, 146.

34. Mitchell, *Gone with the Wind*, 193.

35. *Absalom, Absalom!* has thus proved the primary object of many additional studies of Faulkner's transnationalism, postcoloniality, and/or (anti-)imperialism. See, for example, Ladd, "The Direction of the Howling" (in *Nationalism and the Color Line*); Godden, "*Absalom, Absalom!*, Haiti, and Labor History"; Stanchich, "The Hidden Caribbean 'Other' in William Faulkner's *Absalom, Absalom!*"; Matthews, "Recalling the West Indies"; and Kutzinski, "Borders, Bodies, and Regions."

36. Faulkner, *The Unvanquished*, 210.

37. Faulkner, *Go Down Moses*, 266. It was in the late stages of the preparation of the manuscript for this book that I learned of Sally Wolf-King's discovery of the actual plantation ledger upon which this section of *Go Down, Moses* is based. That Faulkner's fiction proves thereby only to be more intimately connected to nineteenth-century writings about plantations makes one wonder what revelations lay in store. See Cohen, "Faulkner Link to Plantation Diary Discovered."

38. Faulkner, *The Unvanquished*, 341.

39. Faulkner, *Intruder in the Dust*, 41.

40. Faulkner, *The Reivers*, 304. Brannon Costello nevertheless reads *The Reivers* as "a vision of the emptiness and anxiety of the old model of wasteful paternalism" characteristic of a plantation social economy. See Costello, *Plantation Airs*, 91.

41. Faulkner, *The Reivers*, 177, 182. The irony of the second statement is that, to the extent that Ned allows himself to be himself around Lucius, he is in some ways even more like Harris's original Uncle Remus, who behaves differently around the little boy than the white men with whom he comes into contact in the character sketches.

42. Faulkner, *Essays*, 158. Subsequent references are cited parenthetically. For a parallel reading of a similar piece of writing, see Adams, *Wounds of Returning*, 103–5. Adams discusses Faulkner's 1956 article "If I Were a Negro" and its call for what seems like endless "negro" patience while "the white man" works out his response to the demand for black civil equality.

43. Grady, "Against Centralization," 156–57.

CONCLUSION

1. Mencken, "The Sahara of the Bozart," 184–86, 194–95. Subsequent references are cited parenthetically.

2. Indeed Mencken himself alludes to Harris, though only to belittle him: "Once upon a time a Georgian printed a couple of books that attracted notice, but immediately it turned out that he was little more than an amanuensis for the local blacks—that his works were really the products, not of white Georgia, but of black Georgia. Writing afterward as a white man, he swiftly subsided into the fifth rank. And he is not only the glory of the literature of Georgia; he is, almost literally, the whole of the literature of Georgia—nay, the entire art of Georgia" (160).

3. On the idea that Mencken had liberated young southern writers to become serious modernists, see, for example, the entry for "Sahara of the Bozart" in *The Companion to Southern Literature*, 754.

4. One non-American worth considering in this context is Sir George Campbell, an English public figure who toured the South during the late 1870s and published *White and Black: The Outcome of a Visit to the United States* in 1879. Campbell's tour was intended expressly to discover how the white South was handling its race problems so that British colonizers in the Caribbean and elsewhere might better know how to manage their own subjects: "I was . . . led to look particularly into the relations between the black and white races in the Southern States, for the sake of the lessons that might be learned as bearing on our management of British possessions where white and black races are intermingled" (111).

5. Mitchell, *Gone with the Wind*, 47–48.

6. In 1936 Dixon corresponded with Mitchell praising her for the achievement of *Gone with the Wind*. Mitchell responded by acknowledging Dixon as an influence, writing that "I was practically raised on your books and love them very much." See Wood, "From *The Clansman* and *The Birth of a Nation* to *Gone with the Wind*," 123.

7. Harper, *Iola Leroy*, 133.

8. Brown, *My Southern Home*, 221. Emphasis in original.

9. Delany, *Blake*, 135.

10. Griggs, *Imperium in Imperio*, 252, 182.

11. Malcolm X and Haley, *The Autobiography of Malcolm X*, 417. The quotation comes from Haley's 1965 epilogue to the autobiography.

12. Harper, *Iola Leroy*, 88.

13. Chesnutt, *The Marrow of Tradition*, 82, 238. For additional discussions of Chesnutt's anti-imperialism, see Stecopoulos, "The Geography of Reunion" (in *Reconstructing the World*); Goldner, "(Re)Staging Colonial Encounters"; and Wegener, "Charles W. Chesnutt and the Anti-Imperialist Matrix of African-American Writing, 1898–1905."

14. Griggs, *Imperium in Imperio*, 191, 198. The underground/aboveground metaphor is made literal in the novel in the form of "Thomas Jefferson College," a school in Waco, Texas, whose main building allows access to a secret underground complex where the black leaders of the "imperium" meet.

15. Johnson, *The Autobiography of an Ex-Colored Man*, 55.

16. Dunbar, *Lyrics of Love and Laughter*, 148, 152.

17. For discussions of the ways in which Dunbar may subvert the tradition upon which he depends, see Fishkin, "Race and the Politics of Memory: Mark Twain and Paul Laurence Dunbar"; Jones, "Paul Laurence Dunbar and the Authentic Black Voice" (in *Strange Talk*); and Keeling, "Paul Laurence Dunbar and the Mask of Dialect."

18. Grady, *The New South*, 162, 146.

19. The allusions here are to two texts, Stephen D. Cummings's *The Dixification of America* and John Egerton's *The Americanization of Dixie, the Southernization of America*. See also Peter Applebome, *Dixie Rising*.

20. For essays specifically addressing how the South ought no longer to seem a separate space, see Lassiter and Crespino, *The Myth of Southern Exceptionalism*. For the best discussion of how twentieth-century southern literature objects to an image of the South as disproportionately problematic and seeks to highlight the nationality of its problems, see Duck, *The Nation's Region*.

21. Grady, *The New South*, 146.

22. Du Bois, *The Souls of Black Folk*, 145. Subsequent references are cited parenthetically.

23. Faulkner, *Absalom, Absalom!*, 30.

24. In the same passage in which he singles out Thomas Nelson Page for debate, he identifies the more radically white supremacist Benjamin Tillman as worthy of denunciation. Later he would identify "Tom Dixon" alongside "Ben Tillman" as among "the hatefulest enemies of the negro." See Du Bois, *The Souls of Black Folk*, 93, and Lewis, *W. E. B. Du Bois*, 149.

Works Cited

Aboul-Ela, Hosam. *Other South: Faulkner, Coloniality, and the Mariategui Tradition*. Pittsburgh: University of Pittsburgh Press, 2007.

Adams, Henry. *Democracy: An American Novel*. 1880. London: Macmillan, 1882.

Adams, Jessica. "Introduction: Circum-Caribbean Performance, Language, History." In *Just below South: Intercultural Performance in the Caribbean and the U.S. South*, ed. Jessica Adams, Michael Bibler, and Cécile Accilien, 1–21. Charlottesville: University of Virginia Press, 2007.

———. *Wounds of Returning: Race, Memory, and Property on the Postslavery Plantation*. Chapel Hill: University of North Carolina Press, 2007

Allen, James Lane. "The Gentleman in American Fiction." *Bookman* 4, no. 2 (October 1896): 118–21.

"Ambassador to Italy." *New York Times*, June 16, 1913, 8.

Applebome, Peter. *Dixie Rising: How the South Is Shaping American Values, Politics, and Culture*. New York: Times Books, 1996.

Ashcroft, Bill, Gareth Griffiths, and Helen Tiffin, eds. *The Empire Writes Back: Theory and Practice in Post-Colonial Literatures*. 1989. New York: Routledge, 2002.

Austin, Henry. "The Kipling Hysteria." *Dial* 26, no. 310 (May 16, 1899): 327–28.

Avary, Myrta Lockett. *Joel Chandler Harris and His Home: A Sketch*. Atlanta: Uncle Remus Memorial Association, 1913.

Avirett, James Battle. *The Old Plantation: How We Lived in Great House and Cabin before the War*. F. Tennyson Neely, 1901.

Ayers, Edward L. *The Promise of the New South: Life after Reconstruction*. New York: Oxford University Press, 1992.

Baer, Florence E. *Sources and Analogues of the Uncle Remus Tales*. Helsinki: Suomalainen Tiedeakatemia, 1980.

Baker, Barbara A. "Jamming with Julius: Charles Chesnutt and the Post-Bellum–Pre-Harlem Blues." In *Post-Bellum, Pre-Harlem: African American Literature and Culture*, ed. Barbara McCaskill and Caroline Gebhard, 133–45. New York: New York University Press, 2006.

Baker, Charles. *William Faulkner's Postcolonial South*. New York: Peter Lang, 2001.

Baker, Houston A. *Modernism and the Harlem Renaissance*. Chicago: University of Chicago Press, 1987.

Baker, Houston A., and Dana D. Nelson. "Preface: Violence, the Body and 'The South.'" *American Literature* 73, no. 2 (June 2001): 231–44.

Banks, Nancy Huston. "The Brotherhood of All Creatures." *Bookman* 2, no. 5 (January 1896): 405–8.

Baskervill, William Malone. *Southern Writers: Biographical and Critical Studies.* Vol. 1. 1897. Nashville: M. E. Church, 1916. 2 vols.

Bederman, Gail. *Manliness and Civilization: A Cultural History of Gender and Race in the United States, 1880–1917.* Chicago: University of Chicago Press, 1996.

Benítez-Rojo, Antonio. *The Repeating Island: The Caribbean and the Postmodern Perspective.* 1992. Trans. James E. Maraniss. Durham, NC: Duke University Press, 1996.

Benson, Melanie R. *Disturbing Calculations: The Economics of Identity in Postcolonial Southern Literature, 1912–2002.* Athens: University of Georgia Press, 2008.

Bibler, Michael. *Cotton's Queer Relations: Same-Sex Intimacy and the Literature of the Southern Plantation, 1936–1968.* Charlottesville: University of Virginia Press, 2009.

Bickley, Bruce. *Joel Chandler Harris.* Boston: Twayne, 1978.

Bier, Jesse. "Duplicity and Cynicism in Harris's Humor." In *Critical Essays on Joel Chandler Harris*, ed. R. Bruce Bickley, 98–103. Boston: G. K. Hall, 1981.

Binding, Paul. *Separate Country: A Literary Journey through the American South.* Oxford: University Press of Mississippi, 1988.

Birnbaum, Michelle. "Dark Dialects: Scientific and Literary Realism in Joel Chandler Harris' Uncle Remus Series." *New Orleans Review* 18 (Spring 1991): 36–45.

Blotner, Joseph. *Faulkner: A Biography.* 1991. Oxford: University Press of Mississippi, 2005.

Blum. Edward J. *Reforging the White Republic: Race, Religion, and American Nationalism, 1865–1898.* Baton Rouge: Louisiana State University Press, 2005.

Boeckmann, Cathy. *A Question of Character: Scientific Racism and the Genres of American Fiction, 1892–1912.* Tuscaloosa: University of Alabama Press, 2000.

Bone, Robert. "The Oral Tradition." In *Critical Essays on Joel Chandler Harris*, ed. R. Bruce Bickley, 130–45. Boston: G. K. Hall, 1981.

Bonner, Robert E. *Mastering America: Southern Slaveholders and the Crisis of American Nationhood.* New York: Cambridge University Press, 2009.

Bowser, James Dallas. "The Black Man's Burden." *Colored American*, April 8, 1899, 1.

Brantlinger, Patrick. "Kipling's 'The White Man's Burden' and Its Afterlives." *English Literature in Transition, 1880–1920* 50, no. 2 (2007): 172–91.

Brasch, Walter M. *Brer Rabbit, Uncle Remus, and the "Cornfield Journalist": The Tale of Joel Chandler Harris.* Macon, GA: Mercer University Press, 2000.

Briggs, Laura. *Reproducing Empire: Race, Sex, Science, and U.S. Imperialism in Puerto Rico.* Berkeley: University of California Press, 2002.

Brodhead, Richard. *Cultures of Letters: Scenes of Reading and Writing in Nineteenth-Century America.* Chicago: University of Chicago Press, 1993.

Brooke, Stopford. *English Literature; with an Appendix on American Literature by J. Harris Patton.* New York: American Book Company, 1895.

Brown, Sterling. *The Negro in American Fiction*. Washington, DC: Associates in Negro Folk Education, 1937.

Brown, William Garrott. *The Lower South in American History*. New York: Macmillan, 1902.

Brown, William Wells. *My Southern Home*. 1880. In *From Fugitive Slave to Free Man: The Autobiographies of William Wells Brown*, ed. William L. Andrews. Columbia: University of Missouri Press, 1993.

Cable, George Washington. *The Grandissimes: A Story of Negro Life*. New York: Charles Scribner's Sons, 1880.

Campbell, George. *White and Black: The Outcome of a Visit to the United States*. London: Chatto and Windus, 1879.

Cartwright, Keith. *Reading Africa into American Literature: Epics, Fables, and Gothic Tales*. Lexington: University of Kentucky Press, 2002.

Cassidy, Frederic G., ed. *Dictionary of American Regional English*. Vol. 1, *Introduction and A–C*. Cambridge, MA: Harvard University Press, 1985. 4 vols.

Chase, Richard. Foreword to *The Complete Tales of Uncle Remus*, by Joel Chandler Harris. Boston: Houghton Mifflin, 1955.

Chesnutt, Charles W. *The Marrow of Tradition*. 1901. New York: Penguin, 1993.

Cimbala, Paul A. *Under the Guardianship of the Nation: The Freedmen's Bureau and the Reconstruction of Georgia, 1865–1870*. Athens: University of Georgia Press, 2003.

Clymer, Jeffory A. *America's Culture of Terrorism: Violence, Capitalism, and the Written Word*. Chapel Hill: University of North Carolina Press, 2003.

Cochran, Robert. "Black Father: The Subversive Achievement of Joel Chandler Harris." *African American Review* 38 (2004): 21–34.

Cohen, Patricia. "Faulkner Link to Plantation Diary Discovered." *New York Times*, February 10, 2010, *www.nytimes.com*.

Cohn, Deborah N. "Combatting Anti-Americanism during the Cold War: Faulkner, the State Department, and Latin America." *Mississippi Quarterly* 59, nos. 3–4 (2006): 395–413.

————. *History and Memory in the Two Souths: Recent Southern and Spanish American Fiction*. Nashville: Vanderbilt University Press, 1999.

Coleman, C. W., Jr. "The Homes of Some Southern Authors." *Chautauquan* 8, no. 6 (March 1888): 343–45.

Cone, Helen Gray. "Women in Literature." In *Prisoners of Poverty: Women Wage-Workers, Their Trades and Their Lives*, ed. Helen Campbell, 107–27. Boston: Little, Brown, and Company, 1887.

Connolly, Paula T. "Crossing Borders from Africa to America." In *Transcending Boundaries: Writing for a Dual Audience of Children and Adults*, ed. Sandra L. Beckett, 149–64. New York: Routledge, 1999.

Cook, Raymond A. *Fire from the Flint: The Amazing Careers of Thomas Dixon*. Winston-Salem, NC: John F. Blair, 1968.

————. *Thomas Dixon*. New York: Twayne, 1974.

Cooper, John Milton. *Walter Hines Page: The Southerner as American, 1855–1918.* Chapel Hill: University of North Carolina Press, 1977.

Costello, Brannon. *Plantation Airs: Racial Paternalism and the Transformations of Class in Southern Fiction, 1945–1971.* Baton Rouge: Louisiana State University Press, 2007.

Coulter, Charles E. *"Take Up the Black Man's Burden": Kansas City's African American Communities, 1865–1939.* Columbia: University of Missouri Press, 2006.

Cousins, Paul M. *Joel Chandler Harris: A Biography.* Baton Rouge: Louisiana State University Press, 1968.

Cowan, Tynes. "Charles Waddell Chesnutt and Joel Chandler Harris: An Anxiety of Influence." *Resources for American Literary Study* 25, no. 2 (1999): 232–53.

———. *The Slave in the Swamp: Disrupting the Plantation Narrative.* New York: Routledge, 2005.

Cowley, Malcolm, and William Faulkner. *The Faulkner-Cowley File: Letters and Memories, 1944–1962.* New York: Viking, 1966.

Crow, Charles L., ed. *A Companion to the Regional Literatures of America.* Malden, MA: Blackwell, 2003.

Cummings, Stephen D. *The Dixification of America: The American Odyssey into the Conservative Economic Trap.* Westport, CT: Praeger, 1998.

Dainotto, Roberto. "'All the Regions Do Smilingly Revolt': The Literature of Place and Region." *Critical Inquiry* 22, no. 3 (1996): 486–505.

Daniel, Frederick S. "A Visit to a Colonial Estate." *Harper's* 76, no. 404 (March 1888): 517–24.

Davis, Thadious M. *Games of Property: Law, Race, Gender, and Faulkner's* Go Down, Moses. Durham, NC: Duke University Press, 2003.

Delany, Martin R. *Blake; or the Huts of America.* Boston: Beacon, 1970.

Dessens, Nathalie. *Myths of the Plantation Society: Slavery in the American South and the West Indies.* Gainesville: University Press of Florida, 2003.

Dixon, Thomas, Jr. "Booker T. Washington and the Negro." *Saturday Evening Post* 178 (August 19, 1905): 1–2.

———. *The Clansman: An Historical Romance of the Ku Klux Klan.* New York: Doubleday, Page and Company, 1905.

———. *Dixon's Sermons; Delivered in the Grand Opera House, New York, 1898–1899.* New York: F. L. Bussey, 1899.

———. *The Flaming Sword.* Atlanta: Monarch, 1939.

———. *The Leopard's Spots: A Romance of the White Man's Burden.* New York: Doubleday, Page and Company, 1902.

———. *Southern Horizons: The Autobiography of Thomas Dixon.* Alexandria, VA: IWV Publishing, 1984.

———. *The Traitor: A Story of the Fall of the Ku Klux Klan.* New York: Doubleday, Page and Company, 1907.

Douglass, Frederick. *Narrative of the Life of Frederick Douglass, an American Slave, Written by Himself.* 1845. New Haven, CT: Yale University Press, 2001.

Du Bois, W. E. B. "The Burden of Black Women." *Horizon* 2 (November 1907): 3–5.

———. *The Quest of the Silver Fleece: A Novel.* Chicago: A. C. McClurg, 1911.

———. *The Souls of Black Folk.* 1903. New York: Signet Classic, 1995.

Duck, Leigh Anne. "From Colony to Empire: Postmodern Faulkner." In *Global Faulkner*, ed. Annette Trefzer and Ann J. Abadie, 24–42. Oxford: University of Mississippi Press, 2009.

———. *The Nation's Region: Southern Modernism, Segregation, and U.S. Nationalism.* Athens: University of Georgia Press, 2006.

Dunbar, Paul Laurence. *Lyrics of Love and Laughter.* New York: Dodd, Mead, and Company, 1903.

Duvall, John N. *Race and White Identity in Southern Fiction: From Faulkner to Morrison.* New York: Palgrave, 2008.

Egerton, John. *The Americanization of Dixie, the Southernization of America.* New York: Harper and Row, 1974.

Eggleston, George Cary. *Love Is the Sum of It All: A Plantation Romance.* Boston: Lothrop, Lee, and Shepard, 1907.

Ellis, Juniper. "Enacting Culture: Zora Neale Hurston, Joel Chandler Harris, and Literary Anthropology." In *Multiculturalism: Roots and Realities*, ed. C. James Trotman, 155–69. Bloomington: Indiana University Press, 2002.

Entzminger, "Passing as Miscegenation: Whiteness and Homoeroticism in Faulkner's *Absalom, Absalom!*" *Faulkner Journal* 22, nos. 1–2 (Fall 2006/Spring 2007): 90–105.

Evans, Brad. *Before Cultures: The Ethnographic Imagination in American Literature, 1865–1920.* Chicago: University of Chicago Press, 2005.

———. "Howellsian Chic: The Local Color of Cosmopolitanism." *English Literary History* 71, no. 3 (2004): 775–812.

Faulkner, William. *Absalom, Absalom!* 1936. New York: Vintage International, 1986.

———. *As I Lay Dying.* 1930. New York: Vintage International, 1990.

———. *Essays, Speeches, and Public Letters.* New York: Modern Library, 2004.

———. *Go Down Moses.* 1942. New York: Vintage International, 1991.

———. *The Hamlet.* 1940. New York: Vintage International, 1991.

———. *Intruder in the Dust.* 1948. New York: Vintage International, 1991.

———. *Light in August.* 1932. New York: Vintage International, 1985.

———. *The Reivers: A Reminiscence.* 1962. New York: Vintage International, 1990.

———. *Requiem for a Nun.* 1951. New York: Vintage, 1975.

———. "A Rose for Emily." In *The Portable Faulkner*, ed. Malcolm Cowley, 392–402. 1946. New York: Penguin, 2003.

———. *The Sound and the Fury.* 1929. New York: Vintage International, 1990.

———. *The Unvanquished.* 1934. New York: Vintage International, 1991.

———. *The Wild Palms [If I Forget Thee, Jerusalem].* 1939. New York: Vintage International, 1995.

Fetterley, Judith, and Marjorie Pryse, eds. *American Women Regionalists: A Norton Anthology.* New York: Norton, 1992.

Fields, Rufus McClain. "The White Man's Burden." *Southern Cultivator,* March 15, 1904, 19.

Fishkin, Shelley Fisher. "Race and the Politics of Memory: Mark Twain and Paul Laurence Dunbar." *Journal of American Studies* 40 (2006): 283–309.

Flusche, Michael. "Underlying Despair in the Fiction of Joel Chandler Harris." In *Critical Essays on Joel Chandler Harris,* ed. R. Bruce Bickley, 174–84. Boston: G. K. Hall, 1981.

Foote, Stephanie. *Regional Fictions: Culture and Identity in Nineteenth-Century American Literature.* Madison: University of Wisconsin Press, 2000.

Fossett, Judith Jackson. "(K)Night Riders in (K)Night Gowns: The Ku Klux Klan, Race, and Constructions of Masculinity." In *Race Consciousness: African American Studies for the New Century,* ed. Fossett and Jeffrey A. Tucker, 50–63. New York: New York University Press, 1997.

Foster, Stephen Collins, Walter Kittredge, et al. *The Old Plantation Melodies.* New York: H. M. Caldwell, 1888.

Fowler, Doreen. "Joe Christmas and 'Womanshenegro.'" In *Faulkner and Women: Faulkner and Yoknapatawpha 1985,* ed. Doreen Fowler and Ann J. Abadie, 144–61. Jackson: University Press of Mississippi, 1987.

Gaines, Francis Pendleton. *The Southern Plantation: A Study in the Development and the Accuracy of Tradition.* New York: Columbia University Press, 1924.

Gaston, Paul M. *The New South Creed: A Study in Southern Mythmaking.* New York: Knopf, 1970.

Gatewood, Willard. *Black Americans and the White Man's Burden, 1898–1903.* Urbana: University of Illinois Press, 1975.

Gebhard, Caroline. "Reconstructing Southern Manhood: Race, Sentimentality, and Camp in the Plantation Myth." In *Haunted Bodies: Gender and Southern Texts,* ed. Anne Goodwyn Jones and Susan V. Donaldson, 132–55. Charlottesville: University Press of Virginia, 1997.

"Geo. C. Eggleston's Southland Story; Author Preaches Too Much in 'Love Is the Sum of It All'—Advised to Take a Moral Holiday." *New York Times,* September 14, 1907, *Saturday Review of Books,* BR 548.

Gillespie, Michele K., and Randal L. Hall, eds. *Thomas Dixon Jr. and the Birth of Modern America.* Baton Rouge: Louisiana State University Press, 2006.

Gilligan, Heather Tirado. "Reading, Race, and Charles Chesnutt's 'Uncle Julius' Tales." *English Literary History* 74, no. 1 (Spring 2007): 195–215.

Gillman, Susan. *Blood Talk: American Race Melodrama and the Culture of the Occult.* Chicago: University of Chicago Press, 2003.

Glissant, Édouard. *Faulkner, Mississippi.* Trans. Barbara B. Lewis and Thomas C. Spear. Chicago: University of Chicago Press, 2000.

———. *The Poetics of Relation.* 1990. Trans. Betsy Wing. Ann Arbor: University of Michigan Press, 1997.

Godden, Richard. "*Absalom, Absalom!,* Haiti, and Labor History: Reading Unreadable Revolutions." *English Literary History* 61, no. 3 (1994): 685–720.

Goldner, Ellen J. "(Re)Staging Colonial Encounters: Chesnutt's Critique of Imperialism in *The Conjure Woman.*" *Studies in American Fiction* 28, no. 1 (2000): 39–64.

Goldsby, Jacqueline. *A Spectacular Secret: Lynching in American Life and Literature.* Chicago: University of Chicago Press, 2006.

Grady, Henry W. "Against Centralization—Before the Society of the University of Virginia, June 25, 1889." In *Life of Henry W. Grady, Including His Writings and Speeches: A Memorial Volume*, ed. Joel Chandler Harris, 142–57. New York: Cassell Publishing Company, 1890.

———. "At the Boston Banquet." In *Life of Henry W. Grady, Including His Writings and Speeches: A Memorial Volume*, ed. Joel Chandler Harris, 180–98. New York: Cassell Publishing Company, 1890.

———. *The New South.* New York: Robert Bonner's Sons, 1890.

———. "The New South—Delivered at the Banquet of the New England Club, New York, December 21, 1886." In *Life of Henry W. Grady, Including His Writings and Speeches: A Memorial Volume*, ed. Joel Chandler Harris, 83–93. New York: Cassell Publishing Company, 1890.

———. "The South and Her Problems—At the Dallas, Texas State Fair, October 26, 1887." In *Life of Henry W. Grady, Including His Writings and Speeches: A Memorial Volume*, ed. Joel Chandler Harris, 94–120. New York: Cassell Publishing Company, 1890.

Gray, Richard J. *Southern Aberrations: Writers of the American South and the Problems of Regionalism.* Baton Rouge: Louisiana State University Press, 2000.

Greeson, Jennifer Rae. "Colonial Planter to American Farmer: South, Nation, and Decolonization in Crèvecoeur." In *Messy Beginnings: Postcoloniality and Early American Studies*, ed. Malini Johar Schueller and Edward Watts, 103–20. New Brunswick, NJ: Rutgers University Press, 2003.

———. "Expropriating *The Great South* and Exporting 'Local Color': Global and Hemispheric Imaginaries of the First Reconstruction." *American Literary History* 18, no. 3 (2006): 496–520.

Griffin, Larry J., and Don H. Doyle, eds. *The South as an American Problem.* Athens: University of Georgia Press, 1995.

Griggs, Sutton E. *Imperium in Imperio.* 1899. Miami: Mnemosyne, 1969.

Griska, Joseph M., Jr. "In Stead of a 'Gift of Gab': Some New Perspectives on Joel Chandler Harris's Biography." In *Critical Essays on Joel Chandler Harris*, ed. R. Bruce Bickley, 210–25. Boston: G. K. Hall, 1981.

Gross, Theodore L. *Thomas Nelson Page.* New York: Twayne, 1967.

Guerrero, Ed. *Framing Blackness: The African American Image in Film.* Philadelphia: Temple University Press, 1993.

Gunning, Sandra. *Race, Rape, and Lynching: The Red Record of American Literature, 1890–1912.* New York: Oxford University Press, 1996.

Guterl, Matthew Pratt. *American Mediterranean: Southern Slaveholders in the Age of Emancipation.* Cambridge, MA: Harvard University Press, 2008.

Hagood, Taylor. *Faulkner's Imperialism: Space, Place, and the Materiality of Myth*. Baton Rouge: Louisiana State University Press, 2008.

———. "Negotiating the Marble Bonds of Whiteness: Hybridity and Imperial Impulse." *Faulkner Journal* 22, nos. 1–2 (Fall 2006/Spring 2007): 24–38.

———. "'Prodjickin', or Mekin' a Present to Yo' Fam'ly': Rereading Empowerment in Thomas Nelson Page's Frame Narratives." *Mississippi Quarterly* 57, no. 3 (2004): 423–40.

Hale, Grace Elizabeth. *Making Whiteness: The Culture of Segregation in the South, 1890–1940*. New York: Vintage, 1999.

Hall, Stuart. "When Was 'The Post-Colonial'? Thinking at the Limit." In *The Postcolonial Question: Common Skies, Divided Horizons*, ed. Iain Chambers and Lidia Curti, 242–59. New York: Routledge, 1996.

Handley, George. *Postslavery Literatures in the Americas: Family Portraits in Black and White*. Charlottesville: University of Virginia Press, 2000.

Harper, Frances E. W. *Iola Leroy; or, Shadows Uplifted*. 1892. Boston: Beacon Press, 1987.

Harris, Joel Chandler. "Ananias." *Harper's New Monthly Magazine* 76, no. 455 (April 1888): 699–708.

———. *Balaam and His Master, and Other Sketches and Stories*. Boston: Houghton Mifflin, 1891.

———. "Biographical Sketch of Henry W. Grady." In *Life of Henry W. Grady, Including His Writings and Speeches: A Memorial Volume*, ed. Joel Chandler Harris, 9–68. New York: Cassell Publishing Company, 1890.

———. *Daddy Jake the Runaway and Short Stories Told after Dark by "Uncle Remus," Joel Chandler Harris*. New York: Century, 1889.

———. *Gabriel Tolliver: A Story of Reconstruction*. New York: McClure, Phillips, and Company, 1902.

———. *Joel Chandler Harris: Editor and Essayist*. Ed. Julia Collier Harris. Chapel Hill: University of North Carolina Press, 1931.

———. *Nights with Uncle Remus: Myths and Legends of the Old Plantation*. New York: Century, 1883.

———. *On the Plantation: A Story of a Georgia Boy's Adventures during the War*. New York: D. Appleton and Company, 1892.

———. "Provinciality in Literature: A Defense of Boston." In *Joel Chandler Harris: Editor and Essayist*, ed. Julia Collier Harris, 186–91. Chapel Hill: University of North Carolina Press, 1931.

———. *The Tar-Baby and Other Rhymes of Uncle Remus*. New York: D. Appleton and Company, 1904.

———. *Told by Uncle Remus: New Stories of the Old Plantation*. New York: McClure, Phillips, and Company, 1905.

———. *Uncle Remus and Brer Rabbit*. New York: Frederick A. Stokes, 1907.

———. *Uncle Remus and His Friends*. Boston: Houghton Mifflin, 1892.

———. *Uncle Remus, His Songs and His Sayings.* New York: D. Appleton and Company, 1880.

Harris, Joel Chandler, and Eli Shepherd. *Songs and Ballads of the Old Plantation.* Boston: Ticknor and Company, 1888.

Harris, Julia Collier, ed. *The Life and Letters of Joel Chandler Harris.* New York: Houghton Mifflin, 1918.

Harrison, Brady. *Agent of Empire: William Walker and the Imperial Self in American Literature.* Athens: University of Georgia Press, 2004.

Harrison, Hubert H. ("Gunga Din"). "The Black Man's Burden (A Reply to Rudyard Kipling)." *Colored American Review* 1, no. 4 (December 1915): 3.

———. "The Black Man's Burden [II]." In *A Hubert Harrison Reader*, ed. Jeffrey B. Perry, 67–71. Middletown, CT: Wesleyan University Press, 2001.

Hemenway, Robert. "Author, Teller, and Hero." Introduction to *Uncle Remus, His Songs and His Sayings*, by Joel Chandler Harris. 1880. New York: Penguin, 1982.

Hillyard, M. B. *The New South.* Baltimore: The Manufacturer's Record, 1887.

"Henry W. Grady." *New York Times*, December 24, 1889, 4.

Hobson, Fred. *Tell about the South: The Southern Rage to Explain.* Baton Rouge: Louisiana State University Press, 1983.

Hobsbawm, Eric. *The Age of Empire, 1875–1914.* New York: Vintage, 1989.

Hodes, Martha. *White Women, Black Men: Illicit Sex in the 19th-Century South.* New Haven, CT: Yale University Press, 1997.

Holtzclaw, William Henry. *The Black Man's Burden.* New York: Neale, 1915.

Hoganson, Kristin. *Fighting for American Manhood: How Gender Politics Provoked the Spanish-American and Philippine-American Wars.* New Haven, CT: Yale University Press, 1998.

Horne, Gerald. *White Pacific: U.S. Imperialism and Black Slavery in the South Seas after the Civil War.* Honolulu: University of Hawaii Press, 2007.

Howard, June. "Unraveling Regions, Unsettling Periods: Sarah Orne Jewett and American Literary History." *American Literature* 68, no. 2 (1996): 365–84.

Humphries, Jefferson. "Remus Redux, or French Classicism on the Old Plantation." In *Southern Literature and Literary Theory*, ed. Jefferson Humphries, 170–85. Athens: University of Georgia Press, 1990.

Irwin, John T. *Doubling and Incest/Repetition and Revenge: A Speculative Reading of Faulkner.* Baltimore: Johns Hopkins University Press, 1996.

Jackson, Chuck. "American Emergencies: Whiteness, the National Guard, and *Light in August.*" *Faulkner Journal* 22, nos. 1–2 (Fall 2006/Spring 2007): 193–208.

Jacobs, Harriet. *Incidents in the Life of a Slave Girl, Written by Herself.* 1861. Rev. ed. Ed. Jean Fagan Yellin. Cambridge, MA: Harvard University Press, 2009.

Jacobson, Matthew Frye. *Barbarian Virtues: The United States Encounters Foreign Peoples at Home and Abroad, 1876 to 1917.* New York: Hill and Wang, 2000.

Johnson, James Weldon. *The Autobiography of an Ex-Colored Man.* 1912. New York: Penguin, 1990.

Jones, Gavin. *Strange Talk: The Politics of Dialect Literature in Gilded Age America.* Berkeley: University of California Press, 1999.

Jordan, Winthrop. *The White Man's Burden: Historical Origins of Racism in the United States.* New York: Oxford University Press, 1974.

———. *White over Black: American Attitudes toward the Negro, 1550–1812.* New York: W. W. Norton, 1968.

Kantrowitz, Stephen. *Ben Tillman and the Reconstruction of White Supremacy.* Chapel Hill: University of North Carolina Press, 2000.

Kaplan, Amy. *The Anarchy of Empire in the Making of U.S. Culture.* Cambridge, MA: Harvard University Press, 2003.

———. "'Left Alone with America': The Absence of Empire in the Study of American Culture." In *Cultures of United States Imperialism,* ed. Amy Kaplan and Donald E. Pease, 3–21. Durham, NC: Duke University Press, 1993.

———. "Nation, Region, and Empire." In *The Columbia History of the American Novel,* ed. Emory Elliott et al., 240–66. New York: Columbia University Press, 1991.

Kaplan, Amy, and Donald E. Pease, eds. *Cultures of United States Imperialism.* Durham, NC: Duke University Press, 1993.

Keeling, John, "Paul Laurence Dunbar and the Mask of Dialect." *Southern Literary Journal* 25, no. 2 (1993): 24–38.

Kelley, Robin D. G. "Introduction: Looking B(l)ackward: African-American Studies in the Age of Identity Politics." In *Race Consciousness: African-American Studies for the New Century,* ed. Judith Jackson Fossett and Jeffrey A. Tucker, 1–16. New York: New York University Press, 1997.

———. *Yo' Mama's Disfunktional! Fighting the Culture Wars in Urban America.* Boston: Beacon, 1997.

King, Grace. *Monsieur Motte.* New York: A. C. Armstrong, 1888.

"Kipling Had This Celebrity in Mind When He Wrote 'The White Man's Burden.'" *Lexington Morning Herald,* October 10, 1899, 2.

Kipling, Rudyard. *The Complete Stalky & Co.* 1929. New York: Oxford University Press, 1999.

———. *The Letters of Rudyard Kipling.* Ed. Thomas Pinney. Vol. 2, *1890–99.* Iowa City: University of Iowa Press, 1990. 6 vols.

———. "The White Man's Burden." *McClure's Magazine* 12, no. 4 (February 1899): 1–2.

Kodat, Catherine Gunther. "Disney's *Song of the South* and the Birth of the White Negro." In *American Cold War Culture,* ed. Douglas Field, 109–27. Edinburgh: Edinburgh University Press, 2005.

Kohn, Denise, Sarah Meer, and Emily Bishop Todd, eds. *Transatlantic Stowe: Harriet Beecher Stowe and European Culture.* Iowa City: University of Iowa Press, 2006.

Kramer, Paul A. *The Blood of Government: Race, Empire, the United States, and the Philippines.* Chapel Hill: University of North Carolina Press, 2006.

Kutzinski, Vera M. "Borders, Bodies, and Regions: The United States and the Caribbean." In *A Companion to the Regional Literatures of America*, ed. Charles L. Crow, 171–91. Malden, MA: Blackwell, 2003.

Labouchère, Henry. "The Brown Man's Burden." *Truth*, February 1899, 1.

Ladd, Barbara. *Nationalism and the Color Line in George W. Cable, Mark Twain, and William Faulkner*. Baton Rouge: Louisiana State University Press, 1997.

Lanier, Henry W. "'Million' Books and 'Best' Books: A Glance towards the Top of the Fiction American has Read and Produced in Three Hundred Years." *Golden Book Magazine* 4, no. 21 (September 1926): 382–83.

Lassiter, Matt D., and Joseph Crespino. *The Myth of Southern Exceptionalism*. New York: Oxford University Press, 2010.

Lee, Maurice. "Du Bois the Novelist: White Influence, Black Spirit, and *The Quest of the Silver Fleece*." *African American Review* 33, no. 3 (1999): 389–400.

Lewis, David Levering. *W. E. B. Du Bois: The Fight for Equality and the American Century, 1919–1963*. New York: Henry Holt, 2000.

Leyburn, Ellen Douglass. "Satiric Allegory in the Uncle Remus Tales." In *Critical Essays on Joel Chandler Harris*, ed. R. Bruce Bickley, 85–91. Boston: G. K. Hall, 1981.

Light, Kathleen. "Uncle Remus among the Folklorists." In *Critical Essays on Joel Chandler Harris*, ed. R. Bruce Bickley, 146–57. Boston: G. K. Hall, 1981.

Loichot, Valerie. *Orphan Narratives: The Postplantation Literature of Faulkner, Glissant, Morrison, and Saint-John Perse*. Charlottesville: University of Virginia Press, 2007.

Love, Eric T. L. *Race over Empire: Racism and U.S. Imperialism, 1865–1900*. Chapel Hill: University of North Carolina Press, 2004.

Lowe, John. "Reconstruction Revisited: Plantation School Writers, Postcolonial Theory, and Confederates in Brazil." *Mississippi Quarterly* 57, no. 1 (2003): 5–26.

———. "Re-creating a Public for the Plantation: Reconstruction Myths of the Biracial Southern 'Family.'" In *Bridging Southern Cultures: An Interdisciplinary Approach*, ed. Lowe, 221–53. Baton Rouge: Louisiana State University Press, 2005.

Lyerly, Cynthia Lynne. "Gender and Race in Dixon's Religious Ideology." In *Thomas Dixon Jr. and the Birth of Modern America*, ed. Michele K. Gillespie and Randal L. Hall, 80–104. Baton Rouge: Louisiana State University Press, 2006.

Mack, Angela D., and Stephen G. Hoffius. *Landscape of Slavery: The Plantation in American Art*. Columbia, SC: Carolina Art Association, 2008.

Magowan, Kim. "Coming between the 'Black Beast' and the White Virgin: The Pressures of Liminality in Thomas Dixon." *Studies in American Fiction* 27, no. 1 (1999): 77–102.

Malcolm X and Alex Haley. *The Autobiography of Malcolm X*. 1964. Rev. ed. New York: Ballantine Books, 1992.

Martin, Jay. "Joel Chandler Harris and the Cornfield Journalist." In *Critical Essays on Joel Chandler Harris*, ed. R. Bruce Bickley, 92–97. Boston: G. K. Hall, 1981.

Matthews, John T. "Many Mansions: Faulkner's Cold War Conflicts." In *Global*

Faulkner, ed. Annette Trefzer and Ann J. Abadie, 3–23. Oxford: University of Mississippi Press, 2009.

———. "Recalling the West Indies: From Yoknapatawpha to Haiti and Back." *American Literary History* 16, no. 2 (2004): 238–62.

May, Ernest R. "American Expansionism: Some Tentative Explanation." In *American Expansion: The Critical Issues*, ed. Marilyn Blatt Young. Boston: Little, Brown, and Company, 1973.

Mayer, Lewis. "The Spot Where Pocahontas Rescued Captain Smith." Letter. *Century* 23, no. 3 (January 1882): 472.

McCullough, Kate. *Regions of Identity: The Construction of America in Women's Fiction, 1885–1914*. Palo Alto, CA: Stanford University Press, 1999.

McKee, Patricia. *Producing American Races: Henry James, William Faulkner, Toni Morrison*. Durham, NC: Duke University Press, 1999.

MacKethan, Lucinda. *The Dream of Arcady: Place and Time in Southern Literature*. Baton Rouge: Louisiana State University Press, 1980.

McPherson, Tara. *Reconstructing Dixie: Race, Gender, and Nostalgia in the Imagined South*. Durham, NC: Duke University Press, 2003.

Meer, Sarah. *Uncle Tom Mania: Slavery, Minstrelsy, and Transatlantic Culture in the 1850s*. Athens: University of Georgia Press, 2005.

Mencken, H. L. "The Sahara of the Bozart." 1917. In *A Mencken Chrestomathy: His Own Selection of His Choicest Writing* by H. L. Mencken, 184–94. 1949. New York: Vintage, 1982.

Metcalf, John Calvin. "George Cary Eggleston." In *Library of Southern Literature*, ed. Edwin Anderson Alderman and Joel Chandler Harris, 1529. Atlanta: Martin and Hoyt, 1909.

Michaels, Walter Benn. "Anti-Imperial Americanism." In *Cultures of United States Imperialism*, ed. Amy Kaplan and Donald E. Pease, 365–91. Durham, NC: Duke University Press, 1993.

———. "*Absalom, Absalom!* The Difference between White Men and White Men." In *Faulkner in the Twenty-First Century: Faulkner and Yoknapatawpha, 2000*, ed. Robert W. Hamblin and Ann J. Abadie, 137–53. Oxford: University of Mississippi Press, 2003.

———. *Our America: Nativism, Modernism, and Pluralism*. Durham, NC: Duke University Press, 1997.

———. "The Souls of White Folk." In *Literature and the Body: Essays on Populations and Persons*, ed. Elaine Scarry, 185–209. Baltimore: Johns Hopkins University Press, 1988.

Miller, Angela L. *The Empire of the Eye: Landscape Representation and American Cultural Politics, 1825–1875*. Ithaca, NY: Cornell University Press, 1993.

Miller, Ruth, ed. *Backgrounds to Blackamerican Literature*. Scranton, PA: Chandler, 1971.

Mitchell, Margaret. *Gone with the Wind*. 1936. New York: Warner Books, 1999.

Mitchell, Michele. *Righteous Propagation: African Americans and the Politics of Racial*

Destiny after Reconstruction. Chapel Hill: University of North Carolina Press, 2004.

Mixon, Wayne. "The Ultimate Irrelevance of Race: Joel Chandler Harris and Uncle Remus in Their Time." *Journal of Southern History* 56 (1990): 457–80.

Myers, Robert M. "Desirable Immigrants: The Assimilation of Transplanted Yankees in Page and Tourgée." *South Central Review* 21, no. 2 (2004): 63–78.

"The Negro in the South." *New York Times*, May 23, 1899, 8.

Nixon, Raymond B. *Henry W. Grady: Spokesman of the New South*. 1943. New York: Russell and Russell, 1969.

"Nobel Bedfellows." *New York Times*, November 11, 1950, 12.

Norris, Frank. *The Octopus: A Story of California*. New York: Doubleday, Page, and Company, 1901.

———. *The Pit: A Story of Chicago*. New York: Doubleday, Page, and Company, 1903.

North, Michael. *The Dialect of Modernism: Race, Language and Twentieth-Century Literature*. New York: Oxford University Press, 1994.

O'Brien, Michael. *Conjectures of Order: Intellectual Life and the American South, 1810–1860*. Vol. 1. Chapel Hill: University of North Carolina Press, 2004. 2 vols.

Owada, Eiko. "Who Is Joanna Burden? Constructing the Concept of 'Race' in *Light in August*." *Studies in American Literature* 37 (2001): 23–40.

Page, Thomas Nelson. "The Dragon of the Sea." In *Spanish-American War Songs: A Complete Collection of Newspaper Verse during the Recent War with Spain*, ed. Sidney A. Witherbee, 731–32. Detroit: Sidney A. Witherbee, 1898.

———. *In Ole Virginia; or, Marse Chan and Other Stories*. New York: Charles Scribner's Sons, 1887.

———. "Marse Chan." *Century* 27, no. 6 (April 1884): 923–42.

———. "Marse Phil." *Century* 35, no. 6 (April 1888): 896–97.

———. *The Negro: The Southerner's Problem*. New York: Charles Scribner's Sons, 1904.

———. *The Old Dominion: Her Making and Her Manners*. New York: Charles Scribner's Sons, 1908.

———. "The Old South." In *The Old South: Essays Social and Political* by Thomas Nelson Page, 3–64. New York: Charles Scribner's Sons, 1892.

———. *Red Rock: A Chronicle of Reconstruction*. New York: Charles Scribner's Sons, 1898.

———. "Social Life in Old Virginia before the War." In *The Old South: Essays Social and Political*, by Thomas Nelson Page, 143–85. New York: Charles Scribner's Sons, 1892.

———. *Social Life in Old Virginia before the War*. New York: Charles Scribner's Sons, 1897.

———. "A Soldier of the Empire." *Century* 32, no. 6 (October 1886): 948–54.

———. *Two Little Confederates*. New York: Charles Scribner's Sons, 1888.

———. "Two Old Colonial Places." In *The Old South: Essays Social and Political*, by Thomas Nelson Page, 189–232. New York: Charles Scribner's Sons, 1892.

———. "The War with Spain and After." *Atlantic* 81, no. 488 (June 1898): 721–28.

———. "Uncle Gabe's White Folks." *Scribner's Monthly* 13, no. 6 (April 1887): 882.

Page, Thomas Nelson Page, and A. C. Gordon. *Befo' de War: Echoes in Negro Dialect.* New York: Charles Scribner's Sons, 1888.

Painter, Nell Irvin. *Standing at Armageddon: The United States, 1877–1919.* New York: W. W. Norton, 1987.

Pamplin, Claire. "Plantation Makeover: Joel Chandler Harris's Myths and Violations." In *The Great American Makeover: Television, History, Nation*, ed. Dana Heller, 33–49. New York: Palgrave, 2006.

Parfait, Claire. *The Publishing History of Uncle Tom's Cabin, 1852–2002.* New York: Ashgate, 2007.

Peavy, Charles D. *Go Slow Now: Faulkner and the Race Question.* 1971. Eugene: University of Oregon Press, 2002.

Pérez, Vincent. "Remembering the Hacienda: History and Memory in Jovita González and Eve Raleigh's *Caballero: A Historical Novel*." In *Look Away! The U.S. South in New World Studies*, ed. Jon Smith and Deborah Cohn, 471–94. Durham, NC: Duke University Press, 2004.

Perry, Jeffrey Babcock. *Hubert Harrison: The Voice of Harlem Radicalism, 1883–1918.* New York: Columbia University Press, 2009.

Pollard, Edward A. *The Lost Cause: A New Southern History of the War of the Confederates.* New York: E. B. Treat, 1867.

Powell, William S., et al., eds. *The Dictionary of North Carolina Biography.* Vol. 2. Chapel Hill: University of North Carolina Press, 1986. 2 vols.

Rafael, Vincent. *White Love and other Events in Filipino History.* Durham, NC: Duke University Press, 2000.

Railton, Ben. " 'What Else Could a Southern Gentleman Do?': Quentin Compson, Rhett Butler, and Miscegenation." *Southern Literary Journal* 35, no. 2 (Spring 2003): 41–63.

Renda, Mary A. *Taking Haiti: Military Occupation and the Culture of U.S. Imperialism, 1915–1940.* Chapel Hill: University of North Carolina Press, 2001.

Review of *In Ole Virginia*, by Thomas Nelson Page. *Critic* 8 (9 July 1887): 14–15. In *Defining Southern Literature: Perspectives and Assessments, 1831–1952*, ed. John E. Bassett, 165–66. Madison, NJ: Fairleigh Dickinson University Press, 1997.

Review of *Uncle Remus, His Songs and His Sayings*, by Joel Chandler Harris. *Eclectic Magazine* 33, no. 2 (February 1881): 279.

Review of *Uncle Remus, His Songs and His Sayings*, by Joel Chandler Harris. *Publisher's Weekly*, October 1, 1881, 432–33.

Richardson, Riché. " 'The Birth of a Nation'hood': Lessons from Thomas Dixon and D. W. Griffith to William Bradford Huie and *The Klansman*, O. J. Simpson's First Movie." *Mississippi Quarterly* 56, no. 1 (2002): 3–31.

Riley, Benjamin Franklin. *The White Man's Burden: A Discussion of the Interracial Ques-*

tion with Special Reference to the Responsibility of the White Race to the Negro Problem. Birmingham, AL: B. F. Riley, 1910.

Ritterhouse, Jennifer. "Reading, Intimacy, and the Role of Uncle Remus in White Southern Social Memory." *Journal of Southern History* 69, no. 3 (2003): 585–622.

Rivera, John-Michael. "Embodying Greater Mexico: María Amparo Ruiz de Burton and the Reconstruction of the Mexican Question." In *Look Away! The U.S. South in New World Studies*, ed. Jon Smith and Deborah Cohn, 451–70. Durham, NC: Duke University Press, 2004.

Rives, Amélie. *Virginia of Virginia*. New York: Harper and Brothers, 1888.

Roberts, John W. *From Trickster to Badman: The Black Folk Hero in Slavery and Freedom*. Philadelphia: University of Pennsylvania Press, 1989.

Rogin, Michael Paul. *Ronald Reagan, the Movie; and Other Episodes in Political Demonology*. Berkeley: University of California Press, 1987.

Romine, Scott. *The Narrative Forms of Southern Community*. Baton Rouge: Louisiana State University Press, 1999.

———. "Things Falling Apart: The Postcolonial Condition of *Red Rock* and *The Leopard's Spots*." In *Look Away! The U.S. South in New World Studies*, ed. Jon Smith and Deborah Cohn, 175–200. Durham, NC: Duke University Press, 2004.

———. "Thomas Dixon and the Literary Production of Whiteness." In *Thomas Dixon Jr. and the Birth of Modern America*, ed. Michele K. Gillespie and Randal L. Hall, 124–50. Baton Rouge: Louisiana State University Press, 2006.

Rothman, Adam. *Slave Country: American Expansion and the Origins of the Deep South*. Cambridge, MA: Harvard University Press, 2005.

Rousseau, Nicole. *The Black Woman's Burden: Commodifying Black Reproduction*. New York: Palgrave, 2009.

Rowe, John Carlos. *Literary Culture and U.S. Imperialism: From the Revolution to World War II*. New York: Oxford University Press, 2000.

Rubin, Louis D. "Uncle Remus and the Ubiquitous Rabbit." In *Critical Essays on Joel Chandler Harris*, ed. R. Bruce Bickley, 158–73. Boston: G. K. Hall, 1981.

"Rudyard Kipling." *Outlook* 61, no. 9 (March 4, 1899): 490–91.

Russ, Elizabeth Christine. *The Plantation in the Postslavery Imagination*. New York: Oxford University Press, 2009.

"Sahara of the Bozart." In *The Companion to Southern Literature: Themes, Genres, Places, People, Movements, and Motifs*, ed. Joseph M. Flora, Lucinda Hardwick MacKethan, and Todd W. Taylor, 754–55. Baton Rouge: Louisiana State University Press, 2001.

Santiago-Valles, Kelvin. "'Still Longing for the Old Plantation': The Visual Parodies and Racial National Imaginary of U.S. Overseas Expansionism, 1898–1903." *American Studies International* 38, no. 3 (October 1999): 18–43.

Schmidt, Peter. *Sitting in Darkness: New South Fiction, Education, and the Rise of Jim Crow Colonialism, 1865–1920*. Oxford: University of Mississippi Press, 2008.

See, Sarita. "Southern Postcoloniality and the Improbability of Felipino-American

Postcoloniality: Faulkner's *Absalom, Absalom!* and Jessica Hagedorn's *Dogeaters.*" *Mississippi Quarterly* 57, no. 1 (2003/2004): 41–54.

Silber, Nina. *The Romance of Reunion: Northerners and the South, 1865–1900.* Chapel Hill: University of North Carolina Press, 1997.

Singh, Amritjit, and Peter Schmidt, eds. *Postcolonial Theory and the United States: Race, Ethnicity, and Literature.* Oxford: University Press of Mississippi, 2000.

Slide, Anthony. *American Racist: The Life and Films of Thomas Dixon.* Lexington: University Press of Kentucky, 2004.

Smedes, Susan Dabney. *Memorials of a Southern Planter.* Baltimore, MD: Cushings and Bailey, 1887.

Smith, Felipe. *American Body Politics: Race, Gender, and Black Literary Renaissance.* Athens: University of Georgia Press, 1998.

Smith, Francis Hopkinson. *Colonel Carter of Cartersville.* Boston: Houghton, Mifflin, 1891.

Smith, John David, and Thomas H. Appleton Jr., eds. *A Mythic Land Apart: Reassessing Southerners and Their History.* Westport, CT: Greenwood Press, 1997.

Smith, Jon. "Postcolonial, Black, and Nobody's Margin: The U.S. South and New World Studies." *American Literary History* 16, no. 1 (2004): 144–61.

Smith, Jon, and Deborah Cohn, eds. *Look Away! The U.S. South in New World Studies.* Durham, NC: Duke University Press, 2004.

Stanchich, Maritza. "The Hidden Caribbean 'Other' in William Faulkner's *Absalom, Absalom!*" *Mississippi Quarterly* 49, no. 3 (1996): 603–17.

Stanton, Frank Lebby. *Songs of the Soil.* Intro. Joel Chandler Harris. New York: D. Appleton and Company, 1894.

Stead, William T. Introduction to *The Wonderful Adventures of Old Brer Rabbit*, by Joel Chandler Harris. London: Review of Reviews, 1896.

Stecopoulos, Harilaos. *Reconstructing the World: Southern Fictions and. U.S. Imperialism, 1898–1976.* Ithaca, NY: Cornell University Press, 2009.

Stokes, Mason. *The Color of Sex: Whiteness, Heterosexuality, and the Fictions of White Supremacy.* Durham, NC: Duke University Press, 2001.

Stoler, Ann Laura, ed. *Haunted by Empire: Geographies of Intimacy in North American History.* Durham, NC: Duke University Press, 2006.

Stowe, Harriet Beecher. *Uncle Tom's Cabin; or, Life among the Lowly.* 1852. New York: W. W. Norton, 1994.

Streeby, Shelley. *American Sensations: Class, Empire, and the Production of Popular Culture.* Berkeley: University of California Press, 2002.

Stricklin, David. " 'Ours Is a Century of Light': Dixon's Strange Consistency." In *Thomas Dixon Jr. and the Birth of Modern America*, ed. Michele K. Gillespie and Randal L. Hall, 105–23. Baton Rouge: Louisiana State University Press, 2006.

Sundquist, Eric J. *Empire and Slavery in American Literature, 1820–1865.* Oxford, Mississippi: University Press of Mississippi, 2006.

———. *Faulkner: The House Divided.* Baltimore, MD: Johns Hopkins University Press, 1983.

————. *To Wake the Nations: Race in the Making of American Literature*. Cambridge, MA: Belknap, 1993.

Tate, Allen. "The Cornfield Journalist." In *Critical Essays on Joel Chandler Harris*, ed. R. Bruce Bickley, 58–61. Boston: G. K. Hall, 1981.

Tillman, Benjamin R. "Are We to Spread the Christian Religion with the Bayonet Point as Mahomet Spread Islam with a Scimitar." In *Republic or Empire? The Philippine Question*, ed. William Jennings Bryan, 113–27. Chicago: The Independence Company, 1899.

Tourgée, Albion W. "The South as a Field for Fiction." *Forum* 6 (September 1888): 404–13.

Trefzer, Annette. "Postcolonial Displacements in Faulkner's Indian Stories of the 1930s." In *Faulkner in the Twenty-First Century: Faulkner and Yoknapatawpha, 2000*, ed. Robert W. Hamblin and Ann J. Abadie, 68–88. Oxford: University of Mississippi Press, 2003.

Trefzer, Annette, and Ann J. Abadie. *Global Faulkner*. Oxford: University of Mississippi Press, 2009.

Turner, Darwin T. "Daddy Joel Harris and His Old-Time Darkies." In *Critical Essays on Joel Chandler Harris*, ed. R. Bruce Bickley, 113–29. Boston: G. K. Hall, 1981.

Twain, Mark. *Life on the Mississippi*. 1883. New York: Penguin, 1984.

Vlach, John Michael. *The Planter's Prospect: Privilege and Slavery in Plantation Paintings*. Chapel Hill: University of North Carolina Press, 2002.

Wagner, Bryan. *Disturbing the Peace: Black Culture and the Police Power after Slavery*. Cambridge, MA: Harvard University Press, 2009.

Washington, Booker T. *Up from Slavery*. 1901. New York: Signet Classic, 2000.

"A Week of Victories." *New York Times*, May 1, 1898, 1.

Wegener, Frederick. "Charles W. Chesnutt and the Anti-Imperialist Matrix of African-American Writing, 1898–1905." *Criticism* 41, no. 4 (1999): 465–93.

Wells, Chauncey Wetmore. "The Southern American Renaissance." *Yale Literary Magazine* 60, no. 3 (Dececember 1894): 121–25.

Weston, Rubin Francis. *Racism in U.S. Imperialism: The Influence of Racial Assumptions on American Foreign Policy, 1893–1946*. Columbia: University of South Carolina Press, 1972.

Wexler, Laura. *Tender Violence: Domestic Visions in an Age of U.S. Imperialism*. Chapel Hill: University of North Carolina Press, 2000.

"'The White Man's Burden.'" *New York Evangelist*, March 16, 1899, 24.

White, Terence Hanbury, trans. and ed. *The Book of Beasts: Being a Translation from a Latin Bestiary of the Twelfth Century*. 1954. Mineola, NY: Dover, 1984.

Wiggins, Robert Lemuel. *The Life of Joel Chandler Harris*. Nashville: Smith & Lamar, 1918.

Williams, Linda. *Playing the Race Card: Melodramas of Black and White from Uncle Tom to O. J. Simpson*. Princeton, NJ: Princeton University Press, 2001.

Williams, Raymond. *Keywords: A Vocabulary of Culture and Society*. Rev. ed. New York: Oxford University Press, 1983.

Williamson, Joel. *William Faulkner and Southern History*. New York: Oxford University Press, 1993.

Wilson, Matthew. *Whiteness in the Novels of Charles Chesnutt*. Oxford: University of Mississippi Press, 2004.

Wolfe, Bernard. "Uncle Remus and the Malevolent Rabbit: 'Takes a Limber-Toe Gemmun fer ter Jump Jim Crow.'" In *Critical Essays on Joel Chandler Harris*, ed. R. Bruce Bickley, 70–84. Boston: G. K. Hall, 1981.

Wood, Amy Louise. *Lynching and Spectacle: Witnessing Racial Violence in America, 1890–1940*. Chapel Hill: University of North Carolina Press, 2009.

Wood, Gerald. "From *The Clansman* and *The Birth of a Nation* to *Gone with the Wind*: The Loss of American Innocence." In *Recasting:* Gone with the Wind *in American Culture*, ed. Darden Asbury Pyron, 123–36. Gainesville: University Press of Florida, 1983.

Woods, Clyde. *Development Arrested: The Blues and Plantation Power in the Mississippi Delta*. New York: Verso, 1998.

Woodward, C. Vann. *The Burden of Southern History*. 3rd ed. Baton Rouge: Louisiana State University Press, 1993.

———. *Origins of the New South, 1877–1913*. Baton Rouge: Louisiana State University Press, 1951.

Wyatt-Brown, Bertram. *Hearts of Darkness: Wellsprings of a Southern Literary Tradition*. Baton Rouge: Louisiana State University Press, 2003.

X-Ray. "Charity Begins at Home." *Colored American*, March 18, 1899, 4.

Zagarell, Sandra A. "Troubling Regionalism: Rural Life and the Cosmopolitan Eye in Jewett's *Deephaven*." *American Literary History* 10, no. 4 (Winter 1998): 639–64.

Zwick, Jim. *Confronting Imperialism: Essays on Mark Twain and the Anti-Imperialist League*. West Conshohocken, PA: Infinity, 2007.

Index

Page numbers in bold refer to illustrations.
Fictional characters are alphabetized by first name.